Human Interactions

Other Books from Meghan-Kiffer Press

The Real-Time Enterprise
Peter Fingar and Joseph Bellini

Business Process Management: The Third Wave
Howard Smith and Peter Fingar

Business Process Management: A Rigorous Approach
Martyn Ould, Co-published with the British Computer Society

In Search of BPM Excellence
Business Process Management Group

Business Process Management is a Team Sport: Play It to Win!
Andrew Spanyi

IT Doesn't Matter—Business Processes Do
Howard Smith and Peter Fingar

Business Process Management: A Practical Guide
Rashid N. Khan

The Death of 'e' and the Birth of the Real New Economy
Peter Fingar and Ronald Aronica

Enterprise E-Commerce
Peter Fingar, Harsha Kumar and Tarun Sharma

Meghan-Kiffer Press
Tampa, Florida, USA
www.mkpress.com
Innovation at the Intersection of Business and Technology

Human Interactions

The Heart and Soul of
Business Process Management

How people really work
and how they can be helped to work better

Keith Harrison-Broninski

Meghan-Kiffer Press
Tampa, Florida, USA, www.mkpress.com
Innovation at the Intersection of Business and Technology

Publisher's Cataloging-in-Publication Data

Harrison-Broninski, Keith.

Human Interactions : The Heart and Soul of Business Process Management / Keith Harrison-Broninski—1st ed.

p. cm.

Includes bibliographic references, appendices and index.

ISBN 0-929652-44-4 (paperback)

1. Management 2. Technological innovation. 3. Strategic planning. 4. Management information systems. 5. Information technology. 6. Information resources management. 7. Organizational change. I. Harrison-Broninski, Keith. II. Title.

HF58.8..H464 2005   LC Control# 2004118186
658.8'00285-dc21   CIP

Published by Meghan-Kiffer Press

310 East Fern Street — Suite G

Tampa, FL 33604 USA

Any product mentioned in this book may be a trademark of its company.

Meghan-Kiffer Press

Tampa, Florida, USA

Publishers of Advanced Business-Technology Books for Competitive Advantage

Printed in the United States of America. SAN 249-7980

MK Printing 10 9 8 7 6 5 4 3 2 1

To Mum and Dad
who made sure Diane and I had the chances
they missed out on

All music is folk music. I ain't never heard a horse sing a song.
—Louis Armstrong

Table of Contents

Table of Figures

Table of Tables

Acknowledgements

ANATOL HOLT AND HIS TEAM AT ITT, who developed the Role Activity Diagram notation in the early 1980s.

ALL THOSE WHO WORKED ON THE IPSE2.5 PROJECT, my first assignment in the IT industry—what a great start to have had.

TIM TRIBE, who sponsored the initial development of RADRunner while Engineering Director at TCP LifeSystems, and .MATTHEW CLARK, Managing Director of TCP Lifesystems, who gave us the go-ahead.

KELVIN RICHARDS, JOHN ZUCKER AND DAVID HAY OF IBM INNOVATION CENTRE HURSLEY, for the time, energy and goodwill they invested in helping test and productize RADRunner.

FRANCIS HAYDEN, who got it immediately, and not only helped to spread the word, but found the first simple way of describing "it."

PETER FINGAR, Business Process Management pioneer, and enthusiast for new ideas, whose suggestion it was to write this book.

THE OTHERS WHO SAW THE POTENTIAL OF RADRUNNER AT AN EARLY STAGE: David Allmont and Norma Southwood of the UK National Health Service Information Authority, Ron Brown of Computer Sciences Corporation, Philip Wilkinson of Rolls Royce, John Murdoch of York University, John Webb, Nandish Patel of Brunel University, Ken Astley of Loughborough University, Mark Greenwood and Kenan Ilgor of Manchester University, Andy Powell and Rachel Heery of UKOLN, Matthew Dovey of Oxford e-Science Centre, Stewart Green of University of the West of England, Nick Sorensen of The Improvising School, Eddie Zedlewski of EduServ, Patrick Hazlewood of St John's School, Marlborough, Dave Madigan of Glue Ltd, Neil McEvoy of the Genesis forum, Steven Piket and Remy Meyer of Sun Microsystems, Robin Milner, Roger Whitehead, and everyone else who gave encouragement, trust and support when it was most needed.

JUNE AND RON, for being there when I couldn't always be.

BERTIE AND DAISY, for the joy they bring to every single day.

and most definitely not least,

ANN, the real expert on human interactions.

Preface

I first learned of the graphical notation for working activities called *Role Activity Diagrams* in 1987, while working for the software house Praxis Systems plc—at the time a hot house of ideas about how computer systems could be built differently and better. I was then a fresh-faced newbie to industry, with my head full of theory after doing an MSc in Computation at Oxford University, but with no experience of the working world beyond jazz gigs and the usual motley selection of temporary jobs. My first assignment at Praxis was to the IPSE2.5 project, where I was charged with developing a "conceptual model of software project management." Talk about being thrown in at the deep end—not only had I never managed a software project, but I had never even worked on one. At first I had little understanding of what I had been charged with, let alone how to carry it out.

In a more general sense, I also didn't understand for quite some time what the purpose of the project as a whole was. Eventually, however, it became clearer. I realized that we were attempting to understand the nature of work itself. [1]

As with many others who contributed to the IPSE2.5 project, the ideas we dealt with and developed, that had originated a few years before in the USA, [2] made a lasting impression on me. The specific aim of the project was to build an "Integrated Project Support Environment"—a software tool for use by software developers, that did more than provide a programming environment and document repository. We wanted our software to understand what project staff were actually up to when they built applications, and how they communicated with each other as they went about it—the *process* of software development.

And we knew that it was not just about software development. The conceptual model of software project management I eventually developed (following a suggestion from IPSE2.5 lead Mike Tordoff, who actually knew something about the subject) was based on the assignment of Roles such as *Technology, Quality, People* and *Logistics*—an approach that could have been applied in many different domains. Moreover, one could imagine developing any number of different models, for processes other than project management—basically, for use anywhere people were working together to realize individual and shared goals.

Although a commercial product did eventually emerge from IPSE2.5,[3] the project vision was never fully realized for various reasons—a major one being that it was ahead of the technology available to implement it. This was before the Web, at a time when few people even had email.

In fact, the IT industry was then about halfway through a 20-year sea change, driven largely by the pioneering work on object-oriented programming languages and graphical user interfaces at Xerox's Palo Alto Research Center during the 1970s.[4] This work would result not only in window-based operating systems becoming the norm, but also in a world in which software developers dealt not with "programs" but with "objects"— and objects are expected to *talk to each other* as a matter of course.

There is an argument that all the new Internet technologies of the last ten years that have had such dramatic effect on business, from e-commerce to Web services, are a direct result of software becoming more communicative—more *collaborative*, if you like.

But when we were working on IPSE2.5 in the 1980s, none of this was ready yet. Our programs didn't talk to each other in the way we needed them to, and hence didn't permit their users to do so either. We envisioned a free-wheeling world of dynamic processes whose participants could share information and synchronize behavior as needed, but we couldn't make it happen.

I left the project, and in 1989 the company, to go independent. Over the next 12 years I worked for a variety of companies, worldwide, on assignments ranging from systems development to management consultancy. However, I always maintained contact with the niche world of Role Activity Diagrams—using the technique whenever possible for business analysis, working on diagramming software, and hoping all the time for the opportunity to design and build my own enactment software for Role-based processes.

Then, in late 2001, I finally got the chance, thanks to sponsorship from the life insurance software house TCP LifeSystems. By this time, the necessary technologies were available—Internet technologies. After 18 months, an initial version of the *RADRunner* software was finished, tested for scalability and robustness at IBM's labs, certified for large enterprise use, fully documented, and packaged for distribution. I was ready to go—to turn my startup company into a commercial enterprise, and try to cross the chasm.

However, when asked by clients what the software actually did, and why they should bother implementing it, I found it difficult to explain. In fact, I began to find it harder and harder, not easier and easier. What was the *function* of this system? The closest existing category of enterprise software was the emerging field of Business Process Management—but RADRunner didn't look like a normal Business Process Management system. It was, in fact, a *Human Interaction Management System*—process support software focused on the way that people work with each other and with machines, rather than the way that machines work with each other and with humans.

IT standards bodies and established IT vendors were proposing process languages and modeling techniques that weren't even close to the principles on which RADRunner was constructed. Moreover, I had even deviated in many places from the original theory of Role Activity Diagrams on which the software was supposedly based—but had no clear idea why, only an instinctive feeling that these deviations were important to reflect the reality of human activities and interactions. So why, exactly, did I feel that the features unique to RADRunner were important in some way?

People from all quarters, when shown the software, could see immediately that it was innovative—but quite naturally needed a proper justification before investing time, energy and money in implementing this completely new category of software. For a long time, I couldn't answer their questions to my own satisfaction, let alone to theirs. In the end, the search for answers took another 18 months, and would require me to expand my horizons. In order to understand the problem to which I believed a Human Interaction Management System was the solution, it was necessary to recognize that the solution required more than just software— the solution required principles beyond those embodied in the software alone. Additional ideas from the worlds both of business and of academia had to be incorporated, and used to develop a unified theory of Human Interactions—a complete theory of collaborative human work and its management.

This book describes the progress so far in this learning journey—a journey that now requires the engagement of many others if Human Interaction Management is to realize its ultimate promise. The next stages will involve putting into practice the ideas and principles outlined in this book—implementing them, in large-scale projects that reinvent the management and support of human activity within the enterprise. People are already coming on board—for example, various academic research initiatives to this end are currently in progress. What is needed now is for the commercial world to make its own contribution, and participate in the work by trying out the ideas across the board.

The incentives for doing so are explained throughout this book—most of the proposals made are simple enough that common sense will show their immediate benefits. However the theory as a whole is enhanced in the next few years, there is massive competitive advantage to be gained right from the start—even if no software at all is implemented. The theory of Human Interactions offers, in its own right, a powerful way forward for executives and managers at all levels. The varied competitive advantages to be gained from a fresh approach to process management are explained throughout this book. Moreover, most if not all of the techniques recommended have the side-effect of improving working conditions and job satisfaction for people on the ground, which is, of course, a worthwhile end in itself.

Human Interaction Management is a step change in enterprise life. There is more to be discovered about it, and it may eventually revolutionize areas of collaborative activity that are beyond the scope of this book.

The RADRunner system itself may or may not still be around at the end of the road. Either way, this book is *not* a guide to the software, except where experiences in developing and using it are used occasionally to illustrate key points—a detailed guide to RADRunner can be found online if you are interested.[5] The book is not about a particular software application, but about the *ideas* that resulted from the experience of developing and using it. Some of these ideas are not directly related to IT at all, but are about general business modeling and management. Other lessons learned, about software support for human work processes, are presented with the intention of helping others to implement a Human Interaction Management System. The hope is that an entirely new approach to business, and the corresponding field of computer applications, is opening up, and that as many people as possible will join forces to make it successful. This book is by no means just about computer technology, but it recognizes that technology is an important part of the picture, as an enabler.

The IT industry has come a long way since the first Univac II system formally passed its acceptance tests and was put into operation by the US Bureau of the Census in March 1951.[6] Over fifty years later, computer systems have made it into the mainstream of everyday working life. However, computers still have a long way to go before they are genuinely able to support collaborative human activity. To see how far we still are from realizing the potential of computers in the workplace, we only have to observe people everywhere struggling with the software tools supposedly at their disposal. Even those tools that most people are comfortable with, such as email, lead, as often as not, to time being wasted instead of time being saved, and to repeated frustration rather than progressive achievement.

Hopefully these pages will take us a little further toward the goal of a truly helpful workplace—if only to provide a *general framework for understanding work*. Such a framework is a necessary precursor to improving the way that people collaborate and to supporting their work with computers. The benefits will be felt not only by shareholders, directors, and employees of commercial companies, people working for non-profit bodies, and those who negotiate in the social or political sphere, but by everyone who has, in some way, to deal with the world of organized human activity. And who doesn't?

— *Keith Harrison-Broninski,* March 2005

A Note on Style

This book is published in the U.S. Hence spelling is typically Americanized, and the occasional colloquialism that may be unfamiliar to U.S. readers is explained in a chapter endnote. Where the pronoun "we" is used, it generally refers to the shared experience of author and reader, as in "we have seen above that" or "we use an approach based on such-and-such." The occasional usage that differs from this should be clear from the context. In some instances I could have used first person voice, but use "we" as an invitation to agreement on the reader's part – an invitation that the reader may choose of course to decline.

Bibliographic and Web references are generally placed in chapter endnote references. Web site addresses in endnotes are preceded with http:// to clarify their nature—Web site addresses occasionally found in the text, on the other hand, are introduced explicitly as such and hence have this prefix removed for readability. Any misattributions, missing attributions, or errors in interpretation are the author's fault. I apologize in advance, and please let me know corrected details for the benefit of future editions, via email to human.interactions@rolemodellers.com.

Finally, I would like to thank the pre-publication reviewers of this book: Ron Aronica, Ken Astley, Peter Fingar, Francis Hayden, John Murdoch, John Parodi, and Roger Whitehead, for the effort they put in and the valuable feedback they provided. It is with a great sense of relief that I can now claim that the responsibility for any remaining errors either of fact or judgement is no longer mine alone, but theirs entirely.[7]

References.

[1] Snowdon R.A. , 1988, "A Brief Overview of the IPSE 2.5 Project," Ada User, Volume 9, No. 4.

[2] Holt A. W., Ramsey H. R., Grimes J. D., 1983, "Coordination system technology as the basis for a programming environment," Electrical Communication, Vol. 57(4).

Greenspan S.J., 1984, "Requirements Modeling: A Knowledge Representation Approach to Software Requirements Definition," University of Toronto Report

[3] ICL ProcessWise Integrator

[4] Smalltalk

[5] Full RADRunner documentation can be found online at http://www.rolemodellers.com/radrunner. There is also various associated material available on the Role Modellers Web site http://www.rolemodellers.com and the Web forum Role-Based Process Support (http://www.smartgroups.com/groups/roles)

[6] AIEE-IRE Conf., 6-16, December, 1951

[7] Only joking.

Foreword by Peter Fingar

Oh my, what can you say about the 20th century marvel, the World Wide Web? The Web presents an immense opportunity to connect every person, every computer, everywhere, across a company, across trading partners, across the globe. Such connectivity can revolutionize the very ways companies operate, the very ways they conduct business, leading to extreme efficiency and extreme effectiveness. But, even more revolutionary is that such connectivity can transform the very business a business is in.

Now, in the 21st century, Starbucks is no longer just in the coffee business, it's also in the music and Internet services business. Exxon/Mobile is no longer just in the oil business, it's also in the coffee business. IBM is no longer just in the information technology business, it's also in the claims processing business in the insurance industry. The Virgin Group is no longer in just the music and airlines businesses, it's also in the financial services, cell phone, wedding, train, book, gaming, wine, auto, cosmetics, health club, resort and experiences businesses—Sir Richard Branson has been very busy knitting together this tapestry of diverse, customer-pleasing businesses by weaving innovative business processes throughout the fabric of the Web, to the delight of its loyal customers.

What business are you in? Indeed, Virgin and other companies that "get it" understand that they are in the "customer business," aggregating ever more complete solutions for their loyal customers who are, in turn, placing ever more trust in their brands. Industry boundaries have become a blur. Welcome to extreme competition in the 21st century, where customers are gaining supreme power over suppliers and getting what they want, when and where they want it, with greater and greater ease. If your company cannot make that happen, your customers are but a mouse click away from one of your competitors who can.

Yet, with all the opportunity, the Web also posses an immense challenge in that the humans, the very heart and soul of any company, can be overwhelmed by the sheer amounts of business information that can flow through the Web. To harness the Web for business innovation and transformation, breakthrough thinking and new systems will be needed to provide the freedom that workers need so that they are helped, and not hindered, by *the system*. That new way of thinking is Human Interaction

Management, and the capability needed to harness the Web for helping people work better in the wired, flat world of global business is the Human Interaction Management System. In this groundbreaking work, Keith Harrison-Broninski instructs us in how people really work and how they can be helped to work better.

Today's greatest business challenge is to offer total experiences that delight your customers, experiences that exceed their expectations. It's no longer viable to offer commodities, or just the best products or services. Companies must now open a two-way dialog with their customers in order to meet their needs throughout the consumption process, for they don't want your products and services in and of themselves, they want solutions to their needs. In today's fiercely competitive business environment, you must provide the complete experience that delights each and every customer. If you don't do that, you won't be able to compete for the future. If you do do that, you will need the support of the Human Interaction Management System, the breakthrough that changes the rules of business, the breakthrough that changes your relationships with both almighty customers, and the trading partners you must band together with to meet the needs of your present and future customers.

I invite you to join with Keith on a journey that will change your business, forever, by helping your people and your suppliers' people work better to provide extreme value to your customers.

—*Peter Fingar*
Executive Partner, The Greystone Group, and co-author of
Business Process Management: The Third Wave and *The Real-Time Enterprise*

One

The problem of work

KEY POINTS: We explain the subject matter of the book as concerned with *interaction workers*—people who must adapt their working activities as they are carried out, in response to information acquired from other people. Most office workers, programmers, business analysts, financial advisors, project managers, sales people, engineers, doctors, lawyers, politicians, property developers, and town planners are interaction workers. On the other hand, most car mechanics, lorry drivers, session musicians, sculptors, window cleaners, hairdressers, gardeners, plumbers, and composers are what we call *independent workers*—self-directed, working according to guidelines laid down at the start of each activity, without depending so much on continual interactions with others in order for their work to progress.

Interaction workers are, by definition, participants in business processes. The problem that this book addresses is how to understand and manage business processes that are *human-driven* rather than *machine-driven*. We show how the techniques currently available for description and computer support of business processes fail to cater for processes centered on human activity, referring the reader to the essay at the end of the book for details of the argument with respect to technology support.

We look at where existing approaches to the management of collaboration fall down, and illustrate some of the benefits to be gained from Human Interaction Management. Whether or not computer support is implemented, there are concrete advantages in our approach to areas such as control over process change, streamlined communications, employee empowerment, process transparency and quality management.

To show the genesis of the principles in the book, we summarize the differences between human-driven and machine-driven processes, and propose that it is necessary to synthesize a number of different systems and approaches. We outline the approach taken in this book to developing and presenting ideas, and explain what you will *not* find in its pages. This chapter concludes with guidelines for tools to support implementation of the ideas.

All music is folk music. I ain't never heard a horse sing a song.
—Louis Armstrong.

The unhelpful workplace

This book is concerned with human working activities—how people really work, and how they can be helped to work better. Before we start the discussion, however, there are a couple of questions we need to answer:

1. What sort of people are we talking about? Financial advisors? Marketing managers? Landscape gardeners? Tattoo artists? First, we will describe exactly whom the book is talking about. Then we will often refer simply to *workers* later on with this understanding in mind.

2. Second, why should you read this book? Is there a problem with work, and if so, what impact does it have? We will explain why many people struggle unnecessarily with their daily work, and show the sort of effects that this has, hoping to convince the reader that we need to do something about it.

With regard to our definition of *worker*, we are not helped very much by business literature. The standard approach is to make a simple division into *information workers* and *production workers*, but this does not match modern reality very well. Quoting from a typical recent discussion:

"[We can discern] just two sectors of the economy: the first, an information sector, is where people whose prime function is creating, processing, and handling information; the second, a production sector, is where workers are found who chiefly create, process, and handle physical goods.

These distinctions appear reasonable, precise, and empirically valid, but there are difficulties. Not the least is … that 'stating precisely who is an information worker and who is not is a risky proposition.' Indeed it is, since every occupation involves a significant degree of information processing and cognition."[1]

The distinction between an information worker and a production worker is effectively the traditional division into white-collar and blue-collar workers, and these days, it is getting harder and harder to tell them apart. With the allocation of more and more routine tasks to machines, those people left in the enterprise must justify their presence by bringing into play those skills that are uniquely human—observation, assessment, judgement, informal communication, and so on. Modern workers on a factory floor are more likely to be quality checking than assembling. The tradesmen of today need to apply themselves as much to the application of building and safety regulations as to manual craftsmanship. In place of receptionists, companies train customer service agents, who have access to full information about the processes that a caller is engaged in with the company, and the skills to help resolve their query on the spot.

Theorists have tried to deal with this by creating a new kind of information worker, a higher being known as a *knowledge worker*.

"The knowledge worker concept derives its origin from the emergence of changes in the structure of jobs in organizations, this change being brought about by the higher complexity and the increase of information. Cushman et al (1999) and Harris (1999) define these workers as those who 'gather, analyse, add value and communicate information to empower decision-making. The nature of knowledge work is ad hoc, demand driven and creative.' Their jobs are best described as 'decision cycles rather than a fixed sequence or series of well-defined tasks.'

The k-worker must therefore compose with an imprecise definition of the task to perform, its novelty and uniqueness, as well as participate in the formulation of a personalized and adapted response. The tasks also require collaboration with other experts and information sharing. The problems faced are most often complex and unstructured, therefore requiring innovation and knowledge creation for their resolution.

This definition of a knowledge-worker diverges dramatically from the traditional definition of the information-worker, which has inspired the industrial economy of recent years. Drucker (1994, 1999) mentions that the information-worker is considered as one that deals with a simple, well defined and sequential tasks. The information requirements for the task are relatively simple and not necessarily up to date. Furthermore problems have clear solutions because they are recurrent and well structured. The organization around the information-worker does not encourage group work and is focussed [sic] on individual task description and responsibilities.²"

Again, however, this distinction is hard to apply across the board. A fundamental argument of this book is that most business processes in which humans engage are subject to continual change, and that the management of this change is not solely the responsibility of a higher authority. Not only do we all have the innate ability to recognize changes in our environment and adapt our behavior accordingly, but we also need to do so the whole time in order to carry out our jobs, whatever they may be. Anyone who has ever had a building contractor in for house renovation knows that flexibility on both sides is essential for the successful conclusion of the work. Anyone who has worked in engineering knows that the cost and availability of materials have an impact on construction, whatever the designer's original requirements might be. Anyone who has ever worked in a call center knows that different resolution strategies are applied to callers with different problem contexts or different attitudes toward the situation. Intransigence is not helpful to anyone, and is gradually being factored out of the working world for simple practical reasons.

So the knowledge worker concept is not particularly helpful either. Can we just forget distinctions? Are we, in this book, talking about everybody?

Well, no. As you might surmise from the title of the book, we will be looking primarily at what goes on when people work together—*collaborate* to get things done. Interestingly, this appears to *exclude* information workers. Under the definition above—as a person "focused on individual task description and responsibilities"—we are left with production workers and knowledge workers. However, we will make no use of this distinction, which we have already argued is unhelpful, and note it only in passing. If anything, it makes the concept of an information worker even less realistic.

The kind of worker we will discuss is someone whose daily tasks require them to not only to acquire, enhance, and create some understanding about the material world, but also to *negotiate with various others on the basis of this understanding.* Typical office workers, programmers, business analysts, financial advisors, project managers, sales persons, engineers, doctors, lawyers, politicians, property developers, town planners—these are the sort of workers we will discuss. Dental hygienists, car mechanics, lorry drivers, session musicians, experimental physicists, sculptors, window cleaners, hairdressers, gardeners, plumbers, composers, pilots—these, on the other hand, are not generally the kind of worker we are interested in.

As a rule, if you base each task you carry out on a specific request from a specific source, *without* the expectation that the request will change while you carry it out, you are not the kind of worker we are interested in here. If, by contrast, you have to adapt what you do *as you do it* in response to information acquired from other people, we have something to say about your activities. In some professions the distinction will be impossible to make on a general basis, but it comes down to the individual's specific responsibilities, and the situation that they find themselves in—this is true of journalists, for example, house builders, and soldiers. It all depends on how interactive you must be, with how many people, and to what degree this interaction determines the nature of your working activity.

We might best describe the former kind of worker—the fully self-directed kind, that we do not deal with in this book—as an *independent worker*, and the kind of worker we are interested in here as an *interaction worker*. Sometimes in this book we use the term *interaction worker* explicitly, and at other times we refer simply to *worker*—in both cases, however, we mean to signify someone who must adapt their working activities as they are carried out, in response to information acquired from other people.

So, what does an interaction worker actually do all day? Some of their tasks are "real" work—constructing things, repairing things, removing things, transferring things—where the "things" may be *physical* objects such as kitchen units and cars, or *virtual* objects such as documents and money. Other tasks carried out by an interaction worker are not "real" work, but are "about" real work. In order to get to the point, where real work can be done, people use a variety of techniques to prepare for it and organize it beforehand—and while doing it, they carry on using these techniques to interact with those around them in order to check it, deliver it, and maintain it. They read and write emails, create documents, make phone calls, attend meetings, talk to people, research, think, decide, agree, reject, and so on.

What do we have when we take both sorts of activity as a whole? A business process. What an interaction worker does all day is *participate in business processes*. Often they will be active in several processes at any one time—for example, a team member in several projects, supplier to several clients, creator of several designs.

Business processes are a hot topic in today's business world—they are what many companies now compete on. Moreover, organizations of all kinds, even non-profit making ones, are realizing that they can cut costs, perform more efficiently, and adapt more easily to a changing environment if they can get to understand the activities by which they deliver each of their products and services. Such understanding allows those responsible for managing an enterprise to see the forest for the trees, and to appreciate better how the countless tasks undertaken every day on their behalf by both people and machines all fit together.

Moreover, it's not just about business analysis and a different approach to operations. A new category of enterprise software, Business Process Management, has sprung up. Business Process Management not only offers the benefits of workflow in linking individual tasks into sequences, but also goes further by providing automation facilities and a notion of processes that cross *functional silos*—teams, groups or departments within an organization who specialize in one type of activity alone, and who may contribute to multiple processes at any one time. Process management techniques can help workers in functional silos become aware of the different contexts that they are working in, and respond more appropriately in each case as a result. Moreover, a concept of process that crosses functional silos is necessary if processes are to be managed, measured and improved as a whole.

The reader interested in enterprise IT is directed to the essay at the end of this book, which discusses current process support systems, what they can do, and what they can't do. For our purposes in this introduction, it is enough to note that the techniques currently available for both process analysis and computer support are designed for, and most suited to *tasks carried out primarily by machines*. This current form of process management is essential, but what about the foundation for all successful organized activity: *human work?*

After all, as John Seely Brown points out, "processes don't do work, people do."[3] Take away the people from any organization, and you have nothing left. Support for human interactions is the *missing link* in today's enterprise systems. The early commercial adopters of process orientation, and computer-based process support, are more eager than anyone to reinvigorate human-driven work processes, for they have learned by experience that mechanistic processes only take you so far toward performance improvement and innovation. And those other organizations just taking their first tentative steps toward process-based management, along with those who have yet to dip a toe into the water, may well be holding back out of an intuitive understanding that purely mechanistic process management cannot possibly offer all that it promises.

If we are to develop a better way of managing processes, and of supporting them with computers, the descriptions we make of processes—the process models—must take human work into account in a natural way. At present human work is treated largely as an inconvenient but necessary adjunct to the smooth functioning of the machine. Such an approach hardly permits real human work to be properly managed for greater effectiveness, let alone for such work to be augmented by computer systems.

In particular, we cannot deal with human activities by trying to find systems that replace humans—systems that automate people out of the picture. We are nowhere near the (perhaps mythical) stage at which humans have become irrelevant to the daily functioning of the enterprise. To the contrary, business conferences are full of speakers proclaiming the importance of *Innovation! Creativity! Empowerment!* Businesses assert that their greatest asset is their people. Business analysts—and those professional bodies interested in valuing companies—continually seek new ways to measure such assets. The business world generally is taking interest in ideas such as those of Fritjof Capra, who offers an approach to leadership and management that supports the development of creativity within an organization.[4]

This focus on the value of human skills has become accepted across the board in industry. A typical picture presented by business leaders of their organization might be this:

Figure 1: Colleagues with varied skills, improvising harmoniously to satisfy a wide range of customers and gain personal job satisfaction

However, our management practices—and the computer systems that support them—have not kept up. For too many people, the reality of corporate life is more like this:

Figure 2: Management and workers in a more typical corporate scenario

Workers grind away at the coal face, feeling not only that they have unrecognized skills, but also that they are unable to gain traction for the original contributions they would like to make. Managers pile the pressure on, not only in response to pressures they are themselves under (most of them being workers too, after all), but also for lack of any more effective means to track progress and improve efficiency.

This paints an extreme picture, of course—often managers and their staff attempt to resolve such problems informally. But the basic problem is always there. However well-intentioned and co-operative workers and managers may be, neither party has any standard way of forming a complete idea about what constitutes a valuable contribution—what interaction work really *is*. A worker is as likely to feel guilty about spending too long talking to colleagues, or even "just thinking," as their manager is to feel that they should be "getting on with the job." Often, the most important activities in such work have outputs that are very hard to pin down. In the words of Verna Allee:

> "Interest in intangibles and corporate transparency has increased as business thinking evolves from bureaucratic and mechanistic models to more organic perspectives emerging from biology

and living systems theory. Yet, many people working in the intangibles arena, including knowledge management, inappropriately apply traditional business methods, tools, and frameworks to intangibles. This fundamentally different understanding of business and economic activities requires new approaches."[6]

If we are to get the most value from people's activity, it is no use treating them as cogs in the machine. Rather, we need to make the best use of human skills, by facilitating how work actually gets done, by real people. Exposing and supporting the work carried out by people not only benefits the enterprise as a whole, but also improves job satisfaction of the individuals who are its life-blood.

One immediate benefit is that life will then become easier for executives and middle management. At present, managers in general have no formal, generalized way with which to enquire or understand exactly what those who report to them have been doing in the past, or are doing at present. Hence, managing people is something of a black art, which requires reading between the lines of what others say, write and do in order to build a more accurate picture of what is actually going on in an organization. This decreases the ability of management to implement change and track progress—in a sense, it places at least as much power in the hands of those carrying out the work as in those responsible for it, since managers are dependent on an unpredictable and incomplete information flow from those who report to them.

However, equal benefit from a better understanding of human work can be felt by those charged with actually carrying out interaction work (many of whom are also managers themselves, of course). In particular, their communications with others will be streamlined and made more effective, not only by software that supports the transfer of information, but more generally by helping all parties to appreciate the nature and purpose of each interaction.

Moreover, a better understanding of human work naturally leads to proper recognition being given to activities that are often under-valued, and hence allowed insufficient time and resources. Researching, thinking, evaluating, discussing, deciding—these and other such activities may have few *visible* outputs, yet are a crucial part of interaction work. In a sense, such intangible activities are precisely what many interaction workers are employed to do.

In spite of this, people are often given little or no explicit allowance for time in which to carry out these mental activities, funding inadequate to support the resource requirements they generate, and only cursory recognition for their efforts. As a result, people are accustomed to doing such activities in their spare time or—knowing that their managers are unable to formally approve time spent in this way—frequently resort to covering up such time spent at work when reporting on progress. How can this be good for either workers or their management? Giving such activities their proper place is a necessary step toward increased job satisfaction for interaction workers, and can benefit both the work itself and the process of managing it.

In particular, modern enterprises rightly wish to become dynamic, innovative, learning companies. This means encouraging workers and management at all levels to incubate, submit, test and foster new ideas. How can such activities take place when work is perceived—and managed—as if it consisted of pre-defined task sequences? The role of the worker in such a scenario is simply to perform; and that of the manager is simply to resource and measure—neither of which is going to permit, let alone encourage, creativity or true leadership.

Finally, we will see that coming to grips with the true nature of human work isn't about some kind of fuzzy stuff. In recent years, concerns about process implementation related to feasibility, cost, resourcing, and operational quality have become of interest not just to IT staff, but to the boardroom. Not only is there a growing recognition that these issues are fundamental to proper management of the enterprise, but with the wave of recent corporate scandals and consequent appearance of new regulations, *transparency* is a major concern for senior executives.

For example, in the USA the Sarbanes-Oxley Act of 2002 places responsibility for financial accounting squarely on the shoulders of company board members, who may even face a custodial sentence if they don't get it right. Similar statutes are predicted to appear in other parts of the world as well. Tracking and managing financial transactions properly cannot be done without analyzing the *process* that they form part of—and such analysis can only be guaranteed to be accurate if it is founded on formal underpinnings. Such formal underpinnings must take account not only of business processes as originally defined by analysts, but also of how human process definitions change in practice—something that is the province of Human Interaction Management, since it is humans that make such changes. We will show how the theory of human-driven processes provides a way forward for the provision of process reliability and transparency, as well as a powerful new approach for standard features of corporate life such as quality management and commercial confidentiality.

Further, the commercial world is facing up to the demands made by a globalized economy. New competitors to established businesses are springing up in areas of the planet where both labor and materials are cheap, and these new entrants are not content to play second fiddle to any incumbent. They are leveraging new technologies and management techniques at least as efficiently as anyone else does—more so, in many cases, since they are not hampered by legacy systems and entrenched management practices. Hence, established businesses are searching for a competitive edge that differentiates them, and finding it in the supply of personalized services that are based on deep understanding of their customers' behavior patterns. Quoting Pinc and Gilmore, authors of "The Experience Economy":

"Converting the futures price to a per-cup basis, we find that those who treat coffee as a commodity receive about a penny per cup. That's it. When a manufacturer roasts, grinds, packages, and puts those same beans in a grocery store, turning them into a good, the price jumps to between five and 25 cents a cup (depending on brand and package size). Brew the ground beans in a vending machine or run-of-the-mill diner, corner coffee shop, or bodega and that service now sells for fifty cents to a dollar per cup. So depending on what a business does with it, coffee can be any of three economic offerings—commodity, good, or service—with three distinct ranges of value customers attach to the offering. But wait: Serve that same coffee in a five-star restaurant, espresso bar, or ING Direct Café—where the ordering, creation, and consumption of the cup embodies a heightened ambience or sense of theatre, and consumers gladly pay anywhere from $2 to $5 for each cup. Businesses that ascend to this fourth level of value establish a distinctive experience that envelops the purchase of coffee, increasing its value (and therefore its price) by several orders of magnitude over the original commodity.[7]

Just as the Industrial Economy supplanted the Agrarian Economy and was in turn supplanted by the Service Economy, we are now shifting to an Experience Economy. Good and services are no longer enough; they're becoming mere commodities. The developed world's predominant economic offering is fast becoming experiences - memorable events that engage each customer in an inherently personal way. ... companies can [even] use experiences as the basis for a fifth economic offering: transformations, where businesses guide their customers to achieve their aspirations."[8]

Business success in a globalized economy isn't just about the efficiency by which you obtain requirements from customers, then make and supply corresponding products—it's about a form of differentiation that is more sophisticated. When there is little difference between competing companies with regard to cost or delivery time of goods, customers will choose their suppliers on other bases: trust, product quality, brand recognition, personal service, and so on. The coffee cup example above suggests how companies can enhance their offerings by focusing on the means via which they deliver their goods. But how can you get to the "fifth economic offering" described above, "transformations"?

"Guiding customers to achieve their aspirations" is about more than gaining their attention via a congenial trading environment. It is about more, even, than mining supermarket loyalty card data for trends that suggest cross-selling opportunities, or projecting a customer's future demand for an item based on purchases of the item they have made in the past. It's about *engaging with the customer's long-term processes*.

Consider the Western domestic market, for instance—in which people often have more disposable income than time available to spend it. There is a resulting movement toward what might be termed *personal buying services*—suppliers that get to know a customer's lifestyle habits, and proactively suggest the products that they require. Wine dealers, art dealers, dressmakers, booksellers and bankers have traditionally served a moneyed class in this way. In the twenty-first century, diversified companies such as Virgin, Amazon and lastminute.com aim to return to such a model, and hope to use the Internet to implement it. They build on their knowledge of each individual customer's previous purchases to push products of various different kinds forward, rather than waiting for the customers to come to them.

However, such companies still have no way of *binding the customer into a shared process*. For example, you may fly with Virgin for years without anything preventing you switching to other carriers whenever you feel like it— in general, buying via an Internet full of search and price comparison engines just encourages *fickleness* on the customer's part. How can a supplier gain *loyalty* from you—the same kind of loyalty that your personal accountant gets without even needing to try very hard?

The reason one stays loyal to a personal accountant is because the more you deal with them, the more they know about *the way you live your life*—and as their depth of knowledge increases, the harder it would be to transfer it to someone else. Every interaction you have with an accountant embeds him or her further into your personal processes. From the supplier's point of view at least, it is a virtuous circle. How can we extend this principle to the corporate world, and allow suppliers to recreate this kind of engagement with their customers' individual processes?

The answer is not to be found in implementing and automating a networked supply chain. However valuable such efforts are, their aim is simply to improve the mechanistic efficiency with which you operate—to deal better with machines, not with humans. In order to *engage with your customers*—to win their loyalty by binding together your processes and their own—you need to integrate the goals and responsibilities of the humans in their organization with those of the humans in your own. To do this, you need support for Human Interaction Management.

Human Interaction Management allows you to become a fundamental part of the processes by which your customers go about their work—participating on an ongoing basis in their deliberations, negotiations, reorganizations, expansions, evaluations, and so on. The product deliveries that you make, and the payments that you take, are external manifestations of a fundamental integration with the needs of the customer. Such integration isn't just about allowing the customer to specify exactly what they want on a case-by-case basis—it is proactive as much as reactive, and tied intimately into the human-centered processes for which the products will be used.

It is conventional business wisdom that the most profitable business comes from existing customers. In the twenty-first century, where customers are bewildered by choice and seek *understanding* from a supplier as well as low price and efficient delivery, this may be almost the *only* business. Customers will find a supplier that they trust, engage with them, and stick with them. Anyone can compete in this heady new world—but you need Human Interaction Management in order to do so.

Where the problem lies

So, what is involved in amplifying human-driven processes? We need to first understand how to formally describe interaction work. This should lead us naturally to a better understanding of how to manage it. Then—ideally—we must capture this understanding in a computer system.

This calls for a change in kind in business process modeling. In this book we examine the true nature of interaction work, describe how it can be organized more naturally, and show how it can be supported by a Human Interaction Management System.

The discussion presented on the nature of work does not concern the individual, detailed tasks of an interaction worker—writing a document, say, doing a calculation, or giving a presentation. Instead, the discussion concerns the higher level *processes* that give our work shape and structure. We will find a way of thinking about human-driven processes that allows *controlled management of change*—something that we will see is innate in all interaction work. Moreover, this way of *modeling* human work processes—of capturing them formally—will allow us to support them properly with software. Software support is not essential, but makes it far easier to participate in, measure, and facilitate processes that not only involve multiple players, but also evolve continuously throughout their lifetime.

At this point, some readers may be thinking, "Hold on a second. We've got groupware. We've got knowledge management. We've got workflow—sorry, I meant Business Process Management. We *are* the collaborative enterprise. I don't need this." All these technologies are major players in today's business world, and the ideas underlying them are highly pervasive, so we need to look at what they offer if we are to assert that more is required.

Interestingly, each of the above-mentioned technologies is often promoted as *the* solution to human collaboration. But they're very different. Groupware is about messaging and document sharing. Knowledge management doesn't usually do messaging, but does document sharing very well—better upload and search facilities than you get in groupware, essentially. Workflow is different again—it allows people to sequence certain types of activity (data entry or document approval, for instance)—while many current incarnations of Business Process Management permit yet more powerful messaging and automation features (application integration and distributed transaction management, for instance). This situation is depicted graphically, in Figure 3: Using existing collaboration tools. But where in this picture is the work, the human work, for which the person depicted is employed?

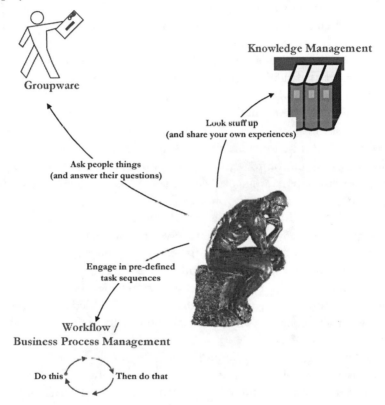

Figure 3: Using existing collaboration tools

It's not there, is it? Even if all the above tools are combined into a single product, from a single vendor, with a unified interface, neither individually nor as a whole, do they "understand" the real work carried out by each individual person—and thus they cannot support it. It is up to the humans concerned to keep track of what they are up to, to decide how to go about it, to locate the necessary resources, and to report on progress to their management.

So, let's suppose you are the manager of a team in the above mentioned collaborative enterprise, and that you are responsible for (to pick a process out of a hat) marketing a range of products. In order to manage your staff, you need to know what everyone is up to at a given time. How do you find out?

You can't get the information from all this so-called collaborative technology. As shown above, it's just not there. Nowhere in the types of software discussed above is there anything that tells you simply and clearly *where everyone is* in the processes they are carrying out—the targets they have met, the blockages they have encountered and what they are doing to work around them, the additional resources they require, their predictions for the next time period, and so on.

To find out these kinds of things, odds are you talk to the people concerned—ask them one by one, or within a team meeting, what they have been doing recently, and what they plan to do next. If you're unable to get hold of them in person for this purpose, you send them each an email asking for a status report, arrange a telephone call, or find some other informal means to get the information you need.

In other words, the basic, essential information any manager requires is not available in any of the computer systems provided for his or her use. Furthermore, the manager's staff is struggling through the work itself without the aid of any consistent and effective means to deal with all the issues that arise daily. Employees chop and change between systems as required, supplementing the work they can do via dedicated operational software applications with any tools that come to hand, from a telephone to a word processor.

Given that an ordinary desktop computer, let alone even an entry-level server, is now capable of processing nearly three billion instructions per second, and communicating at a typical speed of 100 million bits per second, this is hardly an impressive testimonial to our ability to use them effectively.

How can we still be using such primitive means of management, and such a mixed-up approach to work, when such powerful tools are available to support collaboration? Let's hand over for a moment to Loic Le Guisquet of Oracle Corporation:

"To save their knowledge workers from drowning in an ocean of e-mails, faxes and files, many organizations have turned to collaboration tools. They hope to tame the gigantic waves of information engulfing the workplace and sail through the rough seas with the help of these sophisticated tools.

Too often, however, collaboration tools end up being life

jackets thrown to keep everyone (just about) floating. The promise of an environment where work can be carried out efficiently and decisions can be made effectively remains on shores far away.

Knowledge workers find themselves constantly shifting between various collaboration environments and business applications, interrupting the flow of their work to connect to separate tools such as calendar, shared workspaces, content repositories, Web conferencing and instant messaging. The end result of using separate collaboration tools—with their proprietary user interfaces and back-end infrastructures—is that collaboration occurs out of context with the associated business process. Users who want to collaborate must leave their primary business application and log into a number of separate collaboration tools. The collaboration becomes inefficient and fragmented, making the tools inhibitors rather than enablers for collaborative work and decision making.

The incorporation of collaboration as an integral part of business processes across customer, supplier, employee and partner constituencies can only be achieved by creating collaborative platforms; 'unified workplaces', with integrated collaboration tools and business applications. *A unified workplace delivers the promise of collaborative work by putting the tools into the context of a specific business process.* From aircraft design to drug development, from project management to customer service, true collaboration tools have the biggest impact when used as part of a unified workplace."

Loic Le Guisquet, senior vice president EMEA Consulting, Oracle Corporation, quoted in "The Collaborative Enterprise 2004/5," Ark Group special report, p. 20 [my italics]

In other words, collaboration tools, if they are to be genuinely useful, need to understand the *human-driven processes* within which they are used. How is this understanding to be embedded in groupware or knowledge management? How, even, can it be embedded in workflow or Business Process Management, when most things that people do all day—document preparation, physical or virtual meetings with others, research, even such abstract but essential activities as thinking and decision making—find no place in the modeling techniques applied to implement such systems?

Workflow and Business Process Management are intended for process support, of course, but the processes they are conventionally applied to are of a different sort—repetitive sequences of tasks that require human input only here and there, at key points where decisions cannot be made by machines. In order to capture the true nature of human work, we need a new *kind* of process modeling: a technique that is built on entirely different principles than those currently in use.

This is not to say that groupware, knowledge management, or workflow or current Business Process Management systems will then be obsolete. They will actually be more useful then ever, since human-driven process management is fundamentally about *integrating* different technologies. Human Interaction Management will permit existing collaboration tools to realize their true value, by joining them together in a unified workplace based on process understanding. We will see below how information access, interaction, and automation are essential components of human-driven process support, and how they fit together in such an environment.

Furthermore, Human Interaction Management holds out the promise of something few computer systems of any kind achieve: enthusiastic buy-in from users.

As any past sponsor of—or worker on—an enterprise IT system knows, you can deliver the best system in the world, but if the users don't like it, it will be an uphill struggle to prevent your precious efforts from withering unused on the vine. However, as illustrated above, Human Interaction Management Systems should make the life of the interaction worker both easier and more productive. For example, these systems should, at the very least, facilitate the communications interaction workers engage in with others as well as a wide range of other day to day activities, and allow workers to justify and resource the time they spend on activities that have no obvious output. Hence, it should be straightforward to demonstrate to interaction workers how the new system will benefit them personally, and thus gain their acceptance.

Contrast this with, for instance, Customer Relationship Management systems that users often see as simply a burden—after doing the work, who wants to sit there entering details of everything they have just done into a database?[9] Human-driven process management should actively facilitate the activities you engage in, not just passively allow you to record them. It can transform and enhance working patterns, not just monitor them.

How to solve the problem

So, what is the *nature* of human-driven process support? What goes on in interaction work, and hence requires support from a Human Interaction Management System? Let's summarize the fundamental ways in which human-driven processes differ from machine-driven processes:

- *Connection visibility.* In automated processes, the ultimate aim is to render the distribution of data, logic and control arbitrary. That is, traditional approaches to process implementation set out to create a *single virtual space* in which the real location of systems resources can be altered at will without impact on the process participants. This facilitates data center maintenance, and allows cost savings to be made through consolidation of resources. However, in human collaborative situations, quite the opposite is true. A human process creates meaningful *connections* between participants whose skills, responsibilities, authorities and resources are quite distinct and probably very different. To work with people, you need to know *who they are* and *what they can do*. Therefore, collaborative technology must provide a strong representation of *process participants*, the *roles* they play and the *private information resources* that belong to each of them.

- *Structured messaging.* Messaging is an enabling force for human-computer interaction, yet typically results in efficiency losses as well as gains. For example, the volume of email received by organizational workers is an increasing problem—sorting it by relevance and priority alone can consume much of a working day. As they say, the world sometimes appears to be made up of people whose email gets in the way of their work—and people whose email *is* their work. The technologies provided for interaction with our colleagues have no process context, with the result that we have to work out for ourselves what to do with every single message, a time-consuming and thankless task. In the future, our interactions may still take place via email, the Web, or any other standard protocol, but if we are to manage messages better, they must be structured for us, under process control, by software.

- *Support for mental work.* A large part of what humans do has little concrete output—at least, not the kind of concrete output that is easily measured by existing management techniques or computer systems. Yet the mental time and effort invested in researching, comparing, considering, deciding, and generally *responding to information*—turning it into knowledge and ideas—is a critical part of the job of an interaction worker. The ability to turn information into knowledge is a main factor in why we employ one person to do such work rather than another. Yet, this work is not generally tracked in organizations, and, thus, can hardly be managed effectively. Worse, ineffective management of knowledge work often means that employees find it hard to justify the time spent on mental activity, and may resort to doing such work in their own time, covering it up, or simply not doing as much of it as really needed. Hence, rather than being rewarded for their most significant contributions to the cooperative effort, interaction workers are often penalized and made to feel that they should be acting like machines on an assembly line. Human-driven process support must act to change this—to recognize the value of the information processing done in people's heads, and offer ways to manage and recompense mental work like any other form of activity.

- *Supportive rather than prescriptive activity management.* Humans do not sequence their activities in the manner of a procedural computer program—"after doing x, I either do y or z, only depending on the outcome of x." A person that worked like this would *be* a machine. On the contrary, people take action in different ways on different days, in response to their dealings with others, to changes in the state of resources to which they have access, and, if we're realistic, to their mood at the time. People do what they feel to be appropriate at the time, not what someone decided in advance they will do every time. Human activities are prompted by outside intervention, and enabled and validated by circumstances. Only rarely is someone forced into a specific activity. Rather, *they decide* to take action as a result of things they come to know about. This way of working is so intrinsic to human nature that to alter it—as the armed forces seek to do when training new recruits to follow orders without question—requires intensive and often humiliating induction techniques. This may or may not be necessary in the military services for military reasons, but in the everyday workplace we neither wish to alienate our workforce nor to limit their ability to deal thoughtfully and creatively with their responsibilities. This is, after all, why interaction workers were hired. In other words, one should seek to support human nature, and to make the best of it, not to change it.

- *Processes change processes.* Human activities are typically loosely-structured, creative, and exploratory. We are often concerned with solving problems, or making something happen, whether in a technical area (for example, the design of a machine, or plan of a construction project) or generally in business and organizational life (strategy, commerce, human relationship issues, and so on). Such activities routinely start in the same fashion, by establishing a way of proceeding. Before you can design your machine, or develop your marketing plan, you need to work out *how* you are going to do so—which methodology to use, which tools are required, and which people should be consulted. In other words, process definition is an intrinsic part of the process itself. Moreover, this is not a one-time thing—it happens continually throughout the life of the process. As you develop, test and discuss your work, issues arise that drive changes to the way you go about things. This is the norm, not the exception. Hence actions and interactions in human-driven processes must be able to effect *continual change to the process itself.*

Some of the above features (*connection visibility* and *structured messaging*) point strongly to a well-established framework for describing human and organizational collaboration: *Role Activity Theory.* Role Activity Theory is based on the definition of:

- *Users* (humans, organizations or machines)
- *Roles* that users play within processes
- *Resources* private to Roles, required to participate in the process
- *Activities* carried out by Roles to manipulate resources
- *Interactions* between Roles to transfer resources
- *States of a process*, in terms of logical conditions that control the execution and validation of activities.

A simple diagramming technique associated with Role Activity Theory, *Role Activity Diagramming,* has been used for many years by analysts for process modeling. It was a popular technique during the Business Process Reengineering movement in the 1990s,[10] and is the basis of a recent Business Process Management methodology.[11]

However, classical Role Activity Diagrams are not enough. They require both enhancement and extension to support the requirements elaborated above. In particular, *support for mental work, supportive activity management,* and *processes changing processes* find no place in the standard theory. We need to update some key concepts in the theory of Role Activity Diagrams, and integrate the theory as a whole with additional ideas.

These ideas are drawn partly from varied organizational and business theories and partly from work in fields such as biology, psychology, education and learning theory. They also take into account the huge amount of existing research on what might be called "soft" computer science, or *social computing*—work that challenges the conventional interfaces between humans and machines, so as to allow humans to make flexible use of machines, and machines to capture something of human behavior.

However, not only is the work on social computing very scattered, (so that researchers often reinvent the wheel for lack of knowledge of the work of others), but only rarely is it formulated in a manner that allows for practical implementation either via management techniques, or as software for the commercial world (which in the end drives the adoption of technology). Where relevant social computing ideas have made it into the mainstream, they have been treated as a specialized discipline, forestalling new and vital ideas from cross-fertilizing with them. The success of email is a prime example—a technology that nobody can now imagine being without, is not actually very effective in supporting human work. While we all like to be kept in the know, who among us is not drowned in irrelevant information from mailing lists, messages sent to an entire group that not everyone needs to read, requests for information that we don't have the time to respond to and would actually be better handled by someone else, and so on? Spam comes in many forms.

It is necessary to draw together key lines of thinking, old and new, theoretical and practical, and to describe a means of implementation for the synthesis of social computing with mainstream information technology. True human interaction management, and software support for it, can be achieved via a new Role Activity Theory, combined with concepts drawn from social systems theory, organizational theory, cognitive theory, computer science and mathematics to provide a complete modeling framework for human-driven processes.

Such a synthesis brings with it improvement of all kinds to enterprise life. In particular, it gives rise to a new concept of *process management* that caters naturally for the monitoring of, and control over, the most persistent problem in the business world—process change.

In order to make this synthesis, we need to cover deep issues. However, we use plain language, and leave the more heavyweight academic detail and further references to the chapter endnote references. The reasoning and conclusions given below are down to earth—an effort to draw some common sense conclusions from years of deep thinking by many different people, then to apply these conclusions to construct a framework that seems a reasonable match for what we do in our daily work.

Drawn directly from first-hand experience, what follows is a practical guide, not an exposition of abstract theory. High-level discussion, written for business people, is supplemented with technology-focused discussion for enterprise architects and developers, providing them with detailed guidelines for implementing computer support for human-driven processes. How much you read of either aspect of the book is up to you. For convenience, most of the IT-focused material is presented at the end of the book. In other places, technical detail is extracted out into chapter references as endnotes.

Having said this, the reader is assumed to have an interest not only in leading edge business ideas but also in developments at the forefront of Information Technology, even if only at the highest level. Both types of awareness are necessary to a study of human-driven process management, along with a willingness to discuss matters related to areas such as psychology and sociology.

The framework we will build in this book leads naturally to conclusions about processes and their management that have a direct impact on three different areas: business leadership, process modeling and software development. Hence this book speaks to three separate audiences:

- *General business managers*, who need to understand the differences between human and mechanistic processes in order to manage them better.

- *Process specialists and academics*, whose interest lies in how processes might be described formally and depicted via diagrams.

- *The software industry*, which has the task of building process management systems that can properly support human work.

We ask the forbearance of all these audiences, since in each case some of the material discussed will necessarily fall out of their normal sphere of interest. However, we cannot get to the next stage of process understanding without adopting a multi-disciplinary approach. Moreover, we will see that there are ways of understanding human activity that are fundamentally simple and practical. Whether or not new forms of computerized process support are adopted, our approach can help any organization to better understand and control its processes.

As part of the discussion, we will show how our framework can be described using mathematical and logical techniques for purposes of analysis, and supported via computer software. This supporting material is not just for the academics and techies.

The discussion of a formal underpinning for process support goes right to the heart of two major issues involved in modeling human-driven activity—allowing room for creativity, and managing process change. And while our theory can be used simply to manage human activity better, the benefits are magnified if appropriate computer systems are put in place—hence it is important to understand, at least at a high-level, the nature of such systems if you are thinking of building or implementing them.

Hence we recommend that the non-technical reader reads the entire book up to and including the opening part of the chapter concerning computerized implementation of process support. The detailed discussions in the remainder of this chapter and the epilogue can be omitted by the general reader.

Moreover, the book is designed as a single stream of argument, and unfolds in what is intended to be a logical and helpful order. You can dip in here and there if you like—but it's recommended that you wait until a second reading in order to do so. We conclude the stream of argument with a brief summary of the principles and approaches developed in the book—although the ideas presented here are not really reducible to bite-size chunks that can be taken out of context. Like human activity itself, the details are not meaningful unless you understand the whole picture, and are able to put ideas in their proper context.

Where the problem *doesn't* lie

We are concerned here with the nature of human working activity—but, as said above, we are looking at work from a process viewpoint, not attempting to improve the way that *individual* activities are carried out. Neither are we concerned with the nature of enterprise IT per se, nor business analysis in a general way.

Regarding enterprise IT, we do draw from software engineering principles in various places, both in discussion of how to implement human-driven processes and because some of the insights gained from managing complex software developments can also be applied to the management of human activity.

However, there is a much bigger picture that we do not even try to address in this book. For instance, we make no mention of the many fascinating current developments at ground level in programming techniques, and the various new approaches to using, combining, and delivering them. In particular, there are various emerging development techniques that may have specific relevance to process technology, since their aim is to reduce the risks inherent in system construction, by providing a means of control external to the program text itself. In a sense, this can be compared to the distinction between process control and process enactment that we make below—hence, the lessons learned can be applied both to process support system construction, and to process implementation. This discussion may be the subject of a future book. For now, where we touch on technology, we are concerned only with a business-level view of IT—how to use it, rather than how to do it.

Regarding business analysis, to put the principles described in this book into practice (to develop an understanding of the human-driven processes in your own organization, describe them formally, and possibly support them with software) will require the aid of skilled people, in particular business analysts. This book assumes that such skills are available, and does not try to teach how to set up focus groups, conduct interviews, evaluate requirements, prepare documents, and so on.

Moreover, we do not go into detail of how long such an effort will take, and how much you can therefore expect to pay for it, because this depends on a number of factors—the skills and knowledge already available within your organization, the size of the organization, the scope of the processes, and so on. General guidelines on business analysis can be found in many different books. For instance, Ould writes in his original textbook on Role Activity Diagrams, of estimating a process modeling project:

"How long will a modeling project … take? The answer is of course 'it's as long as a piece of string.' But we can parameterize an answer from our own experience:

- We will take about two days on the initial briefing, a sizeable proportion being spent with the process expert. In that time we will start to build up the sketch RADs and role lists as input to the group session in particular and the individual interviews in general.

- Each interview of a senior person will take one to two hours and will require the rest of the day to absorb, derive questions from and so on.

- At least one group modeling session should be planned. Half a day should be assumed. The rest of that day and perhaps the next will be needed to absorb what has been heard and to refine the model, the glossary and the list of issues.

- Further group modeling sessions might be needed, though they might take less time.

- Expect to do an individual interview of at least one representative from each role. More than half of those interviewed will be interviewed twice. Each interview will take up to two hours and will require the rest of the day for absorption.

- Feedback of the 'final' models can be good for the group and preparation for this and the event itself can consume a further day. Overall, preparing and giving feedback across the organization can add 20% to the overall project effort."[12]

To this analysis we would add the caveat that management of human-driven processes (and perhaps all enterprise processes) is fundamentally about change—change to the process participants, change to the process management, even change to the process design can be expected on a regular basis while long-lived processes are in flight. We will see how this can be managed safely as *part of the process itself*—a major focus of this book.

Therefore, with respect to business analysis, it is sensible not to spend too long on initial modelling work. Often it is better to develop a first-cut outline process, and use this as a basis for ongoing process management that caters naturally for refinement, enhancement and extension. Spending a lot of time and money up front on business analysis is very unlikely to be the most efficient use of resources.

The journey through this book

In chapter two we develop ideas on the nature of work, in order to understand our *requirements* of a modeling system for human-driven processes. We look at existing work in various different fields—biology, organizational theory, educational research, cognitive theory, psychology and sociology—and draw together various ideas as underpinning to a small set of principles for *how we go about work*. These principles will form the basis of our approach to describing human-driven processes. We introduce a couple of new acronyms, you'll be pleased to hear.

In chapter three of this book we take these principles, and show how we can provide the basis for human-driven process description via a new interpretation of, and certain extensions made to, Role Activity Theory. Our "new theory of Roles" gives us the *building blocks* we need to capture the principles discussed above.

In chapter four we show how to use these building blocks to describe human-driven processes in their entirety. In other words, we need more than just the modeling constructs alone—we also need *higher-level notions of what happens in a human-driven process,* and a standardized way to describe these notions in Role terms.

In chapter five we assess the *opportunities offered by this new approach,* and discuss the gains to be made from the approach by both the enterprise and the individual. The gains are varied. Among others we discuss improved relations among the workforce, better management of people, fresh approaches to quality, more efficient project planning and stronger protection of confidential information. In all cases concrete recommendations are made—recommendations that can be put in place immediately.

In chapter six we offer *architectural and other technical considerations* for use in the construction of a Human Interaction Management System from these ideas, based on practical experience in developing such a system. Some readers may wish to skip parts of this chapter. However, the issues raised in the opening of the chapter are of general interest and hence this first part is recommended to all readers. It is in the opening of this chapter that the reader is introduced to what a Human Interaction Management System looks like in practice, and we hope that all readers will enjoy experiencing a test ride. After various discussions, the chapter concludes with the definition in technical terms of what a Human Interaction Management System actually *is*—the specification for such a software system—and guidelines on choice of appropriate tools for constructing one.

Chapter seven provides a *brief recap* of the principles and approaches developed in the book, together with suggestions for next steps.

Finally, the epilogue is an essay on the *future of computerized process support* in general, putting the theory and practice of Human Interaction Management as developed in this book into the wider context of general enterprise IT, and explaining its relationship to existing technologies.

The rest of the journey

The effect of this book will hopefully be in three areas:

1. *Involvement from industry* via case studies—as shown throughout this book, there are concrete and significant benefits to be gained straight away from implementing better management of human-driven processes, in many everyday areas such as quality control, confidentiality and project planning.

2. *Investment by software vendors* in developing new forms of process management software—this book provides both principles and detailed guidelines for the construction of such Human Interaction Management Systems (HIMS), based directly on experience with a proven HIMS (RADRunner).

3. *Further development of the theory* of human-driven processes—this book is a starting point for a new approach to understanding human work activity and providing the corresponding computer systems. The current focus of discussion in this area is the Web forum, *Role Based Process Support*, whose purpose is to discuss and synthesize work on human-driven processes (www.smartgroups.com/groups/roles). Members are drawn from varied academic and industry backgrounds, and discuss approaches to social analysis of business processes. If you want to take a look or enter the debate on how to advance computer support of human co-operative work, membership is open to all, and you are encouraged to join.

Tools to support the workplace of the future

At the time of writing, the Human Interaction Management System is not yet widely recognized as a category of software. Hence a specific aim of this book is to help drive the creation of a corresponding marketplace, and to encourage vendors to provide the necessary tools. Current software applications that support the techniques of speech acts, for example, do not support any other aspect of the modeling framework proposed in this book, and hence only provide a part of the feature set required. Similarly, conventional process support systems have an incomplete basis for supporting the human–driven processes we describe. Some process support systems do allow Roles to be specified for process participants, but this is generally no more than a label used to group together a certain set of activities, rather than a fully fledged object in its own right that contains private data, logical conditions based on that data, references to other objects in its process "world," and so on. The feature set provided for Roles in conventional process support systems is inadequate to implement the principles described in this book.

Having said this, computer support *is* available now for human-driven processes, from graphical depiction using Role Activity Diagrams through to complete support for Web-based process enactment. The Human Interaction Management System is a reality today, even if the range of vendors is limited.[13]

As said above, this book is *not* an advert for any particular Human Interaction Management System, but a prod to stimulate the development of new forms of process software—new applications that will permit human activity within the enterprise to be properly supported. Multiple designs for a Human Interaction Management System may emerge, and they may take different approaches to supporting the principles described in this book—it will be interesting to see. However we get there, it is time now for the business world and the IT industry to come together and ensure that, for the first time in 50 years of business automation, computers bend to the needs of humans rather than the other way around.

References.

[1] Webster, F., 1998, "The Information Society," Vol. 10(1), Chapter 4

[2] Roy, M., Falardeau, J., Pelletier, C. "Support Systems For Knowledge Workers: The Need For New Development Approaches," Journal of Knowledge Management Practice, August 2001, http://www.tlainc.com/articl24.htm

[3] "John Seely Brown and Estee Solomon Gray, 1995, "The People Are the Company," http://www.fastcompany.com/online/01/people.html

[4] Capra sees creativity as a process driven by "critical instability." He perceives creativity as being inherent in all living networks and communities and emphasizes the "spontaneous emergence of new order." The concept of emergence offers a radical alternative to an old-fashioned top-down approach to organizational change.

Capra describes the creative process in both individuals and organizations as having 4 stages:

1.   The process of emergence is triggered by a disturbance of the estab-

lished order, whether intentional or unintentional.

2.   This results in a sequence of feedback loops amongst stakeholders, which amplify the trigger events to the extent that some change is necessary to the current state of affairs.

3.   This leads to a point of critical instability: state of uncertainty, loss of control, chaos and doubt.

4.   Out of this state two possible courses of action occur: either breakdown in the existing system or emergence of a new order.

For more details, see, for example, Capra, F, 1997, "Creativity and Leadership in Learning Communities," http://www.ecoliteracy.org/pdf/creativity.pdf

[5] William Gropper, "Sweatshop," 1938 (ink on paper drawing).

[6] Verna Allee, 2002, "A Value Network Approach for Modeling and Measuring Intangibles," http://www.vernaallee.com/library%20articles/A%20ValueNetApproach%20white%20paper.pdf

[7] B.Joseph Pine II and James H.Gilmore, "Create Economic Value with engaging experiences," The Deluxe Knowledge Quarterly, First Quarter 2004

[8] B.Joseph Pine II and James H.Gilmore, http://www.strategichorizons.com/bodyOfThought.html

[9] To make a CRM system effective you must rely on, say, the sales executive doggedly entering data about product, opportunity, target industry and so on for each prospect. And they have to re-enter this information time and time again. No sales staff are tempted by the idea of spending a day on the road then another two hours entering what happened that day into the CRM system. Reward systems are another hazard. Seddon suggests that it will always be difficult to make sales people use CRM systems because "they are incentivised individually. So they don 't want to put their information in the public domain." In this climate, sales people will even falsify data to hide what they re up to. Many CRM installations are designed to monitor the sales staff as much as the customers. Not a happy situation for either the system or the people using it. (http://www.themanufacturer.com/content_detail.html?contents_id=2732&t=manufacturer&header=reports)

[10] See, for example, Ould, M.A., *Business Processes—Modeling and Analysis for Re-engineering and Improvement,* Wiley & Sons, 1995.

[11] *Riva*, see Ould, M.A., *Business Process Management: A Rigorous Approach,* Meghan-

Kiffer Press, 2005.

[12] Ould, 1995, ibid., p.208

[13] With respect to *process depiction*, the simplified Role Activity Diagrams we use to represent human activity can be drawn using any conventional diagramming software. They consist mainly of simple boxes, triangles and circles, connected with straight lines and annotated with text labels.

If you have *Microsoft Visio*, probably the most widely-used diagramming tool, there is a Role Activity Diagram stencil available for free download from Martyn Ould's Web site—this includes all the symbols we use plus many more that are not required to model human-driven activity. The location of the stencil is:
http://www.the-old-school.demon.co.uk/vc/rivastencilv303.vss

If you don't have any diagramming software installed, there is a free open source drawing tool called *Dia* which is perfectly adequate for creating Role Activity Diagrams—it has all the key functionality available in Visio, and allows diagrams to be saved to a wide variety of image formats. The Dia home page, from where the software can be downloaded, is:
http://www.gnome.org/projects/dia/

Dia is described on this page as follows:

"Dia is designed to be much like the commercial Windows program 'Visio.' It can be used to draw many different kinds of diagrams. It currently has special objects to help draw entity relationship diagrams, UML diagrams, flowcharts, network diagrams, and simple circuits. It is also possible to add support for new shapes by writing simple XML files, using a subset of SVG to draw the shape."

Dia installs with a single click on Windows or Linux, and can be used without training by anyone who has used conventional diagramming software in the past. It is possible to extend Dia to support custom diagram types (sheets, in Dia terminology)—hence a Role Activity Diagram sheet could be created containing the necessary shapes, similar to the Visio stencil referred to above. However, the Role Activity Diagram notation is basic enough that this is not necessary—the shapes in the standard Dia sheet are quite sufficient.

With respect to support for *process enactment*, a Human Interaction Management System (HIMS) based directly on the principles outlined on this book is *RAD-Runner*, which is free for evaluation, research and analysis purposes. The software can be downloaded from the Role Modellers Web site:
http://www.rolemodellers.com.

Two

What Is Work?

KEY POINTS: Before we can construct a universal way to describe human-driven processes, we need to impose some order on the apparent chaos of human activity, and seek the fundamental properties of human work. The search leads us to ideas from biology, organizational theory, social systems theory, educational research, cognitive theory, sociology and psychology. The properties and patterns we discover will guide us in the development of a full process description framework.

We start with the well-established computer science concept of *speech acts* to categorize certain interactions between process participants, and place speech act usage within the context of a cyclic, overlapping, nested pattern REACT (Research, Evaluate, Analyze, Constrain, Task). Although this pattern includes activities often considered to have little or no measurable external output, we discuss how it is nonetheless vital to describe and support such activities.

We go on to identify a sub-pattern AIM (Access, Identify, Memorize) of the Research stage, which leads to a discussion of what we might call *human-readable metadata* and its possible uses (such as for searching, harvesting and alerting).

Looking at the subsequent stages of REACT, we find that they are heavily dependent on tool support. In this context, "tools" mean not only computerized support, but also aids in the widest sense, including management support and other forms of human interaction facilitation. Such tools provide the means for individual and workgroup practices and knowledge to integrate with more widely accepted standards of behavior.

We conclude by analyzing the unpredictable and dynamic nature of human activities and interactions. This leads to the proposal that the most effective approach to describing human-driven processes, and thus supporting them with tools, is *suggestive rather than prescriptive*, in that it offers guidance and warning rather than control and regulation. Such an approach moves us away from conventional process modeling techniques, whose heritage in computer programming are biased toward sequencing tasks in a pre-determined fashion. Instead, we move toward a framework for process description based on enablement, interaction and dynamism.

You load sixteen tons and what do you get?
—Merle Travis, "Sixteen Tons," 1946.

How people communicate

If we are to develop principles for understanding interaction work, we must start somewhere. So let's start at the fundamental feature of interaction work, the feature that distinguishes it from what we call independent work—the interaction worker depends on *collaboration with others* in order to proceed. So, if we seek to understand the business processes characterizing interaction work, the processes that we call *human-driven*, a good starting point is to ask: what sort of things go on within a collaborative activity?

This is such a basic question that we need to take a step back from modern business life to seek the answer.

For thousands of years, literate societies have felt the need to devise some means of structuring and controlling the collaborative activity of their citizens—governments, armies, guilds, and so on. We now label any such means of structure and control an *organization*. So, what does *organizational theory* tell us about collaboration?

The principles that have had the most profound impact on the way we think about organizations stem from work carried out from the 1960s onwards by two Chilean biologists: Humberto Maturana and Francisco Varela. Their ideas have been applied in fields ranging from software engineering and artificial intelligence to sociology and psychotherapy.

Maturana and his then-student Varela set out to study cognition—how creatures think. We will look at mainstream approaches to cognitive theory, but focus here on Maturana and Varela's work since it went off on an interesting tangent that has influenced all sorts of other fields. Having started by studying thought processes in general, they ended up not only with a new definition of life itself, but also with a practical approach to understanding *collaboration* that gives us some of what we need to model human-driven processes.[1] Maturana and Varela made two fundamental observations.

First, *everything said is said by an observer.* They started by noting that there is no fixed, objective frame of reference with which to classify all thought.[2]

Living creatures—such as humans—make judgments for all sorts of implicit, non-verbal, emotional, intuitive reasons that are culturally or environmentally specific. We can all appreciate this by thinking about the different social worlds we find ourselves in at home, at work, and in other situations—we deal quite differently with each of these circumstances, for a variety of complex reasons, and think in accordingly different ways. So in order to understand the way an organism thinks, we need to understand the character of its "domain;" the set of relations, interactions, and states within which it operates.

Viewing an enterprise as an organism, for example, we see that its social, cultural, legal, regulatory and business environment is crucial to understanding it. The crucial deduction made from this by Maturana and Varela was that it is necessary to appreciate the differences between external and internal behavior. All living organisms are composed of many interoperating components. So we must distinguish between observing an organism as a whole (external behavior) and observing its components (internal behavior), since each takes place in a quite different environment.

Second, *all knowing is doing, and all doing is knowing.* A living creature's thought processes are intimately tied to its physical nature.[3] How you think about the world determines how you interact with it, and vice-versa—there is a circular relationship between an organism's ideas, and their physical needs and capacities. Hence, rather than focus only on observing a creature's actions, we must discern a creature's form—that is, understand its physical make-up—if we are to understand how it thinks.

Combined with the classification of observable life-forms as either simple or composite, this idea led to a new definition of an *organization*, expressed in terms of the relations between its components—rather than in terms of its actions as a whole or the individual components themselves.[4] This definition reflects the fact that the behavior and make-up of an organization can change, while the organization itself stays essentially the same.

From these insights—how environment is crucial to the understanding of an organism's behavior, and how an organization is defined by its internal structure—came a theory that identified a definitive characteristic of living systems. This characteristic is known as *autopoeisis.*[5] An autopoeitic system is self-producing—it continually regenerates its own components. An animal, for example, is continually making and repairing the basic elements of itself (e.g., skin, blood, and hair), a process driven by interaction with its environment.

This has interesting but limited application to social systems. It is tempting to try to fit human organizations into this scheme, and attempts have been made to categorize them as self-producing. However, it is hard to claim that an enterprise (for example) *produces* its staff. Few modern companies grow their employees in vats, except perhaps those engaged in telemarketing. Having said this, there do seem to be interesting parallels between living systems and organizations as defined above. How can the ideas of autopoeitic theory be used to make the connection?

A step forward was taken by generalizing the concept of self-production. The principle of *autonomy*[6] as defined by Varela is that a system continuously produces a set of *interactions among its components*, rather than the components themselves, where these interactions distinguish the system from other objects around it.[7] In other words, it is the maintenance of discrete internal processes that defines a system, not the creation of its physical components. This is not to say that the internal processes thus produced are stable and unchanging. Intermal processes may evolve, but they always act to differentiate the system from its environment in some way.

Autonomous systems are a more general case than autopoeitic systems. By widening the net in this way, human organizations such as enterprises fall within the bounds of the theory, since there is a convincing argument that social groups are all about maintaining a certain set of relationships between their members. Hence, some useful conclusions from autopoeitic theory can be applied to human organizations.

In particular, we can form a notion of system *identity*—as equivalent to the totality of its internal processes.[8] Such a notion fits well with the modern idea that an enterprise is *defined* by its business processes. Current conceptions of enterprise architecture (such as the BPTrends Pyramid shown in Figure 21) tend to be process-centric. This concept of identity finally leads us to where we need to go—toward an understanding of collaborative activity.

In autopoeitic terms, the defining responsibility of an autonomous system is to maintain its internal processes. This constrains the way that such systems engage with each other. They are considered to do so in a way that ensures that the states of each party's internal processes are brought into mutual alignment.[9] This is not to say that the parties arrive at the "same place," but that they negotiate with each other in order to ensure each party follows a course permitted by their own internal processes. Particular parties may have to deviate somewhat from their previous behavior in order to achieve this, but this is okay as long as the deviations do not disturb the status quo beyond repair (in autopoeitic terms, they should "perturb" rather than "destroy" the system).

From this, we can deduce something very interesting. Communication is not in fact about transmission of knowledge from one party to the other, as common sense would lead us to suppose. According to the maxim that "All knowing is doing, and all doing is knowing," any two parties with different internal make-up will have different perspectives on life, and make different interpretations of any information passed from one to the other. So why bother communicating at all?

Autopoeitic theory asserts that communication is all about the transmission of intent.[10] The purpose of communication is simply to allow the parties involved to synchronize their behavior—so that an interaction can proceed without disturbing each party's internal processes beyond repair (a little is okay, but too much would destroy the stability of the system). For this reason, Maturana refers to verbal interaction as "languaging"—using speech to achieve co-ordination between parties, rather than to transmit symbols assumed to have common meaning for all parties.

In terms of human interactions, this means that *what* you say is not the crucial issue, since each party will make up its own mind about what is going on in the world anyway. The parties have little choice, since judgment is always dependent on perspective. What matters is *how* you say things. Interactions need to:

- Have the right *mechanism*, so as to allow the parties to engage conveniently
- Demonstrate congenial *emotions*, so as to prevent relations breaking down
- Indicate clearly the *intentions* of the parties involved, so as to permit co-ordination of individual behaviors.

These ideas have been influential. The latter, in particular, gave rise in the 1980s to software that allows people to signal to each other the actions they intend to take, and negotiate on their commitments to each other.[11] This was done by implementing what are called *speech acts*—a way of describing human interactions that classifies them by intent, into a fixed set of types. There turn out to be a surprisingly small number of types that recur often in business. Most interactions can be classified as *request/promise, of-*

fer/acceptance, or *report/acknowledgement*. Combinations of such "speech acts" can be built up to make "conversations" that capture much of what goes on in a business activity. A typical negotiation, for example, can be expressed in this way.

The classic process analysis technique based on speech acts focuses on a commonly-found process pattern described by Terry Winograd and Fernando Flores, known as *Conversation for Action*, or just CfA. This is illustrated below in Figure 4: The basic Conversation for Action.[12]

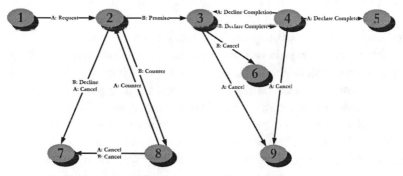

Figure 4: The basic Conversation for Action

The numbered nodes represent "states" of the conversation—places at which the two participants have jointly arrived. Each speech act by either participant leads to a new state of the conversation.

The conversation starts when A requests something from B, specifying the conditions that determine whether A will either accept or reject any item delivered by B—this moves the conversation from state 1 to state 2. B can now:

- Decline the request (moving to state 7), or

- Promise to supply something (moving to state 3), or

- Make an alternative counter-offer (moving to state 8)—A is free to accept, reject or negotiate on this counter-offer.

After reaching state 3, both A and B are free at any time to withdraw from the deal (leading to states 9 and 6 respectively). Alternatively, B can declare that the task is finished (state 4), which A may or may not accept (moving to state 5 or 3, respectively). The conversation is considered ended either at successful conclusion (state 5) or at one of the withdrawal states (6, 7, 8, and 9).

This approach, like others based on it, offers a simple and attractive device for analysis of human-driven collaboration. Software tools to support speech acts have been around for a long time, and have been taken up commercially with some success. Below, we will draw from the technique when constructing a process modeling framework. But, having said this, it is important to appreciate that speech acts are a single viewpoint onto human processes, and only show a small part of what goes on. Like a webcam trained on one part of an office, much of interest is shown, but even more just cannot be seen. The picture of collaboration that speech acts provide is certainly useful, but is not enough on its own to capture human-driven processes, or to support them fully with software. Why is this?

First, speech acts have a tendency to suppress the emotional content of communications—the second of the criteria described above for effective interactions. For example, it can be hard to distinguish between "I will do such-and-such if I can, when I find the time" and "I promise faithfully to do such-and-such." A more damaging example is the difference between "Are you able to do this please?" and "Drop everything and do this now—or else." It can be hard to tell such messages apart when they are received via a software tool, yet the meanings are different in important ways.

As the latter example shows, there is a tendency for unfortunate interpretations of speech acts to be made—biased toward command-and-control rather co-operation. Such misinterpretations can act to damage human relations badly. For example, a report on experimental use of an early software tool based on speech acts[13] for project management in an R&D software laboratory concluded, among other things, that it:

- Had a negative impact on informal organization
- Made communication too explicit for comfort
- Did not effectively support any negotiation on commitments. [14]

In other words, although speech act theory promises to enhance and facilitate communication between process participants, software based solely on speech acts is experienced as tool for *control* rather than *support*.

Second, speech acts alone do not attempt to capture the full details of a process. A particular speech act embodies one of five *illocutionary points*:[15]

- *Assertives*, committing a speaker to the truth of the expressed propositions
- *Directives*, by which a speaker attempts to get a hearer to do something

- *Commissives*, that commit a speaker to a future course of action (some people distinguish sub-categories here, for instance between *intentions* and *promises*)
- *Expressives*, expressing a speaker's psychological state
- *Declaratives*, that by being uttered, make something the case

As the name of the theory suggests, these acts concern communication—and nothing else. Nowhere here does any work actually get done. If we are to model human-driven processes in their entirety, we must find a place for the tasks that move the process forward.

These two concerns are summarized in a paper on the application of speech acts to process modeling by Ian Beeson and Stewart Green of University of West of England.[16] As well as the concerns they note, there are further issues about using speech acts to model human-driven processes.

Third, the first criterion for effective interaction has to do with the *mechanism* of communication. There are many ways in which we express ourselves, and direct verbalization to other people (whether expressed vocally, via email, from a software tool, or any other means) is only one of them. For example, initiating a project, or signing a purchase order, can be interpreted as a speech act. In fact, there is a huge variety of ways, direct and indirect, in which we can express an illocutionary point: we can assign work to someone, publish a document, fail to attend a meeting, ignore something or somebody, sign a deal with a competitor, appoint an auditor, and so on.

Any model for human-driven processes must take account of these means of communication as well as more direct approaches. Otherwise we are trying to fit a square peg into a round hole, by preventing people from communicating in the way they naturally make themselves understood. In short, we need a notion of process that supports indirect as well as direct communication.

We will discuss this issue further when we look at design and management issues for human-driven processes. In particular, we will see how the *user interface presented for an activity* within a process support system can itself be used as a flexible, dynamic and powerful tool for communication from one person to many others. For instance, if a process participant is empowered to change, while a process is running, the design of a screen used by other participants, they can use this as an effective and immediate means of communication without needing to send any direct messages. This approach requires policy constraints to avoid creating mayhem, but it corresponds naturally to the way people have always acted to customize their shared workplace with messages intended for colleagues. The main point is that communication takes place in all sorts of ways when computers are not involved—we should enhance this kind of flexibility, not remove it, once process support systems are brought into the picture.

Fourth, human communication rarely sticks to the subject. When we meet people to discuss something, we invariably get side-tracked at some point. The tangential matters raised in this way are sometimes a waste of time, but often they are the most important of all.

For example, any good sales person encourages wide-ranging discussion when talking with a customer, in the hope that further sales opportunities will manifest themselves—you don't necessarily sell what you have, you sell what the customer is looking for. Another common situation is discussion "round the water cooler"—one member of a project will often bring up something in passing that has direct bearing on the work of another worker on the same project, or a technical matter might be mentioned by one engineer that happens to solve a problem currently plaguing another person working on a totally different assignment. More generally, it is when engaged in free-ranging discussion that people hit on ideas, ideas that perhaps none of them would have arrived at alone.

Constraining negotiation and discussion to the limited range of a set of predefined speech acts virtually eliminates the possibility of such useful tangential interaction. This is not to say that such constraint is worthless—we will see below that it is often valuable in structuring interactions—however, we must take care that its use does not prevent other important interactions from taking place.

Fifth and finally, the theory of speech acts helps us to *label* the communications between parties in a process. It gives us a means of categorizing the elements of conversations. However, it provides no understanding of *why* a specific conversation is structured in a particular way—why certain speech acts are carried out and not others. Without this, a process description based on speech acts is simply symbol manipulation, with no underlying meaning that can be used for analysis or improvement.

It may seem as if such meaning is impossible to embed into a business model or software system. Aren't our reasoning processes so complex, so intertwined with subjective experience, so deeply *human*, that they cannot be captured neatly by a business analyst?

Well, yes and no. Of course we all have motivations and tendencies that are hard to appreciate even by ourselves, let alone a third party. But if we are to understand and manage human-driven business processes rather than simply describe them, we need to understand what is really going on. Fortunately, we need not deal with the full range of human experience—after all, we're not trying to recreate human sentience via artificial intelligence—we simply need to know enough about why people do things, to help them along.

The *why* that we are looking for here is not a big existential cry, a "But why?" to the universe. It is a practical, day-to-day sort of why—as in "For what reason did you do these things, in this particular order?" We usually find it fairly easy to verbalize an explanation to this kind of question—from a simple response such as, "that's how I learned to do it, and it works for me" to a more complex one such as, "there were a number of factors involved, x, y and z—once I appreciated that, the most sensible forward was to do a, b and c."

We are used to explaining ourselves in this way—both at work and at home. So the thought processes are generally familiar, and, hence, it should be possible to say something about them.

So, what is the general case? We are talking here about how we *approach* our work, how we decide what to do then organize ourselves to actually carry out, our work. In other words, when given an assignment, or taking on a job, how do we decide how to go about doing it?

How people decide what to do next

We all go through a simple cycle when carrying out work of any kind. Whether the aim is to start a business, design a machine, deal with a customer service request, or repair a leaking tap, there are five stages involved.

Research   Evaluate   Analyze   Constrain   Task

Figure 5: The REACT pattern

Discussing the stages in turn:

1. *Research*—map out the terrain, investigate the principles, talk to those in the know, locate potential threats, and so on, in order to gain *information* from external sources, and turn it into personal *knowledge*. The external sources may be close at hand—members of a "community of practice," for example, as discussed below. Alternatively, information may be acquired from an impartial expert in the field, a textbook, or a search on the Web. The details are different every time, but the principle is the same. Before you can start to work on something, it is only common sense to find out what you are getting yourself into.

2. *Evaluate*—step back and consider the knowledge thus acquired. Internalize it, in a sense, by making connections between different opinions or facts. Once you have discovered the general lay of the land, you then need to familiarize yourself with it. You may need to carefully read a pile of papers on your desk, or to mull over some advice that you don't yet understand. This stage may take minutes or years, but it is crucial—there is no point doing an investigation unless you make an effort to take on board the information you gathered.

3. *Analyze*—on the basis of your new-found understanding, decide on an approach to the problem. In general, the approach you settle on may result partly from applying logic to reduce the problem to more manageable sub-problems—and partly from an intuitive judgment on what feels "right." The balance varies both with the type of problem and with the type of person trying to solve it. However you arrive at a conclusion, though, the decisions made at this stage are not necessarily a final say on the matter—they are simply a way forward for now; enough to let you proceed further with the work in hand. Sometimes it is hard to be sure whether you are doing the right thing, so you might choose a way forward that hedges our bets—following multiple paths at the same time, in the hope that at least one will work—or decide only on the first few steps, and leave decisions about other steps for later. But you have to make some kind of decision at this point, at least on how to start.

4. *Constrain*—divide the work into separate chunks, and organize them. This may be simply a matter of deciding an approximate order to do them in, or it may be a huge task involving all the techniques of project planning: dependency and impact analysis, critical path definition, resource allocation, budgeting, contingency planning, and so on. How-

ever, you are dealing with human-driven processes here—in which people rarely do things in the order laid down, and rightly see it as part of their work to determine how things should proceed. So this stage is not about defining "workflows," in the sense of ordering activities into strict sequence—it is about laying down the *constraints* that govern the chunks of work, insofar as they can be understood at this point. Typically, constraints are of rather vague form: "before you can promise a delivery date for a product, make sure the component suppliers can meet it," or "it is okay in principle to take on contract staff, as long as you've made a reasonable effort to resource the project internally first."

5. *Task*—you have determined how to break the work into chunks, and handed out these chunks to appropriate people (including yourself, perhaps), so now all those concerned can get on with the *tasks* at hand. For a small job there might only be one chunk, and you might do it yourself. For a large one, this stage may involve many different people and organizations working together to deliver a product or service.

This REACT sequence is general in human behavior—it is the way that people respond to an assignment, fulfill a responsibility, achieve a goal—they *react* to the work they take on.

You may not be very convinced by this yet. For one thing, anyone with experience of executive management will immediately look for the feedback loop—how *measurement* is implemented, and how it leads to *improvement*. For example, a common model for working activity found in business literature is the *Plan Do Check Act* (PDCA) model of Stewart and Deming.[17] This was developed to capture industrial production processes, in which process creation and enactment (*Plan* and *Do*, respectively) are separated cleanly from process monitoring and revision (*Check* and *Act*, respectively). The PDCA model is designed specifically to support the provision of a continual feedback loop between process operation and process evolution.

PDCA, and related models of business behavior, have been influential on the development of modern production techniques. However, they make a basic assumption that is inappropriate for human-driven processes—that *process change is not itself part of process operation*. In human interaction work, by contrast, much of the activity is itself concerned with process evolution. In order to deal with this, we need to develop a more general model of work, one that encompasses *both* process enactment *and* process evolution. Moreover, we need also to allow for the mental activities that are not part of any machine-driven process. We will see later on how REACT can be incorporated into higher-level patterns that deal naturally with both process operation and process change.

Another possible objection may be raised by those with experience of project management. Why does the sequence appear to stop only part of the way through? There is no testing here, no monitoring, reviewing, delivery to or acceptance by the customer. The missing activities are basic in our usual approach to certain kinds of industrial processes—manufacturing a car, constructing a building, even delivering a parcel.

In such cases, there is a point at which we consider the process *ended*, and need to check beforehand that all has gone well. If we are prudent, we check continually as we go along, so as to avoid nasty surprises.

However, human-driven processes rarely terminate in this way. For example, modern enterprises are rapidly moving away from the notion of *delivering one or more products* to a customer, toward that of *establishing a relationship*, that includes delivery of many varied products (as well as warranties, maintenance, refunds, and customer care after the sale). The short-term process of *product delivery*, that ends when the customer signals acceptance, is vanishing, to be replaced by a long-term process of *customer service*. This view applies equally to external customers (third parties who buy from an enterprise) and internal customers—staff within one part of an organization who make requests to those in another part.

Such long-term processes generally have no cut-off point. Why should you drop a customer from your database? The only viable reasons, in most cases, are that they die or go out of business. Even then, there are good reasons to keep their details around. And dealing with internal customers is even more of a drawn-out business, with no end in sight. Hence, the notion of "finishing off" a process with "test, review, deliver and accept" is inappropriate—rather, we need to deal with a *continual cycle* of requests from a customer and responses from the supplier.

Moreover, our definition of customer includes, for example, quality assurance teams, as well as the eventual end users of a product. Recognition of a fault by a quality reviewer does not cause the project to enter some new stage, but instead is one of many ongoing stimuli that may cause a new REACT cycle to take place, generally in parallel with, or nested within, various other existing instances of REACT. Our response to a fault discovered by a reviewer may or may not be different than one discovered by a customer—but either way, we apply REACT when dealing with the problem.

The point is that reviewing, testing, and so on are not different from the work itself—they are part of it, and so is the *rework* that's necessary after uncovering a problem. Software engineering, for example, long ago moved away from the "waterfall" approach to project management, where you gradually dropped down from requirements through specification, design, programming and testing to delivery. Modern software development techniques are designed to support a continual process of requirement change, and the corresponding continual, iterative work necessary to update the software itself.

Human work, in general, is like this. Who ever really clears their desk?

As soon as you've dealt with (or filed away) all your current work, another load descends on you—and much of the load is not "new," but related to what was going on before. Work generates more work, and rework is not a separate thing from work itself.

We have to accept that work processes rarely *end*, and see this as a positive thing—after all, it is the key to being successful as an enterprise, and useful as an employee. If your work comes to an end you are no longer needed—redundant, literally. And every enterprise knows that the most profitable business comes from existing clients rather than new ones. It is not satisfied customers that you want; it is *never-satisfied* customers.

In terms of process modeling, this virtuous circle of never-ending work gives us a way to simplify human processes that often seem terrifyingly complex. We can boil them down to REACT activities—repeated again and again throughout a particular human-driven process. Moreover, the repetitions often overlap—as new requirements come in and new circumstances come to light, which may happen at any time.

In fact, REACT is one part of our theory which applies not only to interaction workers, but to just about all human working activity. Whether or not your work is driven by input from other people, you are likely to go through the REACT stages when carrying it out. REACT is more of a *pattern* than a process in the way we normally conceive of it—it is a way of understanding why people do particular things at particular times.

However, there are some useful things we can say about REACT in terms specific to process modeling. In particular, it is "fractal"—each REACT contains lots of little REACTs, the little ones contain yet smaller ones, and so on. Recall that the *Constrain* stage concerns breaking down the work into more easily manageable chunks, which are carried out in the *Task* stage. Each of these chunks is itself a work assignment, and the persons assigned to it will themselves apply the REACT principle in carrying out their work. Hence, the pattern repeats not only at top level, but at lower levels, too—ad infinitum almost, until the stage is reached where a task can be carried out "almost without thinking."

In fact, saying "almost without thinking" may just hide an application of REACT that is so fast and efficient that we cannot see it happening. There is an argument that even when banging in a nail you actually go through the five stages of REACT.

However, applying Occam's razor, let's keep things as simple as possible, and say that sometimes you just *do* things.

It is worth noting at this point how far we have moved away from a conventional approach to process description. For a start, we are now thinking more in terms of *patterns* than of *task sequences*—an approach we will focus on throughout this book, particularly when we come to look at process improvement. Moreover, we are taking an interest in activities such as *Evaluate* and *Analyze*, for which little allowance is provided in typical business analysis, planning, or budgeting.

One reason that these activities may get short shrift is because their outputs are hard to measure—hence, it is hard to know when and how anyone is actually doing them. However, such mental activities represent real and important effort—in a sense, the most important effort made by interaction workers, and a main reason that they were employed in the first place. If we are to improve, and in a sense, *regenerate*, management of human-driven processes, we must give these activities their due—both reward people for them and allocate resource for carrying them out.

At present, people too often end up having to do mental activities in their own time, even to fund them out of their own pockets—how can this be good either for the work they are charged with, for their own attitude toward their work (and consequent job satisfaction), or for effective management? We will return again to this point in a later section of the book, when we discuss how proper understanding and support of human-driven processes can lead to large-scale benefit for the enterprise, and show how improvement can be achieved simply by better understanding *what is actually going on*—whether or not computer support for human-driven processes is implemented.

This latter point is important. If there is a single thing that we are trying to step away from in this book, it is the perspective adopted by many analysts and thinkers in the business processes arena—that of focusing on IT support. To date, most business process languages and systems are based on ideas originally derived from programming—not only in what they cover (such as the emphasis on sequencing tasks in the manner of a computer program), but in *what they leave out.*

In such a framework, the activities *Evaluate* and *Analyze*, if mentioned at all, are generally dismissed as of little interest, since there is no obvious parallel with programming, or way to implement support via Web screens. Moreover, *Constrain* and *Task* are rarely seen as deeply intertwined in a set of ongoing, overlapping, cycles. To the contrary, they are called "process modeling" and "process enactment," and assigned to "managers" and workers" respectively.

As you will have seen by now, we challenge all these views.

There *are* ways to provide support, via computers, for *Evaluate* and *Analyze*, and, in particular, to provide visibility of their progress to management and colleagues, and to support them with the necessary resources (which may simply involve allocating them enough time for the effort). Even if computers are not used to support such activities, it is vital to recognize that the activities are taking place for all sorts of reasons. We will discuss these reasons in greater depth when we look at improving human processes.

Moving on, *Constrain* and *Task* cannot be properly carried out or managed if they are seen as steps in a chronological sequence, carried out by different classes of employee. Recognizing that processes change on a regular basis is not enough when it comes to human activities—after all, human activities are in continual flux, changing all the time, not only in their general nature, but also in a case by case basis, and throughout the life of each case. This may sound daunting to analyze, but it must be possible to work with, because what we are describing is the real world as it exists—in which we generally manage to get our work done, eventually. Hence, we must all have some conception of these principles in mind already, or we wouldn't be able to cope. We just need to transfer the informal ideas we have to a formal system about which we can all agree.

Let's pause for a moment, and recap what we have covered . We have:

- Seen how communication between people and organizations can be structured in terms of a small set of request/response pairs— *request/promise, offer/acceptance,* and *report/acknowledgement*—that can be used to describe the fundamental elements of negotiation.

- Considered the limitations of such "speech acts" with respect to a complete framework for describing human-driven processes—limited emotional range leading to misinterpretation, failure to model action as well as conversation, not allowing for typical communication mechanisms that people use, artificially constraining conversation, and not providing enough understanding to aid analysis for improvement.

- Presented a pattern for human work (REACT) that deals, at least, with the latter of these reservations, by giving us more insight into *why* we structure our activities the way we do.

As we move on, we will discover more about what is going on within the REACT pattern, and how we can fill the remaining gaps in our new approach to describing human-driven processes.

How people find things out

We start by recognizing that the first stage of REACT is unique. The nature of Research is different in kind to that of Evaluate/Analyze/ Constrain/Task, in that the flow of information is largely *inward* to the worker. In all other stages, the individual human worker contributes something of their own (a synthesis, a decision, a plan, some other working activity)— there is information going *outward* from the worker.

Of course, the act of choosing what to research, and how, is in a sense a flow of information *from* the worker—just as, in the other stages, we receive continual input from colleagues and those others with whom we come into contact. Figure 6 is thus simplified for clarity. However, there is a good reason to consider Research as a separate case. Because we are essentially just looking for input, that activity implies different mental processes.

When we engage in research, we put ourselves into a receptive state of mind. We are looking to be influenced, and hoping to receive guidance. In a sense, we are *abdicating responsibility* for the moment—a vital step to take if we are to truly learn from those around us, and from what has gone before.

This is not to say that we somehow act *irresponsibly* when researching, nor that we have forgotten the duties incumbent on us from the work we have taken on. Quite the opposite; it takes more effort and mental resilience to open yourself to new ideas and working practices than to stay with what you know already. Making this effort shows that you are committed to doing the job well, and doing so should be rewarded.

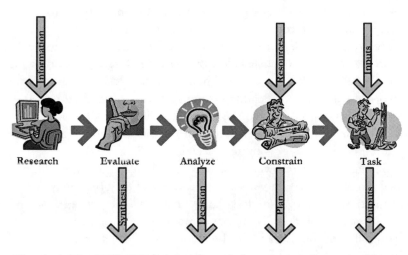

Figure 6: The REACT pattern, extended to show information flows

When you open yourself to outside influence, what you are doing is re-sisting the temptation to rush to judgment, as fools do. You are recognizing that *more haste is less speed,* and—crucially—that you don't know or under-stand everything. For one thing, other people's ideas and experiences have much to offer, and you need to at least make some kind of effort to find out what. For another thing, the situation may not be as simple as it seems.

Suppose, for example, that you are a distributor of domestic heating equipment, and are approached by a building contractor with a large order for radiators. They know exactly what they want, and are prepared to pro-vide the money up front. Surely the sensible thing is to take the cash, dis-patch the goods and move on to the next deal?

Not always. An experienced sales person will start to ask more about the situation before agreeing to supply the goods. Then they will go away and find out for themselves whether or not the goods requested are indeed appropriate. It is possible that the radiators specified by the contractor are the wrong ones, for some reason—too tall, not powerful enough, etc—and it is much better to find this out now than to have an upset customer on the telephone in a month, berating you for being unable to supply new radia-tors in time for them to meet their construction deadline. It may not really be your fault, but it is better to avoid problems than to have to solve them.

But more importantly, learning more about the type of building project, either from colleagues or written reference materials, will reveal other interesting possibilities. Perhaps there is also the opportunity to sell other materials that will be required (details of which perhaps the contractor did not realize), or to demonstrate that your firm has experience valuable enough that you can sell installation or consultancy services along with the goods themselves. Possibly, even, a better solution for all parties would be an expensive under-floor heating system rather than standard-priced radiators— this system might save the contractor time and thus money due to reduced labor costs, increase the value of the properties they are constructing, and result in a bigger contract for you, the supplier.

Sometimes research will involve extended investigation, which may be carried out in conjunction with other people, and the effort may last weeks or months. Suppose you are designing a boat. It is only sensible to compare and contrast existing designs, try out some of these in practice, and familiarize yourself with the demands to be made of your boat and the conditions to be encountered on its voyages. A pleasure yacht for use in the Mediterranean has different design requirements from an Arctic trawler—and, in each case, people have built such vehicles before, so you may as well learn from their experience.

Of course, such research takes time, time in which you could be selling to other people, or getting on with building your boat. It may even directly cost money, if reference materials have to be purchased. So it is always a trade-off. What we need to recognize here is that:

- Research requires placing yourself in a working mode different from other activities—receptive rather than proactive, if you like.

- Research has its own constraints—typically arising from the balance between the resources you are able to invest in it, and estimated future benefits.

- The Research stage is important. Even if you only do it in a cursory way, you should at least nod in the direction of assessing a new territory before you set foot in it.

All this is common sense, yet research as a distinct stage is very often left out when people attempt to analyze *work processes*. We must avoid this mistake, and try instead to deduce what we can about the mechanisms involved, in order to better manage and support real-world work processes.

We are not trying to describe the detailed activities of a professional researcher, but in a general way, we are describing how we each of us makes an effort to find out what is involved in a piece of work we have taken on—how we find out what we feel we really should know in order to carry out the work successfully.

This process—of gaining *information* from external sources, and turning it into personal *knowledge*—may seem very different in different fields. Surely supplying heating equipment is different from designing a boat. Yet all research has some common features that we can model. A useful general model of research can be found in the work of UKOLN: A centre of expertise in digital information management, providing advice and services to the [UK] library, information, education and cultural heritage communities.[18]

In particular, we will make use of the work done by UKOLN on behalf of the UK academic community[19] to help develop an "integrated set of networked services that allow the [UK academic] end-user to discover, access, use and publish digital and physical resources as part of their learning and research activities."[20] UKOLN's analysis of what goes on when an academic seeks information from external sources will guide us to some more general principles.

Note the distinction between digital and physical resources in the quote above. The intention is to distinguish between (say) materials available in a database or on the Internet, and printed books or papers. We need to generalize this, since Research in the sense we mean typically includes, or may even just consist of, talking to other people. However, the simple framework devised by UKOLN provides us with a useful model for any kind of research activity.

We draw, in particular, from the paper by Andy Powell and Liz Lyon on the "DNER Technical Architecture,"[21] that presents a framework capturing the manner in which people go about searching for reference material.[22]

Note that we are *not* concerned here with the technical detail of such searches—the approach we describe could be implemented via any combination of search engines. Remember that we are also interested in human interaction as a means of information discovery. We are trying to get at the *process* by which people locate the information resources they require.

The basis of the approach taken by Powell and Lyon is to appreciate that before you can even start researching, you need a means to do it— some access to *services* that point you at information sources. Such services may be personal—the help of a librarian, for example—or electronic, such as a software application. In either case, you may need authorization to use the services concerned. You may even need to pay, for which funding will be required and need to be justified to your management.

Powell and Lyon then recognize the distinction between information resources themselves and the "collections" in which they reside. For an academic paper, a collection might be a database or Web site. For a commercial product, it might be a printed catalogue. For expert information, it might be the organization where that the expert in question works. Before you can access the information itself, you need to find out where it lives.

Moreover, sometimes knowing the location of the information is enough for the moment. You might only wish to identify the people you will need to consult later on, or to provide project staff with a list of appropriate reference sources.

What we see is an iterative process that moves from initial interaction with DNER services (authenticate and buildLandscape), through discovery of resources (survey, discover), through accessing those resources (detail, request, authorize, access), to their use (useRecord, useResource). It is worth noting that the discovery phase results in the end-user having some metadata about a resource in which they are potentially interested. That metadata record may be an end in itself. For example, if the end-user is a lecturer, he or she may add that record to a course reading list and share it with his or her students. The access phase results in the availability of the resource itself. [23] This process is depicted in Figure 7: High-level DNER process.[24]

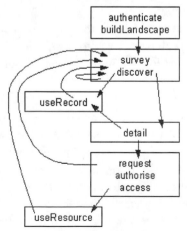

Figure 7: High-level DNER process

We rephrase Powell and Lyon's approach here for convenience, dividing it into three stages (see Figure 8), named as follows:

1. *Access* discovery services. Decide where you will go to obtain information, and obtain any necessary authorization. This might be permission to contact someone, login details for a database, or funds to use some kind of finder agency.

2. *Identify* resources required. From the service(s) above, choose resources likely to be of interest. At this stage, you will have only cursory understanding of their content—what matters is that they seem likely to be useful.

3. *Memorize* [optional] information obtained from particular resources. It is important to focus on committing information to memory, even if the information is only that chapter of a book contains information you will need later on. Unless you have memorized information gathered at this first stage of REACT, it is no use in the following stage, *Evaluate*—you cannot synthesize ideas you have forgotten, or need to look up in order to understand. This stage is all about *internalizing* the ideas in question.

This simple, high-level sequence, AIM (Access, Identify, Memorize) can be used to describe any research activity. Similar to the way we apply REACT to human work in general, we now have a pattern that we can use to structure the particular activities of information discovery.

Moreover, AIM offers clues as to how we can manage, and provide computer support for, the work concerned. In particular, the second stage—Identify—is the hardest to accomplish successfully. In a world full of people and information, how do you know who to spend your time talking to, or what to spend your time reading?

Powell and Lyon propose a computerized solution based on the use of *metadata.* This is *data about data*—overview information that describes briefly the content of a particular information resource, and categorizes that content so as to help you understand what you will gain from studying it. They see three main facilities that metadata can permit:

1. One-off queries,

2. Periodic extraction of all information likely to be of general use, and

3. Enablement of services to proactively let potential users know of updated information resources that may be of interest.

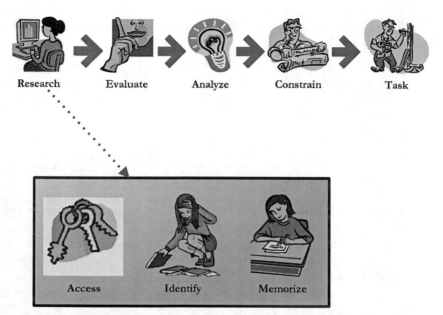

Figure 8: The REACT pattern, extended to show the AIM sub-pattern

In order to allow end users to discover resources across multiple collections offered though multiple content provision services, those services need to expose metadata for machine to machine (m2m) use. Metadata about the available resources needs to be exposed to facilitate searching, harvesting and alerting:

- *Searching* involves sending a query from one service (the client) to another service (the server) with results being returned to the client. This must be done in such a way that both the client and the server share an understanding of what the query means and how results are to be structured.

- *Harvesting* involves regular gathering of metadata from one service (the server) to another (the client). Again, the client and server must share an understanding of how the metadata being harvested is structured.

- *Alerting* is conceptually different from harvesting, in that metadata is pushed from the server to the client. In practice however, alerting mechanisms are typically implemented using a regular (and frequent) harvesting process. [25]

Powell and Lyon go on to discuss possible mechanisms for implementing computer-based support for use of metadata, via the use of portals and what is more generally known as the "semantic Web." [26] We will return to computer support of human activities below, but for now we are concerned more with the general framework. What can the principle of metadata offer us about the human activities of research?

In fact, most information collections make some attempt to provide metadata. Books have indexes; libraries have card catalogs; Web sites have search facilities, or at the very least a guide to their contents. From the point of view of machine interpretation, this is often too unstructured to be of use—a computer program is unlikely to be able to interpret English language text from a Web site. However, we are not dealing with machines here. We are interested in the structure of human processes: human interactions with each other, with machines, and with reference material.

Hence, appreciating that we use "informal metadata" tells us a lot about how human-driven processes operate. Before we request access to a collection, we use information about it to decide whether or not its contents may be of value to us—and this information comes in many different forms.

In particular, we are often as guided by intuitive, emotional responses to information sources as by rational judgment. For example, we may decide which organization to approach for help on the basis of trust—who seems the most respectable, the most established, the most "expert?" Alternatively, we may prefer to use material from a trade publication with a style that conforms to that which we view as our own—whether that style is formal, informal, or conforms to some other criterion.

This analysis tells us that we need to allow for some form of *human-readable metadata* when we model human-driven processes. In other words, our process descriptions must take account of the fact that we all make lists of things we have found, or may in the future find, useful—and these lists are quite separate from the things themselves.

Taking a simple example, one often comes across articles, papers, Web links, or other documents that seem of interest—from an email, perhaps, or in discussion with a colleague. However, it is generally not convenient to read the document immediately. So it would be sensible to make a note of the reference for later use. This could be done, perhaps, via a yellow sticky on your desk, or a shortcut on your computer desktop. The idea is to provide a convenient visual reminder to review the document at some time when you have a few minutes free. The stickies or shortcuts are effectively human-readable metadata.

Such a scheme might work okay after a fashion, but the list is in no way tailored to the different activities of one's daily life. It is just there all the time, without anything to link to a particular working activity (in my case, writing this book, consultancy work, software development, music composition, or some personal task such as booking a family holiday). Moreover, the list tells you nothing about the content of each document, or why you thought it useful in the first place. What is needed is an equally convenient means of storing the links, but a means that locates each link in the context of a specific activity you are engaged in, with some useful metadata attached to remind you why you should bother reading it at all.

Going further, even if one stores the list on a computer (as shortcuts rather than stickies, say) there is no way to use the shortcut list *actively* within a process. Recall the suggestion made by Powell and Lyon that metadata could form the basis of facilities such as *searching, harvesting* and *alerting*. Their proposal is for automated tools that make use of machine-readable metadata, but we can generalize this to human-readable metadata. The activities they describe—looking through a list, collating references to document that seem of interest, forwarding a reference to a colleague—are ones that we all do regularly. Hence, we should take account of these when describing human-driven processes, so as to provide better support for them when managing them and building software to support them.

It *is* possible to use a combination of existing technologies to achieve this aim. For instance, take *harvesting*. Suppose you are a marketer in a team responsible for promoting a new breakfast cereal, and that you know of various new regulations in the food and advertising industries that have direct bearing on the work of the team. Your content management system may allow the creation of links to documents of various forms concerning these regulations, and subsequent export of these links as a list. If so, one could then email the list to a colleague or group of colleagues, perhaps as background reading that you consider essential. But there is no *process context* here. First, creating and sending the list is a laborious procedure requiring manual hooking together of software systems—this should be catered for naturally by software intended, after all, to support collaboration. Second, there is no visibility of this work to management, and no way to know whether the recipients ever used the list, or if they did, whether it was helpful.

Similarly, *alerting* is a typical action taken by project workers. Suppose for example that you are a structural engineer, working in a large team on a new airplane wing. You come across something that may impact the project, and circulate it—perhaps you email a Web link to other designers, referencing a trade journal item that warns of a possible defect in a new material you have all discussed using here and there in the wing. How do you know whether your colleagues have read the item, or if they have, what their opinion is? You cannot even know whether any of them intend to go ahead with use of a possibly dangerous material. Alerting may be part of Research, yet is no less an important *process step* and as such, it must be tracked and responded to.

In both these cases, human-readable metadata is a key element. If you could "mark up" the list of nutrition links as "essential background reading," or the trade journal item as "danger—read now," this would help your colleagues to know how to respond, and prompt your management to track their responses.

You can try to achieve something of this without need for specialized process support, or management understanding. For example, you could simply send an email saying "danger—read now." But we are all drowning in email, and without a process context such an email blends into the background with the other 800 daily messages insisting you read them now, including the time of the fire alarm drill, planned downtime on a server you rarely use, and policy changes with regard to travel expenses. It is necessary to ensure that such a message is received as *part of a particular work process*, so that you can immediately understand its relevance, deal with it as part of your work rather than an interruption to it, make a response that is logged as part of the process by the system, and allow your manager to track the issue automatically.

In many cases, it would be possible to use machine-readable metadata to do this. You could create levels of "severity," for instance, that dictated how the recipients should process the messages received. In the example above, the "danger—read now" message could be used in a process support system to prevent any other activity by each project worker until the news item had been read. This would be a further enhancement, but is not a *necessary* one—if we can't trust people to respond to messages appropriately, why are we employing them?

The key thing for which we need a process context is to ensure that:

- The recipients get some form of message that *tells them how to respond*, rather than just another set of Web links with no supporting information to explain why they are important.

- *Responses made by the recipients are tracked* and form part of the ongoing process.

We will return later to the AIM pattern and associated techniques—human-readable metadata, searching, harvesting and alerting—when we consider how to model human-driven processes at a high level, and will discuss various gains that it brings both to management and to computerized support of human activity. For now, though, we have gained enough understanding of Research to move on to the rest of the REACT pattern.

Once we have found the information we seek (Research), what do we do with it? We internalize it as knowledge (Evaluate) and use it to make decisions and solve problems (Analyze, Constrain, Task). What can we say about these latter activities? Are there general properties of human thought, as applied to work assignments, that give us a basis for describing them methodically?

Our aim is to manage them better, and possibly facilitate them with software. So what we are looking for is some structure, or pattern, to the way we think about carrying out the work we are charged with—the way we decide what to do, then work out how to do it. If we can find such a framework, we have a way forward.

How people work things out

As you might expect, there is a long tradition of research into human decision-making and problem-solving activity, known generally as *cognitive theory*. This has essentially had three stages. We discuss each stage here in chronological turn, since following the development of ideas will help to clarify the elements of day-to-day human work that we are looking for.

The first approach to cognitive theory was the *information processing* approach. This treats human reasoning as akin to the operation of a computer program, in that both are complex systems based on the manipulation of abstract symbols.[27] In organizational terms, problem-solving at work is analyzed in terms of search processes that select an appropriate "program" from an organization-wide repository of techniques.

The information processing approach gave rise to some useful Artificial Intelligence techniques.[28] However, the approach was never really appropriate to describe human thought. Tempting as it is to frame parallels between the human brain and a computer, and whatever aspects these two systems may have in common, it is simply not realistic to suppose that we go about our work in the same way that a computer executes a stored program—following pre-scripted instructions line by line. Even when we try to stick to fixed procedures, events conspire to lead us off the path—and if you are unable to cope with this, you will almost inevitably fail in your job.

Ask any hardware maintenance engineer, project manager, or sales person whether they follow the rule book to the letter when taking on a new assignment. A particular individual, if they are minded to do so, may try to stick to the rules whenever possible—but if you want to make things go well, you have to adapt to the circumstances you encounter. This is so instinctive to human nature that most of the time people do not even realize they are doing it—cutting corners, cannibalizing old work for use in a different situation, and adding in tweaks here and there as required. People make continual adjustments, mostly but not always minor, to keep things running smoothly. Accepting this naturally leads to the question: how does a person know what adjustments to make? Saying "experience" is to give part of the answer, but on its own this does not tell us enough. How does someone gain, retain, and know when to use this experience?

Enter a second approach to cognitive theory: the *situated action* approach. This remedies a major deficiency in the information processing approach—that is, failing to take account of *context*.

Experimental evidence shows that problem-solving behavior varies widely depending on the environment in which it is carried out. As a result, researchers inspired by sociological theory developed the principle that personal knowledge and problem-solving are closely tied up with both your inter-relations with others and the "artefacts" that you use—the tools of your trade, as found in your specific working environment.

In organizational terms, this led to the notion of a *community of practice*—a group of people bound together by informal relations, who share a work pattern and work place. Around these the group naturally develops certain common mental constructs: language, understanding of their work context, and meanings attached to tools. These shared ideas are rarely made explicit, but learned on the job by newcomers as they observe more experienced people, and are used in group problem-solving via the telling of "stories" that draw on accumulated wisdom to seek parallels with newly-encountered situations.[29]

These are powerful ideas, and have had major impact on the way we understand organizations. In particular, many of the sophisticated knowledge management and groupware tools currently in commercial use were originally developed to support the sharing of stories as described above, and to aid with their application to problem-solving.

However, such tools have limitations, particularly with respect to our goal here—of modeling work formally as a *process*. For a start, groupware and knowledge management encourage informal relationships between collaborators. This is worthy, but has the unfortunate side-effect of limiting efficiency gains possible through better management of the work. Moreover, we need to impose structure for a further reason—in order to understand the inter-relationship between work carried out locally and more general patterns of behavior.

Examples of general behavior patterns are those regulated by trade organizations, documented in educational and training material, mandated by institutional policy, accepted by society, and regulated by government. Organizations are moving all the time toward *standardization*—both internally, as they strive for better quality practices, and across specific industries via common trading standards. The latter trend is evident particularly in the move in some sectors toward individual companies structuring their own processes around standard industry frameworks.[30]

There is a general principle at work here. These recent business initiatives actually derive from deep-seated human behavior patterns. As Wenger writes in *Communities of Practice: Learning, Meaning and Identity*:

> "What transpires is that knowing is defined only in the context of specific practices, where it arises out of the combination of a regime of competence and an experience of meaning. Our knowing—even of the most unexceptional kind—is always too big, too rich, too ancient, and too connected for us to be the source of it individually. At the same time, our knowing—even of the most elevated kind—is too engaged, too precise, too tailored, too active, and too experiential for it to be just of a generic size."[31]

Without taking into account a wider, standardized notion of process, we cannot properly address the *institutionalization* of human-driven processes. It is the search for institutionalization that has driven most process improvement initiatives (e.g., Six Sigma and the Capability Maturity Model).

Institutionalization must also concern us if we are to better support and manage human-driven processes.

We find some answers in the third and most recent approach to cognitive theory: the *socio-historical approach*. This attempts to tie together local context with wider cultural and institutional norms.

Drawing from psychology, a key idea is that human cognitive processes are mediated not only by the physical tools we use (writing materials, computers, and so on) but also by language and external symbolic representations such as books, training manuals, diagrammatic representations of procedures, and so on.

Another important notion is that of the *zone of proximal development*. This describes the way we learn to accomplish tasks as first to copy others in their use of tools without understanding, then, as we come to understand the reasons for the learned behavior, to internalize the procedure, often to the point where we find it hard to explain verbally. The longer term transmission of knowledge is "crystallized and saved in the physical and conceptual tools of the trade and in the social organization of work."[32]

From our point of view, the socio-historical approach offers a way forward in our quest for supporting human-driven processes. Lorenz summarizes it as follows:

"The historical-cultural approach to cognition implies that the routinised and problem-solving behaviors of organizational members are emergent features of their interaction in carrying out distributed tasks with the help of external and internal mediating devices ... Meanings are not given by the language of the text but rather come about through the task performer's experience in carrying out the task, which involves coordinating the mediating artifact with the task environment. For this reason, language and verbal texts rather than being thought of as instances of codified knowledge are better thought of as coordinating tools used in task performance ... mediating devices typically set up constraints that serve to control behavior indirectly by allowing the actor to evaluate his or her behavior and to judge whether or not it is appropriate."[33]

In other words, tools not only determine the behavior of those who use them, but are the medium for implementing social and institutional norms. So we need to focus on tools—by which we mean not only computerized process support, but *any aids given to the worker*. By this, we include reference material, support from management, interactions with colleagues, and access to resources of various domain-specific kinds.

However, the tools we require must neither offer a set of predetermined steps to follow (as would be suggested by the information processing approach to problem-solving), nor be devoid of meaning (as implied by situated learning theory, that suggests that meaning is held only in shared human understanding). The tools must capture common assumptions and practices, and act as a kind of Jiminy Cricket for those who use them—issuing prompts and gentle reminders when required, warning of potentially dangerous or unacceptable behavior, easing communication between the parties in a process, and providing short cuts where possible.

Hence, our description of process—our process modeling—should assume we require only *advice* on what to do, and that we only wish management (whether human, or implemented via a computerized process support system) to step in when some important code of conduct has been violated. Corresponding Human Interaction Management Systems must support and enforce control on behalf of the organization, while facilitating human work by providing the resources necessary for the people concerned to carry out their tasks as they see fit.

Moreover, to allow for inevitable adjustments to circumstances, the process description system must be flexible enough to allow each person carrying out a process to do it differently—differently, not only from their peers, but also from the last time they did it themselves. It must even be possible to change the process as you go along.

Having said this, we still want to make the most of any computer support available. Hence, it must be possible to specify how various activities are to be facilitated when they are chosen, including optional automation of the details. Often, for instance, there are simple sequences of activity that we carry out regularly in a fixed order, such as adding a document back to the knowledge management system after updating it. This might involve a repetitive set of steps that human-driven process support can automate on our behalf.

Putting it all together

To conclude and summarize this chapter:

- We see value in using speech acts to *categorize* certain interactions between process participants, but not to *frame* entire processes. As discussed, speech acts do not allow much of what goes on in human work to be described or supported effectively.

- In contrast, we analyze processes in terms of a *cyclic, nested, fractal* pattern REACT (Research, Evaluate, Analyze, Constrain, Task). This pattern includes activities often considered to have little or no measurable external output—we make the point that it is nonetheless vital to describe and support such activities.

- We identify a sub-pattern AIM (Access, Identify, Memorize) of the Research stage. We go on to discuss the nature of what we might call *human-readable metadata*, and its possible uses (such as for *searching, harvesting* and *alerting*).

- We understand that the subsequent stages of REACT are heavily dependent on tool support, where by *tools* we include not only computerized support, but also aids in the widest sense, including management support and other human interaction. It is the tools that provide the means for individual and workgroup practices and knowledge to integrate with more widely accepted standards of behavior.

- Bearing in mind the unpredictable and dynamic nature of human activities and interactions, we propose that the most effective approach to describing human-driven processes, and thus supporting them with tools, is *suggestive* rather than *prescriptive*, offering guidance and warning, rather than machine-like predetermination of task sequences and data structures, with high-level control and regulation provided to keep things on the straight and narrow. This moves us away from conventional process modeling techniques (that have a heritage in computer programming and are hence biased toward sequencing tasks in a pre-determined fashion) toward a framework for process description based on *enablement, interaction* and *dynamism*.

To date, the main attempt to capture and support human interactions formally in the business world has been via use of speech acts alone, in isolation from other process modeling techniques. We have discussed the deficiencies of this approach above, and we conclude by noting how the approach to process understanding and support developed in this chapter remedies these deficiencies:

1. Deficiency of Speech Acts alone: *Turning a process from a collaborative activity into a dictatorial one.* With a process support system that *suggests* actions

rather than *prescribing* them, it will be possible to put in place a genuinely co-operative framework for interactions. Later on we'll see how it is possible to place a high-level structure on human interaction that is based on the notion of agreements on *how the process will work from now on*, rather than on one party committing to supply specific deliverables.

2. Deficiency of Speech Acts alone: *Allowing only for communication and not for action.* Guided again by the insights of cognitive theory, we focus on tool support—by which we mean all forms of aid to the worker, not just those that are computerized—rather than on interaction alone. Hence, we are able to describe, manage and facilitate *tasks* as well as *conversations*.

3. Deficiency of Speech Acts alone: *Assuming all communication is direct.* Our approach to interaction is to recognize that it is it is not the framework into which the entire process must fit, but dynamic behavior inspired by process needs at the time. In other words, we do not equate the process with a particular pattern of interaction. This might be necessary for machine interactions, but is unnatural for human ones, in which people have an intuitive ability to interpret the actions of others. We need to take indirect communication into account, and we will see later how an awareness of the process as a whole in its current incarnation can help both to facilitate indirect communication and to clear up the problems that indirect communications sometimes cause.

4. Deficiency of Speech Acts alone: *Preventing tangential discussion.* Our process descriptions are essentially the *basis* for behavior, not its entirety. We neither prevent arbitrary discussion, nor deny its importance. On the contrary, any process support system we put in place will allow unexpected interactions to influence the process itself in any way that the participants and their management see fit.

5. Deficiency of Speech Acts alone: *Describing processes rather than understanding them.* We start from *the inner structural patterns of a process* (in terms of REACT, and within its first stage, AIM), not from its external manifestation in terms of particular communications. Conversations are often nothing more than the outward and transient means by which an underlying pattern of behavior is implemented. It is the underlying patterns that we need to understand, describe and support.

In the next chapter we take these principles, and seek the *building blocks* required to capture them—the basis of a description language. We will show how we can provide the basis for human-driven process modeling via a new interpretation of, and certain extensions made to, the framework known as Role Activity Theory. This will give us the means we require to provide *suggestive rather than prescriptive* process description and support.

This is not all we will need, however. In a subsequent section we will move on to show how to use this "new theory of Roles" to describe human-driven processes in their entirety. In other words, modeling constructs are not enough—we also need *higher-level notions of what happens in a human-driven process*, how you can manage it, and a standardized way to describe these notions in Role terms. From this we will gain a means of integrating speech acts with the REACT pattern and its AIM sub-pattern, and show how this integration gives us a means for controlling process evolution.

But first things first. Our next step is to determine the fundamental constructs of human-driven processes. We will see that these can be found in a set of ideas that originated in the early 1980s—with a few new ones stirred into the mix here and there.

References.

[1] The reader interested in discovering more about autopoeitic theory would do well to start at Randall Whitaker's Web site http://www.enolagaia.com, which includes tutorials as well as links to further material. Whitaker also gives an overview of the application of autopoeitic theory to social systems at http://www.acm.org/sigs/sigois/auto/AT&Soc.html.

[2] *An observer is a ... living system who can make distinctions and specify that which he or she distinguishes as a unity, as an entity different from himself or herself that can be used for manipulations or descriptions in interactions with other observers.*
Maturana, H.R., "Cognition," 1978, in Hejl, Köck, and Roth (eds.), "Wahrnehmung und Kommunikation," Frankfurt: Lang, p. 31

[3] *Cognition is a biological phenomenon and can only be understood as such; any epistemological insight into the domain of knowledge requires this understanding.*
Maturana, H.R., "Biology of Cognition," 1970, Biological Computer Laboratory Research Report BCL 9.0., Urbana IL: Univ. of Illinois

[4] *The relations that define a machine as a unity, and determine the dynamics of interactions and transformations which it may undergo as such a unity, constitute the organization of the machine.*Maturana, H.R., Varela, F.J., "Autopoiesis and Cognition: The Realization of the Living," 1980, Boston Studies in the Philosophy of Science [Cohen, Robert S., and Marx W. Wartofsky (eds.)], Vol. 42, Dordecht: D. Reidel Pub. Co., p. 77

[5] *An autopoietic system is organized (defined as a unity) as a network of processes of production (transformation and destruction) of components that produces the components that:*
(i) through their interactions and transformations continuously regenerate and realize the network of processes (relations) that produced them; and
(ii) constitute it (the machine) as a concrete unity in the space in which they [the components] exist by specifying the topological domain of its realization as such a network.
Varela, F.J., 1979, "Principles of Biological Autonomy," New York: Elsevier (North Holland), p. 13

[6] and the related notion of *organizational closure*

[7] [Autonomous systems are] ...*defined as a composite unity by a network of interactions of components that through their interactions recursively regenerate the network of interactions that produced them, and realize the network as a unity in the space in which the components exist by constituting and specifying the unity's boundaries as a cleavage from the background...*
Varela, F.J., "Autonomy and autopoiesis," 1981, in Roth, Gerhard, and Helmut Schwegler (eds.) "Self-organizing Systems: An Interdisciplinary Approach," Frankfurt/New York: Campus Verlag, pp. 15.
[Systems exhibit organizational closure if...] ...their organization is characterized by processes such that the processes are related as a network, so that they recursively depend on each other in the generation and realization of the processes themselves, and they constitute the system as a unity recognizable in the space (domain) in which the processes exist.
Varela, F.J., 1979, ibid., p.55

[8] This is expressed via the principle of *structural determination*:
The organization and structure of a structure-determined system ... continuously determine:
(a) the domain of states of the system, by specifying the states that it may adopt in the course of its internal dynamics or as a result of its interactions;
(b) its domain of perturbations, by specifying the matching configurations of properties of the medium that may perturb it; and
(c) its domain of disintegration, by specifying all the configurations of properties of the medium that may trigger its disintegration.
Maturana, H.R., 1978, "Biology of language: The epistemology of reality," in Miller, George A., and Elizabeth Lenneberg (eds.), "Psychology and Biology of Language and Thought: Essays in Honor of Eric Lenneberg," New York: Academic Press, p. 34

[9] Interaction between systems is effectively ...a history of recurrent interactions leading to the structural congruence between two (or more) systems.
Maturana, H.R., Varela, F.J., 1987, "The Tree of Knowledge: The Biological

Roots of Human Understanding," Boston: Shambhala / New Science Pr., p. 75

[10] So long as language is considered to be denotative it will be necessary to look at it as a means for the transmission of information, as if something were transmitted from organism to organism, in a manner such that the domain of uncertainties of the 'receiver' should be reduced according to the specifications of the 'sender'. However, when it is recognized that language is connotative and not denotative, and that its function is to orient the orientee within his cognitive domain without regard for the cognitive domain of the orienter, it becomes apparent that there is no transmission of information through language. It behooves the orientee, as a result of an independent internal operation upon his own state, to choose where to orient his cognitive domain; the choice is caused by the 'message', but the orientation thus produced is independent of what the 'message' represents for the orienter. In a strict sense then, there is no transfer of thought from the speaker to his interlocutor; the listener creates information by reducing his uncertainty through his interactions in his cognitive domain.
Maturana, H.R., 1970, ibid

[11] The Coordinator was designed to give workers a channel for communications specifically tailored to the generation, negotiation, and tracking of 'commitments' for action. Messages were structured in accordance with Winograd and Flores' 'conversation for action' model and John Searle's formalization of the British philosopher John Austin's theory of 'speech acts'. In addition to facilitating operational coordination, use of The Coordinator was intended to promote enterprise learning: 'People's conscious knowledge of their participation in the network of commitment can be reinforced and developed, improving their capacity to act in the domain of language.'
http://www.acm.org/sigs/sigois/auto/AT&Soc.html

[12] Diagram based on fig. 5.1 in Winograd & Flores, 1986, "Understanding Computers and Cognition," Ablex, Norwood, NJ, p. 65

[13] The Coordinator, from Action Technologies

[14] Armenise, P. and Dottarelli, R., 1991, "Experimenting with a Language/Action Perspective based tool in the software process.," Proceedings of the 1st European Workshop on Software Process Modeling, 53-58

[15] Searle, J.R., 1969, "Speech Acts," Cambridge University Press, Cambridge.

[16] "a confusion between imperatives and regulatives in speech act theory, carried through into CfA analysis, has produced an unbalanced model of interaction which overemphasizes the role of the initiator of the interaction and underemphasizes the role of the partner at the other end ... the overemphasis on direc-

tives and assertives reflects a fundamental error common across the fields of business modeling and systems analysis, namely a systematic overplay of direction and management at the expense of agreement and interpretation—an idea that once decisions are made and instructions are given their meanings are clear and uncontestable and their execution unproblematic. Whereas the real achievement of organizations lies in their ability to carry out complex tasks intelligently even though meanings and priorities shift continuously and execution and operation present constant challenges …A reconstruction of the CfA approach is called for which would take it toward a more general exchange model, and root it more truly in a participative model of organizations." What seems to be needed, to gain benefit from a CfA type of analysis in alliance with RAD modeling, is a more general theory and model of exchange, which incorporates the insights of speech act theory but in which communication is generalized toward cooperation and which perhaps can encompass actions as well as communications about action."
Beeson, I., Green, S., 2003, "Using A Language Action Framework To Extend Organizational Process Modeling"

[17] See, for example, http://www.balancedscorecard.org/bkgd/pdca.html

[18] See http://www.ukoln.ac.uk/

[19] Much of the work described here was funded by the *Joint Information Systems Committee:* The Joint Information Systems Committee (JISC) supports further and higher education by providing strategic guidance, advice and opportunities to use Information and Communications Technology (ICT) to support teaching, learning, research and administration (http://www.jisc.ac.uk)

[20] http://www.ukoln.ac.uk/distributed-systems/jisc-ie/arch/

[21] Powell, A., Lyon, L., 2001, "The DNER Technical Architecture: scoping the information environment," UKOLN, University of Bath, http://www.ukoln.ac.uk/distributed-systems/jisc-ie/arch/dner-arch.pdf

[22] *The Distributed National Electronic Resource (DNER) … is a managed information environment for accessing quality assured Internet resources from many sources.*
Powell, A., Lyon, L., 2001, ibid.

[23] Powell, A., Lyon, L., 2001, ibid.

[24] Powell, A., Lyon, L., 2001, ibid.

[25] Powell, A., Lyon, L., 2001, ibid.

[26] Portals are able to gather metadata records from remote content providers using the Open Archives Protocol for Metadata Harvesting … This allows them to

build local databases that contain copies of the records provided by remote content providers. The OAI protocol provides a mechanism for sharing metadata records between services. Based on HTTP and XML, the protocol is very simple, allowing a client to ask a repository for all of its records or for a sub-set of all its records based on a date range. There is no search facility within the OAI protocol. By default, the exchanged records conform to Dublin Core. However, it is possible to define richer record syntaxes if necessary. As in the case of searching, the portal will obtain protocol-specific details of available OAI repositories from the service description service. It is also likely that we will see OAI aggregator services becoming available. Such services will aggregate metadata records from several repositories, making them available for harvesting by others. Finally, portals will be alerted to new resources using RDF Site Summary (RSS) ... RSS is a Resource Description Framework (RDF) ... application for syndicated news feeds on the Web. News items are described using Dublin Core-based descriptions and then exchanged as RDF/XML files. Although originally developed for 'traditional' news content, press-releases and the like, RSS can be used to exchange metadata about any frequently updated material. Again, RSS does not provide any mechanism for querying a remote service. It simply provides a mechanism for regularly gathering an RSS 'channel' from a content provider to the portal. Powell, A., Lyon, L., 2001, ibid.

[27] See, for instance, Newell, A. and Simon, H. ; 1976, "Computer Science as Empirical Enquiry: Symbol and Search," Communications of the AMC, 19 (3)

[28] In particular, the *connectionist* theory (in which knowledge is represented by a network of parallel processes storing relations between inputs and outputs) was a direct input to the development of neural nets, which have been able to handle previously intractable problems such as face recognition.

[29] See, for instance, Brown, J.S., Collins, A. and Duguid, P. ; 1989, 'Situated Cognition and the Culture of Learning', Education Researcher, 18, 32-42

[30] For example, the Supply Chain Council's SCOR (Supply Chain Operations Reference) and the TeleManagement Forum's eTOM (e-business Telecom Operations Model).

[31] Wenger, E. ; 1998a, Communities of Practice: Learning, Meaning and Identity, Cambridge University Press, Cambridge

[32] Hutchins, E. ; 1995, Cognition in the Wild, MIT Press, Cambridge, MA

[33] Lorenz, E., 2001, "Models of Cognition, the Contextualisation of Knowledge and Organizational Theory"

Three

A New Theory Of Roles

KEY POINTS: In this chapter, we introduce the Role Activity Diagram notation that we will use as building blocks in our approach to modeling human-driven processes. No familiarity with the technique is necessary in order to follow the discussion, which shows how the six standard object types (*Roles, Resources, Activities, Users, States* and *Interactions*) are the basic components of everyday collaborative activity.

Our use of Role Activity Diagrams involves making several changes to the standard use of the notation—and we propose that our altered notation is adopted in place of the standard usage, at least for the modelling of human-driven processes. Our changes involve a new interpretation of how to understand the diagrams, as well as of certain particular symbols. In general, we make enhancements and extensions in the following areas:

- *Process participation.* To model human-driven processes effectively enough to support improvement, we need to understand better the nature of people, organizations, and machines as process participants. In particular, we must be able to characterize the Roles in a process, and the Users that play them, by adding various attributes not found in the standard notation. We also require a better technique for modeling relationships—both on a personal basis as Users, and within a process context as Roles.

- *Process management under process control.* You must be able to use a Role to define, start, stop, monitor, and generally manage processes and their associated users. This requires that we support the definition of process objects of all forms as information resources within Roles, and allow them to be passed from one Role to another via interactions.

- *Activity enablement and validation.* Humans typically jump from one activity to another, repeating and interleaving activities as they see fit. If we are to facilitate people's work rather than constrain it unnaturally—and if we expect to gain acceptance for any process support system we attempt to implement—we must support this behavior, while simultaneously permitting appropriate controls to be placed on the process. This leads us toward an approach to process definition based on the use of logical conditions that enable and validate both activities and Roles—and this leads us away from process modeling based on sequencing of tasks (as is usual).

- *Activities are not atomic, but composed of multiple lower-level tasks.* It is a modeling issue whether or not to expose a particular task on a Role Activity Diagram as a fully-fledged activity, but there are some simple principles that can be applied. For example, tasks are often unpredictably repeated and interleaved, to the point where it would be hard to find a typical order to draw them in if shown separately. Unless some logical and standardized dependencies can be found for the tasks, they may as well be grouped together inside a single activity.

- *Interactions are not generally synchronous.* A closer match to real life is to view them as formed of multiple channels for sending and receiving resources, where each channel has a sender and one or more recipients. A sender may donate an item into a channel when they are ready, and recipients may take it out in their own time.

All the world's a stage,
And all the men and women merely players.
They have their exits and their entrances,
And one man in his time plays many parts
—Shakespeare, "As You Like It" (II, vii, 139-142).

Show and tell

In this chapter we will define our terms—give names to the fundamental building blocks needed to describe human-driven processes. This alone is not enough to fully support the requirements outlined in the last section, such as the REACT pattern. For that we will need to construct higher-level approaches to process modeling, such as *separation of control* and *agreements* among process participants, and we will provide these higher-level approaches in a later section of the book. For now, we start with first principles, and seek some way to break down the complex web of human activity discussed so far into simple atomic elements suitable for describing human-driven processes.

The main trick in doing this is to know where to start—what to choose as our *first* building block, since we hope that the others will then follow naturally. Should we start by looking at the *tasks* people carry out? At the *information* they use and generate? At the *access permissions and approval rights* they have? At the *interactions* they have with each other? At the *deliverables* they produce?

We need all these concepts somewhere in our framework. And they are the *foundation* of most notations for process description. However, our interest is in human-driven processes, and most process description techniques fall down in this area. For instance, Coplien and Harrison write, after 10 years research into working practices within software development organizations:

> "... the core processes of architecture, design, implementation and validation are poorly understood from a task perspective. We have found that task ordering changes rapidly in a high-technology development organization, so it can't be counted on as a stable component of process structure. One large organization we studied surveyed its developers and found that 80% of them were working under officially granted process waivers instead of the official common process, largely because the project's process standard didn't capture the essential, stable structure of the process."[1]

Software development is typical of the kinds of activity we are concerned with—human-driven, team based, and adaptive. It *is* possible to describe such activity in process terms, but the conventional starting points for process modeling are unhelpful. So, where should we start?

By our definition of human-driven processes—as concerned with interaction work, rather than independent work—their fundamental nature is *collaborative*. What is the most basic aspect of human collaboration? When we agree to join a team, project, committee, or organization, what is the first question that any of us naturally asks? Apart, that is, from "How much will I get paid?"

There is a simple and universal question that enables us to understand at least in outline what we are letting ourselves in for, and to make an initial assessment of whether or not we wish (or are qualified) to get involved. Above and before all else, we need to know, "What is my *Role* in the proceedings?"

Each of us understands at a deep level that any collaborative activity— whether it is a supply chain, a marketing program, or a mammoth hunt—is based on the division of the participants into Roles. Roles tell us such basic things as who signs the checks, who approves the final deliverables, who gets to throw the spears (or catch them)—and who is to blame if it all goes down the spout.

In business life, process Roles may be played by individuals or by organizations—even sometimes by machines. In other words, there are different types of actors, or *Users*, that play, or take on, Roles. This means that, in practice, some Roles are carried out in a different way from others—shared between people inside an organization, for example, or composed largely of automated tasks. However, this makes no difference to our instinctive perception of the process. We still locate ourselves in a collaborative activity by identifying our own Role(s) in the proceedings, and those of the others we are working with, whatever their nature.

So, what exactly do we get from knowing our own Role, and knowing about the other Roles in a process? Various important pieces of information include:

- A means of partitioning the work into separate *groups of activity*
- An understanding of each participant's individual *goals*, which may be different from the shared goals of the process as a whole (if such shared goals exist at all)
- A way of subdividing *responsibility* within the process, so that everyone knows who is taking care of what
- A guide to *who knows what* about the different things going on—where the information lies within the process
- *Who we can talk to*—for reporting, access to information, requests for resources, delivery of outputs, and so on

Imagine, for example, that you are engaged by a government agency to help in an investigation into cost reduction. Before you can start work, you need to know with whom you will be working, what you will do as opposed to what they will do, what is expected of you in terms of deliverables, where to go for the information you need, and so on. All this is very different if you are the *Project Manager*, as opposed to a *Business Analyst*, as opposed to an *Accountant*.

Of course, knowing that you are the Project Manager (say) does not by itself give you all the information you need. The name of a Role is not enough—it must be fleshed out with the details of how that Role is to op-

erate, and how it collaborates with the others around it. But without knowing your Role, you cannot even get started—and knowing your Role at least
gives you a basic idea of what will be expected from you.

Hence, we will take as our starting point for analysis of human-driven
processes the division of a process into Roles. We will then see how we can
add a small number of other concepts that, taken together, give us all we
need to "model" human-driven processes—that is, to build *formal descriptions*
of processes that allow shared understanding by participants, and effective
management by the organizations concerned. The process models we construct in this way will not only be intuitive—relating directly to people's
instinctive understanding of what is going on—but powerful enough to
allow computerized support, if we so wish.

However, before we start adding concepts to our basic ones, of Role
and User, we need a way of *visualizing* processes. Without some kind of
mental image of what is going on in a process, we will find it hard to grasp
it in overview—to picture the shape of things. We need a simple diagramming technique for process depiction.

We will present this diagramming technique before explaining in full
the different elements of our modeling framework, since it will help the
reader to relate the concepts to one another. Not all the concepts we introduce for process modeling are included in the notation, but that doesn't
matter—all we seek from the graphical notation is an informal aid in grasp-
ing the general outline of a process. Where the graphical notation lacks necessary detail, we will find other ways to supplement the model.

Our aid to visualization of processes is based on a notation for process
depiction called *Role Activity Diagrams* (RADs).

Role Activity Diagrams are an established approach to business analysis, originating from work carried out in the USA during the early 1980s,[2]
taken up by the UK government-sponsored IPSE2.5 project during the late
1980s,[3] and used fairly widely by Business Process Reengineering analysts
during the mid-1990s. However, for lack of tool support from major vendors, Role Activity Diagrams never made it into the commercial mainstream of business analysis, and are currently a niche approach used mainly
by academics.

This situation is viewed by those familiar with Role Activity Diagrams
as a pity, since the main alternatives adopted for process description are
software design techniques, and hence not really suitable for business-level
description of activity. Not only are software design techniques confusing

for business people to read, but they force the user into a process modeling approach that is biased toward providing IT support, rather than toward describing human behavior.[4]

Role Activity Diagrams, on the other hand, are not intended for describing software—they show how people work together to accomplish their individual and shared goals. The notation originally arose from a study of collaborative work carried out at the US telecommunications firm ITT during the early 1980s, that looked at how people work together to build software. It turned out that the principles developed could be applied to any sort of coordinated human activity.

As a result, Role Activity Diagrams have been found useful as a means of documenting all forms of organizational procedure, in a way that anyone can understand—whether or not they have an IT background, and regardless of where they work in the organization. Most people can learn to read the notation in a minute or two. The meaning of most Role Activity Diagrams is generally clear almost immediately, whether or not you have an interest or any training in business analysis—something that makes them very suitable for our purposes here.

However, despite their advantages, there are good reasons why Role Activity Diagrams in their standard form haven't acquired widespread tool support, and hence remained a niche approach. We will see that the original notation requires extensions and enhancements of various kinds in order to provide the foundation we need for process support. We will discuss and highlight these alterations as we take a tour around the notation. For now, it is enough to say that the notation, as it is currently used, *appears* to provide an effective means for depicting processes—but the processes thus shown bear only indirect relationship to reality. We will retain, and even enhance, the ease of use inherent in the notation, while adapting the notation to provide it with a stronger formal basis.

In particular, Role Activity Diagrams, in their current form, could not be completely supported by a computer system, which is part of the reason why tool support has been lacking. In order to actually build a Human Interaction Management System, for instance, some of the alterations made to the standard notation were *necessary* as well as desirable. Hence, we propose that the altered Role Activity Diagram notation described in this book is adopted in place of the standard usage, at least for the modelling of human-driven processes.

With regard to the standard notation, there have been two main reference books published on Role Activity Diagrams, both by people who played a significant role in the IPSE2.5 project. The first book was published in 1995 by business consultant Martyn Ould,[5] then still of Praxis Systems plc, and the second in 1999 by Professor Brian Warboys and his team at the University of Manchester *Informatics Process Group*.[6] The first book, by Ould, is based directly on Role Activity Diagrams, and was the main influence on business analysts who chose to take up the notation for use in re-engineering. The later book, by Warboys et al, is a more general discussion encompassing wider issues of organizational theory and information system design. However, both books describe the same notational conventions.

We will present only a subset of these conventions here, because we do not need them all for the purposes of this book. As we will see, even though it was intended originally for describing human collaboration, the Role Activity Diagram notation to date has been used with mechanistic processes in mind. Hence, over the years people have extended the original notation with symbols that are too precise—too specific about *what happens when*—for use in the description of human-driven processes. We need to allow more flexibility, which means that much of the now-standard notation is not necessary for our purposes. Moreover, we will change some basic assumptions about the meaning of certain symbols, and these changes will make some other symbols obsolete.

Hence, we will take from the Role Activity Diagram notation what we need, changing it as necessary here and there, and leave out much of the standard symbol palette. For the purposes of this book, this has an incidental advantage of making a background in business analysis unnecessary. The notation we will use is small enough that this book is still suited to a readership with a general interest in better organizational management, not just in process modeling per se.

A sample Role Activity Diagram is shown in Figure 9: Example Role Activity Diagram
(fragment of an Engineering Design process).

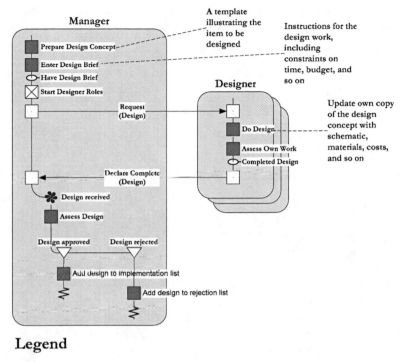

Figure 9: Example Role Activity Diagram
(fragment of an Engineering Design process)

This figure represents a dummy process in the engineering design domain. It depicts a manager constructing a design concept and brief, assigning some designers to the work, passing each one the same brief, receiving back the completed designs, then approving/rejecting each design for further processing. The diagram omits any interactions between designers, as well as the actions to be taken on approval/rejection. However, it includes the main notational elements we will need, of which there are only a few.

Although the figure includes a legend naming the elements of the notation, we do not provide a full guide to the notation at this point, preferring to work in a logical order through the concepts inherent in our conception of a Role Activity Diagram, introducing the various graphical symbols one by one as we go along. As we describe the elements of the notation, we'll focus on the six core types of object within a Role Activity Diagram:

- *Roles* that users play within processes
- *Resources* private to Roles—information and other items required to participate in the process
- *Activities* carried out by Roles to manipulate resources
- *Users*—the humans, organizations or machines that take on Roles
- *States of a process*, defined in terms of logical conditions that control the execution and validation of activities.
- *Interactions* between Roles to transfer resources and synchronize behavior.

We will conclude by summarizing the differences between our use of the notation and the standard approach.

Before we start, though, we make some general comments about the diagramming notation.

We have the ability to make free text *notes* on the diagram—these are shown above as attached by dotted lines to the object they describe. This is used simply to augment the graphical symbols, as a convenient place to put additional description. The notes have no functional importance.

However, these notes could be used by a process support system as the basis for help text. More generally, they should be used in preference to external documentation as the means of annotating a diagram with additional information. It is best to keep all understanding about a process in a single place, if possible—once there are multiple documents involved, they will almost inevitably get out of step with each other at some point.

Another symbol of general interest is the *lightning strike*, shown above and beneath both "Design approved" and "Design rejected." This simply shows where we omit detail, either because the diagram in question is an overview or because we do not know yet what should be done there.

We may *never* know, at least not at process definition stage. As we have discussed, much of a human-driven process is determined during enactment of the process itself—part of the work for which people are employed is to determine how things should be done appropriately in each case they come across. Whether you are a project manager, sales person, marketer, or architect, you need to be able not only to prepare plans and follow procedures, but also to devise, on the fly, ways of handling situations as they arise.

Hence, the process designer cannot know in advance, god-like, everything that is to happen—at the initial stage, it is more important to focus on placing appropriate general constraints on the operation of the process. We will see below how we can build such constraints into the fabric of a process for management purposes, as well to ensure that the process conforms to general policies, guidelines and/or regulations.

Having said this, what *can* we say in advance? And how do we show it on a diagram?

Roles

The *vertical, rounded rectangles* are *Roles*—we often color these with a yellow fill. However, any use of color within a Role Activity Diagram is optional and has no significance. We use yellow for Roles since it makes the strongest contrast with black, and can be distinguished even if you are color-blind. Roles are generally depicted with rectangles containing rounded corners.

Technically the Roles represent divisions of *responsibility* within the process. For simplicity, though, they can be thought of as each corresponding to a *type of process participant*.

Note the word *type* in the last sentence. A Role shows a general sort of behavior (Manager, Designer), rather than a specific participant who has that behavior. For example, there may be many actual Designers within a real process—to indicate this, the Role rectangle in question is shown with others layered behind it. However, the number of Designer Roles shown by this layering is only suggestive; it may not correspond to the number used in a production process, because at the modeling stage, we may have no way of knowing how many actual Designers there will be. The number of Designers could well change during the life of the process, for one thing.[7]

Similarly, the diagram does not show the person, organization or machine who will play, or take on, each Role. The User of a Role is a critical concept in the modeling of human-driven processes, and one that we will discuss at length, but it is not part of the Role Activity Diagramming graphical notation. There are good reasons for this. For one thing, we generally don't know who the players will be at the modeling stage—a process diagram shows a general type of behavior that may have many instances in real life, each with different people or organizations involved. Moreover, the players can—and generally do—change during the life of the process. A Manager may delegate his or her work to someone else while he or she goes on leave, for instance, or hand over the Role entirely on promotion or re-assignment.

However, we will find it necessary to say things about the User of a Role. In general, we need to specify user-specific process criteria such as "the User of a Designer Role must have certain qualifications," or "the User of a Manager Role must be at a certain level within the organization." Users need to be trained and develop their skills, something that may be an important ancillary or even primary objective of a particular process instance—whereas Roles just get assigned to Users, and modified as necessary. Moreover, some Roles have it as part of their duty to add, modify and delete Users, so they need to know about them as prt of their information resources.

A Human Interaction Management System, for instance, must allow a Role to define, and tell other Roles, about objects that represent Users— these can be humans, organizations or machines. In fact, it is also necessary to support the use of information resources that represent other kinds of process object—Roles, for instance, or interactions—since only in this way can computer-supported processes become adaptive on-the-fly in the way that process in real life naturally are.

It is a limitation of the graphical notation that Users (and information resources generally) are not shown as visibly as Roles. However, there is always a trade-off between power and simplicity—the more expressiveness you want in your diagrams, the more complicated they become. We choose for now to leave them simple, and add the remaining detail of process models in other ways—in particular, via a Human Interaction Management software tool that has a full-strength underlying process modeling "language," and the means to drill down into objects shown on a diagram to provide additional information. One purpose of this book is to explain how to construct and use such software tools. From a graphical notation, we seek mainly a way of depicting processes that allows the reader to grasp almost instantly what is going on.

Leaving Users aside for the moment, and returning to what *is* shown on the diagram, a Role is often used by analysts to represent a job within an organization, or a specific aspect of someone's job. However, this use is not always correct. Most people play many Roles as part of their job— sometimes more than one within a particular process. Even in the above fragment, it is possible that both Roles shown could be played by the same person—in a very simple example of the process, one individual might write the concept and brief then do the design itself. Conversely, some Roles may not be part of any person's actual job at all, just a sort of behavior taken on by different people at different times—chairperson in a committee, for example, that may rotate around an organization over time.

Hence, Roles are not jobs so much as *behaviors*—different ways of engaging with the world around us. Everyone has many such ways of acting. The division between home and work is a basic one, although this alone does not tell us enough. Even at home people all play multiple Roles—wife, mother, daughter, friend, school governor, hockey team member, book club organizer, and so on. At work there is just as much variety, but it can be harder to break down what your own behaviors are. As we have seen, your job description does not tell you, so you won't find them on the organization chart. You won't even find them on a matrix management chart, since many behaviors are not related to management at all, but to such floating but vital activities as *committee membership* and *mentoring*.

This high-level, human-oriented concept of Role has various attributes that we need in our framework. Consider the archetypal process *Complex Sales*, in which multiple parties within an organization work together to carry out a large-scale sales activity. Given below are typical attributes of the Roles concerned:

- *Goals* (the *Account Manager* tries to make his or her personal target quota)
- *Responsibilities* (the *Technical Support* must answer questions correctly and in a timely fashion)
- *Interests* (the *Sales Director* wishes to keep track of key sales)
- *Agreements* (between vendor and client there exist contracts, specifications, informal understandings, etc)
- *Private information resources* (the *Account Manager* maintains varied information about the client)
- *References to other Roles* (the *Sales Director* knows who his or her *Account Managers* are, each *Account Manager* knows how to get hold of the *Marketing* department if required)
- *Capabilities* in terms of actions that can be carried out (only certain *Account Managers* can grant high levels of discount)
- *Process authority* (*Marketing* has the final say on what promotional literature can be distributed)

Although these are not shown on a Role Activity Diagram, and some do not appear in the standard literature, we will need such attributes in our framework. As we develop an understanding of the principles underlying our building blocks and their use in process modeling, we will show how each property described above can be captured:

- The goals and responsibilities of a Role can be expressed as a *terminating condition* and *always condition* respectively.

- Interests and agreements are *information about process*, which can be stored in a Role along with other private information resources.

- Similarly, references to other Roles can be maintained within a Role.

- Capabilities and process authority are implicit from the activities belonging to the Role.

For now, though, we are discussing the framework at a high level only. A process such as *Complex Sales* includes a number of Roles that inter-relate in subtle and complex ways. How can we start to analyze it? In what way can we work out the Roles we each play at work?

Resources

A vital clue is that these behaviors are based not simply on activities to be carried out, but also—and perhaps even more essentially—on the *information required in order to carry out such activities*. A simple way to think about Roles is in terms of files—not documents on a computer, but old-fashioned box files.

People naturally keep related items and papers together, if they can manage it. If the objects in question are on a computer, they group them into directories, folders or branches on a tree. If the objects are physical rather than virtual (atoms rather than bits), they put them in the same box. If and when such systems break down, it becomes hard to carry out the work to which the objects are related—and if this has happened at all, it often means that the work has *already* gone astray, and that things generally are in a muddle. This tells us that proper division of information is linked intimately to proper division of behavior.

Based on this principle, a reasonable way to start dividing up behavior into Roles is by dividing up the information used in each one. This applies whether you are an analyst trying to understand a specific business process, or an individual trying to understand their separate responsibilities within an organization. A reasonable mental image of a Role is a *desktop* or an *office*, containing a specific set of documents and other items (keys to machinery, rubber stamps, communication devices, symbolic badges of status, etc.).

Taking this paradigm further, we can say something very interesting about Roles. Their information is *private*. You do not expect other people to come up and remove—or even read—documents on your desktop without explicit permission. In other words, others do not have access to information resources within one of your Roles. If and when you wish to share information, you do so by sending it to someone, or by showing it to them.

Moreover, once you have shared information in this way, allowing people to take it away for their own use, you do not expect their copy of the information to remain the same as your own. You might email them a draft of a memo, then carry on working on the original, for instance, or send a status report on a certain date that carries on being updated daily at your end. This assumption is absolutely basic to human behavior. We all like—and need—to remain in control of the information we use.

There are many reasons for this. For one, sharing information with someone is to release it from your control to some extent, and we need to prepare for this—make sure that we are happy with what goes out—before letting it go. For another, much information is sensitive, and we need to make sure that only the right people see it, at the right time, with the right guarantees of security. There are also implied commitments made by sharing knowledge. For example, telling a supplier that you are looking for a partner on an important project might well give them the idea that they are being considered as the potential partner, with the result that they invest time and money in preparing for the project. It would be irresponsible, and detrimental to future relations with the supplier, to give them such information if you had no intention of giving them any chance to bid when the time came.

Understanding that the information each Role uses is *personal* to that Role has yet deeper significance. Information takes different forms on different desktops. Almost the first thing that anyone does on receiving a spreadsheet, for example, is to reformat it to show the rows and columns they are particularly interested in, perhaps with highlighting or filtering in places. They may also add additional data that was not included in the original spreadsheet—information they are privy to that possibly was not available to the originator of the spreadsheet, or information they generate while working: the status of each item, for example, or just free text notes.

The spreadsheet example is just that—an example. The principle that data formats vary between Roles applies to almost any form of data held within a Role. Even structured data that comes from a computer system is no exception.

The original application for which the RADRunner Human Interaction Management System was created was to act as the central coordination agent for a life insurance system made of independent components. These components communicated via Web service calls—requests for actions to be carried out, and information to be retrieved, made via Internet protocols. What we found was that the messages and data returned from such Web service calls into a Role varied greatly in format over time—not only as the Web service implementations changed, but even on a case by case basis, since some claims possess information that others don't (different types of evidence, for example). We also found that error conditions were best handled by understanding that the data returned had a different format. Hence the Human Interaction Management System allows data structures within a Role to vary over its life—the original data structures built into the Role definition are simply a starting point.

As we have found, and will find again, this seems to introduce a great deal of complexity into the management of human-driven processes. However, as with much of the discussion in this book, we are not attempting here to prescribe how to go about things, but simply to describe the way things already are. Humans do not feel any need to store information in exactly the same way as their fellows—to the contrary, we all seem to strive to make our own information sources as different from our peers as we possibly can. We personalize our desktops, organize our filing cabinets, structure our file systems, ... not just to assert individuality (although that is part of the reason) but because human work is based on information. People find it hard to use information unless it is available in a form convenient for them personally, and we all seem to have different needs in this respect.

If one tries to ignore the natural variety of ways people rearrange information to suite their purposes by imposing a fixed, universal structure for all data, people just work round it. They make notes in free text documents, scribble on hard copies, use fields on a screen for purposes they were not intended ... with the result that information floats around an organization in an untraceable and unmanageable way.

It is better to recognize that we all need at least the *ability* to make our data slightly different in format from that of our peers, and provide the means to do this from the start, ideally in a computer system for process support. Then people will—hopefully—use the facilities provided and keep data where it belongs, rather than scattering it about in a way that not only makes life harder for themselves, but makes handover to someone else in the organization a convoluted and error-prone task.

If a central repository with data held in a standard format is also required, for audit or query purposes perhaps, this can also be provided, as an extract akin to a data mart. Such a "process mart" must be maintained, however, from *within the process*—for example, using a repository Role to hold standardized extracts from various other Roles—so that the management of information within the process mart is done under process control, and the relationship between privately held data and centrally held data made explicit. Only in this way can the humans participating in a process work as efficiently as possible, without being hampered by the demands of centralized data control.

This approach to data storage is fundamentally different from that assumed by current enterprise systems, of all types. The general assumption in enterprise IT is that any and all business data should "live" in a centralized corporate repository, such as a database, data warehouse, file server, document/content management system or directory. Storing data in this way allows retrieval, maintenance and analysis tools to conceal its actual location from the business user, which makes it much easier for IT staff to maintain that data and keep it consistent.

From the point of view of computerized process support, a process activity can make use of any such repository by invoking a tool to access it. This has been viewed as a fundamental enabler for process support systems, because it makes it possible to *define processes without having to manage the data they operate upon*. The aim and principle has been to keep process and data separate.

Stemming from ideas originally put forward by Michael Jackson in the early 1980s,[8] a process is typically viewed as the sequence of activities used to transform a particular collection of business data. Moreover, each "instance" of the process—each case of the process that occurs during business operations—uses a data collection *with the same structure and format*. As a result, you can keep the current state of each such data collection in a database, getting it out when required to move a particular process instance forwards. Since the process itself is the same for each data collection, you just need to "load" a particular data collection into it in order to do some "processing." This works because—and only because—the data structure and format is the same for each instance.

This approach may or may not work well for mechanistic processes— and we are certainly not advocating the removal of all structured data from enterprise life. Relational databases, for example, have been an enabler of immense importance for organizational administration systems, and for data analysis techniques based thereon—few large organizations could now function without them. There are many situations in which data structures can be determined in advance, and safely assumed to remain constant for at least a while. However, we have seen that this approach to data description is inappropriate for human-driven processes. It leads only to people bypassing the system to make their own personalized data stores, which are then under no process control whatsoever—unlike private data belonging to a Role, which is an integral part of a business process.

This discussion so far has led us to an understanding that the vertical rectangles on a Role Activity Diagram, the Roles, represent types of behavior—not people, not jobs, not even parts of jobs, but *typical ways for people to participate in a process*. Moreover, each of these behaviors is fundamentally tied to a particular set of *highly personalized information*.

In a human-driven process, personalized information is essential, and it is instinctively understood by a User to exist within in the context of a specific Role. This way of storing information is more appropriate to human-driven processes than using enterprise repositories.

Note that traditional data storage issues do not go away. Content management technologies, for example, deal with such issues as versioning, indexing and searching of documents, and it is necessary to replicate some of this functionality within a Role. However, there is generally no need for such heavyweight solutions. For a start, there is no need for access control, since by definition the information within a Role is available to the User of that Role, and just to them—information required by others, for example for management reporting purposes, is sent to them explicitly when required, via an interaction. Similarly, while a Role may need to keep all versions of a particular document that it possesses, or just certain versions, access to the document is not shared between multiple parties, so there is no need for full-scale configuration management. The main requirement is for easy retrieval of the document you are seeking, whether from a list of different documents, or from a list of versions of the same document. We will see when we come to look at implementing computer support for human-driven processes how this can be done.

A data storage issue new to human-driven process support is the need to cater to resources that are not "just" information, but physical objects: keys to machinery or buildings, printed documents representing insurance policies or share certificates, promotional material such as marketing freebies, and so on—atoms rather than bits, as computer techies say.

We will term such physical, non-virtual information resources *offline entities*. An offline entity is an object that does not exist in a software system, but is merely represented within a software system. We need to keep track of such objects since they form a vital part of the operation of the process, and their presence or absence within a Role makes a big difference to what that Role can achieve. However, we also need to recognize that they must be treated differently. We will see when we come to discuss interactions between Roles some of the ways in which offline entities behave differently than resources that are pure information.

Resources in general are the basis for all process modeling. Any activity within a Role can be described in terms of some kind of *operation* on a resource—whether it is to create, access, modify or remove it.—and interactions between Roles are generally concerned with *sharing* resources.

So, what is the nature of the activities within a human-driven process?

Activities

On a Role Activity Diagram, the shaded square boxes within a Role are the *activities* that it can carry out, in order to advance toward its goals. The process is considered generally to unfold downward from the top of the diagram—although as we will see, in practice things are not usually this simple. People, unlike machines, rarely do things the same way twice. They jump about, loop back, repeat and interleave actions—generally we do things as and when we see fit, rather than according to some pre-defined script. People also have a tendency to introduce new actions if they are necessary, or dispense with ones that are not required in a particular instance.

Consider, for example, a simple sales process. The sales person may be furnished with a procedure manual, or policy booklet, describing how the company wishes them to go about their work. However, any sales person worth his or her salt is unlikely to stick rigidly to the process as laid down, since this would be to waste potential opportunities. Sales is fundamentally about human relationships: reading between the lines, changing tack according to the customer's needs and budget, negotiating carefully, anticipating future requirements, following up off-the-cuff comments in the hope of additional work, and so on. All this means that the sales people redesign their own processes as they go along—this is a fundamental part of their job, and their skill in doing it is at least part of why they are employed.

This is not to say that there is no abstract logic to human activity. None of us would be able to work together in large organizations if this were true. The point is just that activities as shown on the diagram of a human-driven process depict not what people actually do when they carry out a process, but instead archetypal behavior—a kind of average, or lowest common denominator, of typical practice. This has great value, since it allows us to define in advance a basis for process management and possible computerized support. However, it should not be taken as gospel when it comes to carrying out work itself. In particular, any support system for human-driven processes must *treat change to the pre-defined process as the norm*, not an exception to it.

So how are we to interpret the sequence of activities on a Role Activity Diagram, if they can be done quite differently when it comes to process enactment? We will see that the notation, if interpreted a certain way, actually gives us a combination of power and flexibility that is just what we need. Based on the description of *states of the process*—shown as the *vertical lines* that connect activity boxes, sometimes annotated with an oval label (e.g., "Have Design Brief" or "Completed Design")—we can provide a framework to control how activities are carried out that supports people in their work without preventing them from doing it in the most sensible way.

Leaving aside for the moment the manner in which activities are controlled, we will look more closely at what goes on inside an activity. What is happening within, say, "Do Design?"

The short answer is: a number of different things. It is likely that one or more software tools will be used—not only Computer-Aided Design (CAD) tools but also applications that retrieve reference material, calculate costs, and perhaps specialized products having to do with materials design or 3-D simulation. Even if only one multi-purpose product is available, it is unlikely that the designer will sit down and complete the work in one sitting. There are a number of different things that need to be achieved—*tasks* to be carried out—before the work is finished.

If this is true, why is the activity shown in a single box on the Role Activity Diagram? Why not break it into several?

While this is often a difficult decision to make in modeling, there are some simple principles that can be applied. In some cases, the tasks may be unpredictably repeated and interleaved, to the point where it would be hard to find a typical order to draw them in if shown separately. Unless some logical and standardized dependencies can be found for the tasks, they may as well simply be grouped together.

Interestingly, there are other cases where task order is highly predictable, yet it is still appropriate to group the tasks together into a single activity. Suppose a particular set of tasks is to be carried out in a fixed sequence, one after another, without anything being done in between. They may as well be listed inside an activity definition, in their set order, since nothing is gained by exposing them at Role level. This is particularly useful if computerized process support is available and the tasks concerned can be automated. A Human Interaction Management System, for instance, can be configured to carry out such a sequence of tasks in the background, without disturbing the user at all, if and when appropriate.

As we have seen with resources and Users, the division of an activity into tasks is not shown in the Role Activity Diagram itself, but must be added either via a process modeling system that allows activity detail to be added, or as plain text (e.g., in the activity description). We choose to keep the notation itself simple, preferring ease of use for non-technical readers over expressive power.

We continue our tour of the notation with the two symbols within a Role that we have not yet described—the box containing a cross, and the branching headed either by an asterisk or by triangles—and will complete it by discussing the horizontal lines that represent communication between Roles.

Users

The *box containing a cross* represents an action that starts one or more Role "instances"—it uses the definition of a *Role type* to create *real Roles*, each assigned to a person (or organization, or machine) as User. In the example Role Activity Diagram, there is such an action called "Start Designer Roles," that uses the definition of a Designer Role to create one or more real Designers in the process.

Starting Role instances generally, but not always, also includes assigning them to Users. It may even include creating the User, in the sense of making a new login available within a process support system, or granting access to a person already existing within a corporate directory. Neither of these actions is necessary—a Role instance could be started for later use, and left dormant in the meantime. However, it is usual to start the Role when it is needed, and for it to be activated, it needs a User.

A special case of a Role being assigned a User is for it to be assigned a "machine" user. This is done when a Role can be entirely automated—for example, it may act simply as a repository of information within the process, perhaps filtering it and sending specific pieces of information out to other Roles as required. This might be appropriate for an insurance claim handling process, in which claims are received via the Web and distributed automatically to agents specializing in the appropriate type of case. Alternatively, it could be that a particular Role can be used in either automated or manual mode. Continuing the insurance example, simple cases could be handled automatically, but more complex ones assigned to a human for processing.

We will discuss Role automation later on in the book. Automation is a necessary part of computerized support for human-driven processes—since any enterprise system should aim to do as much as possible on behalf of the people who use it. However, automation in a human-driven process requires a level of sophistication beyond that available in most current systems. In the *Automation* section below, we look at the different levels of automation support required, and show how these can be implemented.

In general, because we are dealing with human-driven activity, our concept of User must cater effectively to individuals and organizations as well as machines. Hence we need to include the personal characteristics that have direct and indirect impact on process enactment. We can illustrate key attributes of human-driven process Users by looking again at the archetypal *Complex Sales* process:

- *Identity* (a *Sales Director* will not entrust a key account to just anybody—he or she needs to know that an appropriate person is taking on the Role)

- *Physical location* (the time zone of the user assigned to *Technical Support* may be important if phone calls in office hours are required)

- *Virtual location* (if it is necessary to contact the *Sales Director* at short notice, his or her mobile number and email address must be known)

- *Relationships* with others (it would not be sensible to assign to a client an

Account Manager who is known to get on badly with someone in his or her organization; conversely it is wise to build upon existing working relationships where possible)

- *Behavioral tendencies* (a client whose preference is for extended and repeated meetings preparatory to purchase should be assigned an *Account Manager* with the necessary patience)

- *Capabilities* in terms of knowledge and experience (the user assigned to *Technical Support* should have the necessary skills)

- *Organizational authority* (a major client may feel slighted unless his or her *Account Manager* has a senior position in the vendor's organization)

Unfortunately, Users do not appear on a Role Activity Diagram, and hence neither do these attributes, important as they are. We could extend the graphical notation, but we make the trade off for clarity against expressive power, and choose to avoid cluttering up diagrams with too much detail—they can get complex enough just showing Roles.

Nevertheless, Users and their properties are an essential aspect of human activity—since they represent the humans! We will return to them throughout this book, showing how the nature of human participants in a process can be captured and used in a process—not only when we discuss a high-level modeling framework, but also when we come to discuss how human-driven processes can be improved.

States of a process

The remaining set of symbols contained within a Role (we will discuss interactions between Roles later) is the notation for "branching." In the example Role Activity Diagram, Figure 9, this is shown in the Manager Role in several places. For instance, there is a kind of looping shown after "Declare Complete (Design)," wherein each design received is processed by the Manager. Also, underneath the activity "Assess Design" there are two small *triangles*, labeled "Design approved" and "Design rejected." Beneath each of these triangles the process continues, although in our example Role Activity Diagram we do not include the details of what happens next.

It looks as though the Manager makes a choice after "Assess Design"—which path to take next, approval or rejection? And this is one conventional interpretation made of branching in a Role Activity Diagram (the other possibilities being to follow both paths in parallel or to loop repeatedly). The branching notation is known as *refinement*, and the various standard forms are:

- *Case refinement*, which shows a decision made by the User of the Role, perhaps based on the value(s) in some data object(s) they have access to—this decision then determines their future course(s) of action.

- *Part refinement*, which shows a point at which the process splits, taking more than one path at the same time—the future paths are considered to execute simultaneously.

- *Iteration* (sometimes known as *replicated part refinement*), which shows a sequence of activities repeated for each element in a collection.

These concepts of branching may seem intuitively reasonable, but they are some of the things we will change about the notation.

Let us consider case refinement first. In real life, it is only rarely that we find ourselves at a decision point such that, if we take a particular path, all activities on the other, alternate, path are forever out of the question. The norm is that we recognize that a certain state of affairs exists, and as a result plan to take a certain set of activities. However, the situation may change, or we may come to understand it better, with the result that we may decide that other activities are in fact more appropriate. What we do, time and again in working life, is make *provisional* decisions:

- A sales person may have a go at selling something by talking up its high quality, and if this doesn't work well enough, switch to a focus on cost comparison with competitors.

- A house builder may try putting under-floor heating into new houses, but if becomes too expensive, cut the losses and change back to conventional radiators.

- An office outfitter may start buying furnishing fabrics from discount suppliers via the Internet, only to find that inappropriate or low quality goods are sent, and turn to ordering material over the telephone from reputable manufacturers.

Making provisional decisions is ubiquitous in working life, and we need to allow for it in the way we model case refinement. However, the conventional understanding of the notation—in which you are *committed* to a branch once you have chosen it—does not allow for this at all. Consider, for example, the engineering design example shown in Figure 9, and suppose there was a new activity on the "Design rejected" branch, called "Describe potential safety problems." This is shown in Figure 10: Engineering Design Process (fragment), extended.

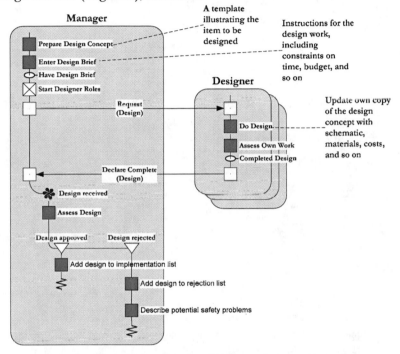

Figure 10: Engineering Design Process (fragment), extended

The Manager is unlikely to use this activity if he or she has approved the work—but may need to as a result of circumstances. For example, implementation of an approved design may reveal safety problems that were not spotted at first. Corrective action is unable to remove the safety hazard, and the design must be rejected after all. What the Manager needs to do is "jump across" to the rejection branch of the refinement, in order to describe the safety problems. But this cannot be done using the conventional interpretation of the notation—once you've started moving down a branch, you're stuck on it for good.

We could try adding the "Describe potential safety problems" activity to both branches, as show below in Figure 11: Engineering Design Process (fragment), extended differently.

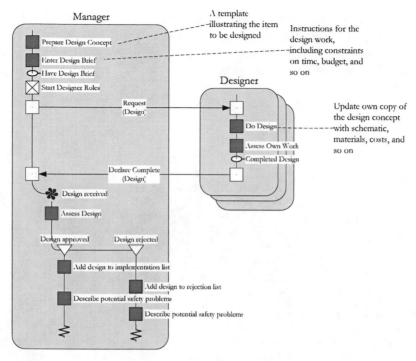

Figure 11: Engineering Design Process (fragment), extended differently

However, this doesn't capture what we want to say, since it suggests that it is acceptable for an *approved* design to have potential safety problems. This would contravene regulations. Let's try removing the activity from either branch, and placing it higher up, say under "Assess Design," as shown in Figure 12: Engineering Design Process (fragment), extended differently again.

But this isn't right either. Here the assumption is that the Manager *always* has to describe potential safety problems, which as a rule will be unnecessary, and again suggests that a design that has safety problems can still be approved.

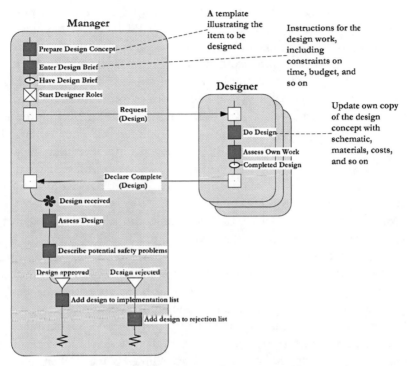

Figure 12: Engineering Design Process (fragment),
extended differently again

The problem is that, once we have started down the approval branch, there's no way to jump onto the rejection branch. The Manager is committed to a specific course of action, and doesn't want or need to be. If managers didn't have a Role Activity Diagram to work from, or a process support system based on such a system, they wouldn't feel constrained in such a way. It is one thing to show how things should go in principle, and another to prevent people from taking an alternative route through the process if it turns out to be necessary. The whole aim of modeling a human-driven process is to indicate the likely way in which the process will unfold, which means putting the activity where it is most suited. We just need to allow the process participant to make judicious changes to the archetype, if it is necessary in practice.

We could deal with this *particular* example by judicious process construction—for example, a design-assess-implement loop that could be repeated as necessary—if we knew in advance that this *particular* issue was likely to crop up. The point is that, when we start out, we cannot possibly predict all the issues that are likely to crop up. Problems of any kind can strike at any point in a human-driven process, and if you try to cater for them all in advance, the complexity of your process design will spiral out of control—and you'll never think of everything anyway. The simplest, safest and only truly practical approach to human-driven process design is to define the *process you expect to take place*, using a notation that allows appropriate flexibility during process enactment. This alone will not always be enough—we also need a method of applying the notation that supports *ongoing process change*, since some events may require flexibility beyond any that can be built into a notation—but we leave the description of such a method until the next chapter.

So, the most natural place for "Describe potential safety problems" is on the "Design rejected" branch, but we need to allow the User of the Role to make use of this branch if and when it becomes necessary. We must not insist that, after the branch point, they commit themselves to using only the activities on the chosen branch—that having once approved the design, they cannot later on reject it and start treating it accordingly.

Moreover, this discussion shows that *part refinement* is as unrealistic as *case refinement* in human processes if each branch is understood to represent a specific sequence of activity. People *do* sometimes perceive themselves as having genuinely separate streams of activity—but if these are truly distinct, they are better modeled as different Roles. If one has a set of activities to carry out that are within the same Role, and hence can make use of the same information resources, it is an artificial constraint to insist that they be divided into separate "sequences."

To see this with respect to part refinement, suppose that after assessing a design, the Manager has to:

1. Complete an employee appraisal for the Designer concerned, circulating it to the employee and *his or her* colleagues for comment in the process.

2. Respond to the Designer with comments, and obtain feedback.

3. Log the design in a corporate content management repository, adding his or her own notes, concerns and references to related work.

These activities make use of the same information resource (the design in question) so the most natural modeling approach is to put them in the same Role. And as with the example above ("Describe potential safety problems"), the clearest approach to modeling them is to put each one on separate branches—all of which are intended from the start to be carried out simultaneously.

The revised Role Activity Diagram is shown in Figure 13: Engineering Design Process (fragment), further extended.

However, there is no reason to suppose that a Manager will actually do the activities at different times. A human is not a computer program, whose activities must be defined in advance as taking place in a specific order, or in parallel "threads" that somehow communicate—a Manager is a person, with an innate ability to do their work in a sensible way (or they wouldn't have got the job).

So it is quite likely that the Manager will realize, without being prompted, that the activities are inter-related—and save time in carrying them out by using the same meetings, emails and telephone calls to acquire, distribute and record the information required by each activity. As with much human work, in practice different work items are connected to each other at a deep level, and we understand instinctively that the best and quickest way to get things done is to kill two birds with one stone. Managing human processes, and supporting them with software, in a way that insists they be divided up into separate streams only hinders efficient operation of the organization. Our aim is always to facilitate the way people work naturally, and take advantage of human cleverness in organizing their own work, not place artificial restrictions on it at the whim of a business analyst.

Finally, coming to iteration, the example Role Activity Diagram shows an asterisk symbol labeled "Design received"—the *asterisk (*)* indicates that the activities below are to be carried out *for each* design received. The conventional—and obvious—interpretation of this symbol is to assume that you have a list of items—designs, in this case—and that the activities below indicate how each of them should be treated in turn.

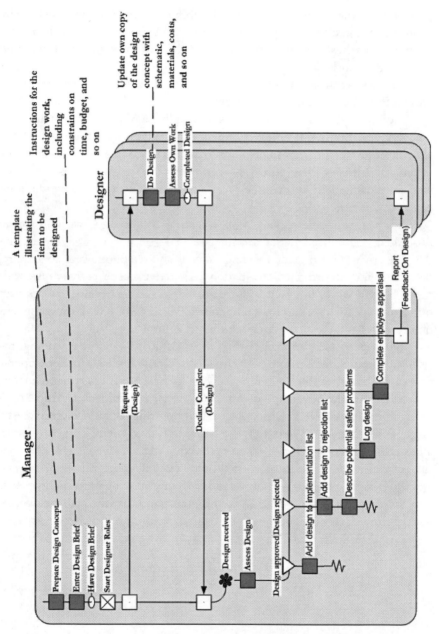

Figure 13: Engineering Design Process (fragment), further extended

Despite the apparent simplicity of this interpretation, it is not really appropriate for human-driven processes. This kind of iteration is a programming notion, based on the standard "for" construct found in most programming languages. To start with, the assumption underlying such a construct is that the list is ready for processing when you come to do the loop itself—that you have all the elements of the list before you start processing it. However, this is rarely true in most human-driven processes.

In our engineering design example, the Designers are likely to submit their designs one by one, over an extended period of time—and the Manager is likely to start processing the first ones to be received before all of them have arrived. Apart from the obvious efficiency gains to be made by working in this way, some designs may never be submitted at all, so it would not be sensible to wait too long before starting to assess the ones that have been sent in.

The construct we need is more of the nature of: "once a new design becomes available, process it as follows." The iteration construct is there to show typical activities to be taken for each design, rather than to instruct the User that they should repeat a specific activity sequence at a certain point, as if they were a machine.

Moreover, the User may well process certain designs before others, regardless of the order in which they are received, for all sorts of reasons—perhaps some are less complex than others, and can be dealt with more quickly, or some are obviously inappropriate and can be rejected immediately in order to cut down the list to a more manageable size. Hence, we cannot even rely on the order of receiving designs as a guide to the manner in which they are processed.

So, we claim on the one hand that branching is useful for modeling—since it clarifies things to show different activities in separate streams, whether these are alternatives, simultaneous, or repeated. Yet we claim on the other hand that to take the branching literally when it comes to process enactment is restrictive and inefficient. How can we make an interpretation of the branching notation that is meaningful and helpful, yet allows the user to pick and choose the activities they require from more than one branch?

To answer this, we must look back at the origins of the Role Activity Diagram notation. Role Activity Diagrams were originally derived from a more general type of process diagram called a *Petri net*, originating in Carl Adam Petri's 1962 dissertation "Kommunikation mit Automaten." Quoting from Wil van der Aalst's Web tutorial on Petri nets (from which is also taken Figure 14: A classic Petri net):[9]

"A Petri net consists of *places* and *transitions*. We indicate a place using a circle. A transition is shown as a rectangle. [The figure below] shows a simple Petri net, consisting of three places (*claim*, *under_consideration* and *ready*) and three transitions (*record*, *pay* and *send_letter*). This network models the process for dealing with an insurance claim. Arriving at the place *claim*, it is first recorded, after which either a payment is made or a letter sent explaining the reasons for rejection ….

Places can contain tokens. These are indicated using black dots … the place *claim* contains three tokens. The structure of a Petri net is fixed; however, the distribution of its tokens among the places can change. The transition *record* can thus take tokens from the *claim* input place and put them in *under_consideration*. We call this the *firing* of the transition *record* …

The state of a Petri net is indicated by the distribution of tokens amongst its places. We can describe the state illustrated [as there being] three tokens in *claim*, none in *under_consideration* and none in *ready*."

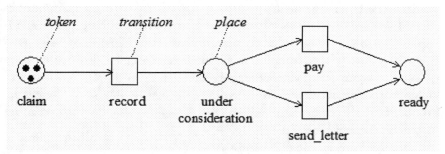

Figure 14: A classic Petri net

There is a lot more to Petri nets, which have been extended in all sorts of ways since their original formulation—the interested reader can find further details on the Web.[10] For our purposes here, it is enough to note that Petri nets are a visual technique not only with great expressive power—much more than a flowchart, for example—but they can also be represented mathematically, in order to deduce things about the processes they depict.

A Role Activity Diagram was originally conceived as a special case of a Petri net—tokens are considered to move between activities as the process unfolds.[11] This formalism has certain implications, of which some are valuable to us in the modeling of human-driven processes.

A strength of Role Activity Diagrams is their focus on *states of a process*—equivalent to the places in a Petri net—and their consequent recognition that an activity may take place as result of the process state, rather than simply because another activity considered to be "preceding" has just been carried out.

For instance, after completion and acceptance of a design, the operation of the process may depend in all sorts of ways on the nature of the design—how many components it has, what sort of components these are, the interfaces made use of, the materials required, and so on. A Role Activity Diagram makes explicit how the various subsequent activities are conditional on these attributes, and thus tied closely to the information contained within the Role—not just to the simple fact of a design having been completed.

However, not only is the detailed use of states rather complex with Petri nets, but the Petri net paradigm also brings with it other assumptions that have held back use of the Role Activity Diagram notation.

In particular, the guiding principle of Petri nets (as with other graph-based modeling techniques) is that you cannot go from place A to place B unless there is a connection between them. Hence, in Role Activity Diagram terms, there is an implicit assumption that immediately after carrying out a specific activity you can only carry out certain other activities—those connected to the previous activity by a vertical line or branch. As we have seen, there *is* a notion that there may be separate streams of activity within a Role, carried out in parallel—these correspond to multiple tokens in a Petri net. But the principle still applies—each token "lives" inside a particular stream, and inside that stream, you have to do things in the order prescribed by the process diagram.

This restriction gives Petri nets their power, and we will find it very useful later on, when we come to modeling human activity at a higher level. However, the approach is too restrictive when applied to the detailed activities shown in a Role Activity Diagram. As we have discussed throughout this book, humans see no need to be hampered in this way—to the contrary, in order to carry out our work as effectively as possible, we need the right to jump about between activities, repeating and interleaving them as we see fit. If we need to do something at a specific time, we will try and do so regardless of whether the process designer anticipated a need for such an action at that point. To prevent people doing so, for example via a process support system based directly on places and transitions within a Role, will only result in people bypassing the system when they need to—which benefits neither the process participants or the organization they belong to.

So, we are not proposing to remove from human-driven processes a basis in Petri nets. We simply claim that Petri net theory has not been applied at the right level. When we come to discuss a higher level of modeling, we will see that there is more natural and powerful way to apply Petri nets to human activity. Moreover, we will also show that the new formalism currently competing with Petri nets for mindshare in the process modeling world—the *pi-calculus* of Robin Milner[12]—can also be applied, giving those interested in mathematical formalism or software development a choice of approaches.

At this point, however, we are looking at the detail of what goes on inside a process, and therefore will not go into alternative approaches to formal, mathematical representation of human-driven processes. Once we have covered more ground, and introduced higher-level modeling concepts, we will deal with such formal matters, in *Reasoning about processes*, where we show how they give us a way forward for the analysis and control of process change.

Returning to Role Activity Diagrams—we propose to take away their low-level basis in Petri nets, so we need to replace this with a new understanding of what goes on inside a Role. In particular, we will show that there is an alternative approach that gives us the flexibility we need without taking away meaning from the process model.

Above or below each activity on a Role Activity Diagram is a vertical line. In Petri net terms, this represents a transition, from a preceding activity or to a subsequent one—technically, there should be an oval label on each such line, describing the state of the process at that point, although these labels are often omitted.[13]

We propose to change the interpretation of these lines, as follows:

- The vertical line entering an activity from above is its *precondition*—a logical statement about the information resources in the Role which, if true *at any time whatsoever*, means that the activity can then be carried out.[14] Note the italics—the vertical line above an activity has always been interpreted as a precondition, but in the standard interpretation the use is quite different. In particular, suppose there is another, "upper" activity above the line—using the standard interpretation, the precondition of the "lower" activity is only ever evaluated, and the lower activity potentially carried out, if the process has just finished the upper activity. We remove this restriction.

- The vertical line leaving the activity from below is its *postcondition*—a logical statement about the information resources in the Role which is guaranteed to be true on completing the activity. Again, this has always been the conventional interpretation of the line below an activity, but postconditions were rarely used by modelers. However, in the modeling of human-driven processes they are a powerful tool for exercising control over free-flowing, adaptive human activity. We will see how postconditions can be used to prevent people doing things that they are not supposed to, by insisting that any activity that would cause a postcondition to be violated is *automatically undone*.

The use of preconditions means that an activity can in theory be carried out at almost any time. In fact, the only time you know it definitely *cannot* be carried out is immediately after an activity that has a contradictory postcondition. At all other times, the option is there to do the work if the state of the Role permits it, and the User of the Role sees fit. This approach permits the process definer to control operation of the process as necessary, without hampering the efficiency of its operation by Users.

For example, the precondition of an activity such as "Describe potential safety problems" could simply be that a design exists. This allows it to be used whenever necessary, but prevents it from being available at inappropriate times. In particular, we could then put the activity on the "Design rejected" branch, where it sits most naturally, safe in the knowledge that the Manager can use it if they see fit even after approving the design.

Similarly, the use of postconditions to control activity execution gives the process definer the ability to set standards that the process Users must conform to, yet does not restrict them from taking an individual approach to their work.

For example, the postcondition of an activity such as "Do Design" could mandate that certain elements of the design existed—a schematic and outline costs, for example—yet not require that every detail was completed. For example, the designer may submit a design for which they are unable to specify exactly the materials that should be used—perhaps they know the requirements that the material must satisfy, and are able to make an educated guess that such-and-such a plastic would work, but suggest that expert advice be taken and tests carried out before committing to its use in production.

One immediate implication of this interpretation is that we must change our understanding of what it means to show two activities, one above the other, connected by a vertical line. This no longer implies that the lower activity is carried out after the upper activity. What it says, is that after completing the upper activity, we will be ready to carry out the lower activity. However, after completing the upper activity we may also be ready to do many other things, depending on the preconditions to the other activities in the Role—some of which may well be implied or even equal to the postcondition of the upper activity. Similarly, we may be in a position to carry out the lower activity at various points, not just after completing the upper activity. Exactly when we come to be in a position to carry out the lower activity depends partly on the postconditions of other activities in the Role—some of which may imply or even be equal to the precondition of the lower activity—and partly on state changes that are not captured in the notation. We may arrive at a position to carry out the lower activity at various times other than just after the upper activity, since not every state change of the Role can or should be described explicitly via a postcondition—the modeler attempts to capture in postconditions only those state changes that are important for purposes of control. Most activities in a Role will have effects on the Role state beyond those that are described explicitly in their postcondition—this is an inevitable feature of the richness of human behavior, and not a problem for process modeling as long as we adopt an appropriate approach to notation.

The approach described here—based on the use of logical statements as pre- and postconditions to activities—allows the process definer to ensure that company policies, industry standards, and statutory regulations are adhered to, while giving full reign to the individual expertise of those carrying out the work. In the example above, later activities in the process would be concerned with verifying the safety of materials used—whether or not these materials were specified in detail within the original design. Not only can the process evolve naturally to deal with unforeseen eventualities, as we will see later, but also the User of the Role is permitted to interleave, repeat, and jump "back" to previous activities as and when required, since we can put the necessary control structure in place via careful use of pre- and postconditions.

In terms of computerized process support, the system will not allow an activity to be started if the precondition is false, or to complete if the postcondition is violated. For example, a Human Interaction Management System only shows to the User those activities within their Role(s) that have a true precondition at the time. Moreover, the system will not permit the effects of any task within an activity to be saved unless the postcondition is true. If the User tries to complete an activity in a way that would leave it with a false postcondition, the system will automatically undo all the work done during that activity.

If used correctly, this does not mean that human work will be lost. For instance, the postcondition "All parts of a design exist" should not be applied to an activity such as "Draw up blueprint," but rather to an activity such as "Submit design for production." The idea is to help Users do things correctly, automating as much as possible, not to prevent them doing their work stage by stage in a natural way.

Returning to branching, we see that this interpretation of Role Activity Diagrams permits a quite different use of refinement within a Role—interpreted in terms of *process state rather than activity sequences*:

- We replace both *case refinement* and *part refinement* with a single refinement symbol, the triangle pointing down (conventionally part refinement is shown via a triangle pointing up).

   o If the triangle is labeled with a condition, like "Design approved" or "Design rejected" in the example shown, this is taken to be an addition to the precondition of every activity below the triangle. It indicates that any activity on the branch in question may be taken, at least in principle, as long as both the precondition of the branch *and* the precondition of the activity itself are true. If there is no condition attached to the triangle, we assume that any activity in the branch can be taken at the User's discretion. Where we have nested refinements, we follow the same principle, and insist that the activity can be taken only if the condition at the head of each refinement containing an activity is true, as well as the precondition of the activity itself. What this means in our example, is that as soon as the design is rejected, any activity on the "Design rejected" branch becomes immediately available. There is no need to "jump" over to a different branch. We do not locate the user at a specific place (or places) in the Role according to their previous actions, as is done in a Petri net—rather, we use *the current situation as it stands* to determine what should be done next.

o   Any branches that are available—have no condition attached, or a condition that is true at the time—can be followed in parallel. In other words, the User can pick and choose among the activities in the various enabled branches, interleaving the activities as they see fit in order to get through the process as efficiently as possible. Referring to Figure 13, showing activities on additional refinement branches, it would be entirely possible to carry out activities on several branches at the same time, interleaving them as convenient and appropriate.

- We interpret the *iteration* symbol—a label preceded by an asterisk—as meaning that in principle the sequence of activities beneath should be followed for each item in the indicated collection, but assume that the User will choose the time, order and manner of doing so. We allow iteration to be used in combination with other branches if desired—i.e., you could have one branch that repeats, and others that just execute once (or not at all, depending on the condition at the top). In terms of our example, this means that we can interleave work on the various designs as we desire. As they arrive from the individual Designers, they will be added to a collection. The Manager will get designs out of this collection one at a time in the order he or she sees fit, do some processing on each one and then put the design back. There is no constraint on the Manager to deal with the designs in a specific order, or to complete processing on a design once it has been started.

Our approach to iteration is essentially the same as in standard Role Activity Diagram theory, since the use of different tokens in a Petri net can simulate the kind of interleaving of behavior described above. However, our approach to case and part refinement—abolishing them in favor of a single refinement notion based on division of state as opposed to activity sequences—is dramatically different. It provides a combination of power and flexibility not available with the original Petri net based notation.

Moreover, such power and flexibility are not available in other process modeling notations either. To date, all major process modeling notations are based either on:

- *Graph theoretical approaches*, for example Petri nets or activity diagrams in the UML[15], which take as a first principle that from a particular node, you can only move to another that is connected; or

- *"Block-structured" programming languages*, for example BPML[16] or

XLANG,[17] which are based on the combination of activities into sequences—even if these sequences can be executed in parallel, at a detailed level the basic idea is to follow one activity with specific other activities.

We replace both these approaches with an entirely different approach—to allow depiction of a process in a manner familiar at first glance to anyone (somewhat like a basic flowchart), but to interpret this depiction in a way that combines expressive power with freedom of execution. This allows us to satisfy the criteria developed in the preceding section, when considering the general nature of human work:

> Bearing in mind the unpredictable and dynamic nature of human activities and interactions, we propose that the most effective approach to describing human-driven processes, and thus supporting them with tools, is suggestive rather than prescriptive, offering guidance and warning, rather than machine-like predetermination of task sequences and data structures, with high-level control and regulation provided to keep things on the straight and narrow.

In order to simplify our approach for the process definer, as well as for the User of a process, we make the assumption that if a vertical line is *not* labeled with a oval shape, the corresponding precondition or postcondition is just "true"—i.e., neither is asserted as part of the process definition.

On this basis, experience in implementing process models with a Human Interaction Management System shows that a simple and effective approach to process definition is to leave all but the most essential pre- and postconditions empty at the start. Then try out the process. It will soon become clear where such conditions need to be added, and where they would be too restrictive.

Where conditions *are* needed, they are defined in terms of the information resources of the Role. What does this mean, exactly? How can such logical conditions be constructed and used?

At the simplest level, a condition can be made about whether a particular resource is *present at all*—for example, "a design exists."

Statements can also be made about the *status* of a resource—e.g., "the design has been approved"—or its contents—e.g., "the design includes a materials specification."

Logical statements can be made about the *details* of an information resource as well as at a high level. For instance, the statement "the design materials include plastic" might serve as precondition for an activity to engage a specialist in plastics onto the project, or the statement "design valid until Dec 2010" might warn that the regulatory guidelines followed will expire on that date.

This examination of resource details could be used to *loop over the contents* of an information resource, examining each one in turn. For example, suppose the design in our example is for an aircraft wing. The process model might be extended to include an activity sequence that looked at each part of the wing design, and added the interfaces it specified to an overall list for use by designers of the other aircraft components.

A computerized support tool for human-driven processes will allow the modeler to construct such conditions based on the details of the information resources within a Role. A Human Interaction Management System not only allows the elements of each resource to be included in conditions, but also allows *simple conditions* to be combined into more sophisticated *compound conditions* using conventional logical operators (AND, NAND, OR, XOR and NOT). This makes it possible to express conditions of arbitrary complexity, ranging from "materials list complete AND interface list complete" through to a lengthy statement that encapsulates company policy about suitability of a design for production release.

A main strength of Role Activity Diagrams has always been their emphasis on describing the states of a process, in terms of the objects used within it. This not only makes it possible to control and validate activities as described above, but also allows high-level control to be placed over the Role as a whole.

For example, recall from the description of Role attributes given above that it necessary to describe, as part of a process model, both the *goals* and the *responsibilities* of a particular Role. This can also be done using logical conditions:

- The goals of a Role can be expressed via a *terminating condition* for the Role—a logical statement that when true, signals to the User and to any process support system that the work of the Role is done, and the Role can be safely terminated. For the Designer in our example, this might be "Final acceptance received from Manager OR Final rejection received from Manager." In a computerized process support environment, this may mean that the Role will be removed from the system automatically. Alternatively, the termination of the Role can be left under manual control if desired. Note that this approach means that a Role can be ended at any point in its lifecycle—if the terminating condition becomes true, why hang around trying to complete outstanding tasks that are no longer required?

- The responsibilities of a Role can be expressed via an *always condition*—a logical statement that must never be violated. In practice, this means that when the User tries to complete an activity, not only is any post-condition on that activity evaluated, but also the always condition of the Role as a whole. If *either* is false, the effects of the activity are all undone. An always condition is a simple way to ensure that a Role upholds its duties, whether these duties pertain to its specific nature (a Manager, for example, might have an always condition such as "assessed designs must have some reason given for approval/rejection"), company policies (for example, quality standards), or statutory regulations (such as export compliance).

For now, we will move on from states of a process, returning to them when we come to discuss the implementation of a human-driven process support system. We have yet to deal with the last remaining construct in the Role Activity Diagram notation—interactions between Roles—where again we will make changes to the standard interpretation.

Interactions

The *horizontal lines* on a Role Activity Diagram show where two or more Roles interact. In our original example, Figure 9, there were two interactions: one for the Manager to provide the Designer(s) with a design brief from which to prepare a design, the other for each Designer to return a design for assessment. The further extended example, Figure 13, shows an additional interaction used by the Manager to provide feedback to a Designer.

An interaction is generally used to the exchange of information, although interactions are sometimes employed simply as a means of synchronization—to ensure that the parties concerned are all aware that a particular point in the process has been reached, such as a project milestone.

As a result of the original background in Petri nets, interactions between Roles are traditionally considered to be *synchronous*—they can only take place if both parties are willing and able to participate at the same time.

Ould explains,

> "An interaction can be two-party—involving two roles—or multi-party, involving a number of roles. However many parties are involved, interactions are always *synchronous*; that is, both role instances must be ready for the interaction to take place before it can start, it starts at the same moment for each party, and it completes at the same moment for each party at which point they enter their respective new states."[18]

With this interpretation, a Role Activity Diagram interaction is more like a telephone call than an email. There is no way for one party to send something in advance of the other party being ready to receive it.

Both telephone calls and email have their strengths. However, insisting that both parties to every interaction in every process are there at the same moment not only introduces delays, but is simply unrealistic. These days most of us deal much more by email than via the telephone, since we can get our work done faster if we don't have to wait until the other party is ready every single time.

Moreover, the usual interpretation of interactions for purposes of process support is that they are *directional*. Although there is no precise definition of interaction semantics made in the literature, by convention an interaction either involves no data at all being passed, or it passes data:

- From one Role to another (a purchase order, for example);
- From one Role to many others (distribution of meeting minutes, for example); or
- From many Roles to one (status reports to a manager, for example).

Again, this is an unnecessary restriction when it comes to human-driven processes. Consider an interaction that represents a project team meeting, an absolutely typical and everyday part of organizational life. It is likely that all parties will have something to contribute—in general, team members will bring a status report for their part of the work, while the project manager or secretary will also supply the meeting agenda—and all parties will take away most of the information concerned. This could be modeled as a series of separate interactions, but to do so would make an activity that is essentially simple and easily understood into something that is unnecessarily complex.

Hence, we change the interpretation of interactions within a Role Activity Diagram. Rather than being a one-off, atomic action we consider an interaction to be composed of a number of separate *channels*. Each channel is like a communication pipe, attached to a single sender Role and to one or more recipient Roles. The sender Role contributes an item of data into the channel when ready, and the recipient Roles each then take the item out at their leisure.

In the simplest case, there is one channel, with one sender Role and one recipient Role, and the item is empty. The use of such an interaction is simply for the sender to indicate to the recipient that they have reached a certain point, or that something particular has happened. For example, this could be used by a public relations firm to let their client know that they have sent out promotional material to the press.

Another simple case is the sending of a message from one party to another. Like an email, this just consists of the sender supplying a piece of information, and the recipient picking it up when they are ready. Again, only a single channel is required.

A more complex case might be the project team meeting referred to above. Here everyone has something to send, and other things to receive. Each sender in this case has their own channel, to which most if not all of the other team members are connected as recipients. The interaction can be made as sophisticated as desired—not everyone could receive everything, for example.

This approach is sufficiently simple and general to allow almost any form of communication between process participants to be described.

For one thing, it is possible to support a very common case—the repeated use of a single interaction. It is characteristic of human collaboration that people negotiate to clarify a request before it can be accepted. A single line on a Role Activity Diagram labeled *Request (such-and-such)* might therefore turn into an exchange of messages before the request is accepted. A Human Interaction Management System may allow this as the norm. If the interactions have been set up to be repeatable, the conversation can be launched and kept open as long as necessary—until all parties indicate that agreement has been reached, which will then disable the preconditions of the interaction on all sides and prevent further message transmission.

It is even possible to simulate the synchronous behavior of the traditional approach to interaction definition. To do this, the interaction is defined such that each party to it:

- Sends an input;

- Receives all inputs made by others; and

- Is unable to continue their work until all inputs from the others have been received.

Then the interaction effectively synchronizes all parties, just as in the conventional approach to interpreting a Role Activity Diagram. In the simplest case, with two parties, this just means having two channels in the interaction—one for each Role to send something to the other.

Our interpretation of interactions is founded on the passing of data from one Role to another. Hence we need to understand in more detail what this implies.

For a start, the data transfer can leave the original in the sender—or not. Since Roles are considered to own their information resources, this makes a big difference. If the sender wishes to retain the original data for later use, as they will often do, both sender and recipient end up with copies of the same document— that, over time, may well diverge in content as one or the other is edited or changed in some other way. Both the process definer and the process participants need to be aware that this is a possibility, and allow for it. For example, the process could identify one Role as the ultimate owner of the data and holder of the master copy, with the ability at appropriate points to include any changes made by others, and thus ensure consistency.

This issue arises specifically from the nature of Roles as having *private* information resources, rather than drawing them from a common corporate repository when required. It introduces additional complication, but this complication is one that already exists, in real life—like it or not, people will make personal copies of the same data, and edit these copies as they see fit, so the process must support this behavior. Suppose you are a member of a committee working to draw up a new standard, of some kind—you will note down your ideas when they occur to you, probably by marking up your own copy of the draft specification. Unless the process support system allows you to do this, you will simply bypass it, which is what we are trying to avoid.

An even deeper issue is introduced by the existence of the same object in multiple Roles. We saw above in our discussion of *Resources* that the format and structure of a data item within a Role may well change over time. How is this to be resolved, if Roles can pass data to one another? Surely the recipient must expect data of a certain type, in order that they have the ability to process it—to use the appropriate reader application to open the document, for example—or access *properties* that he or she needs. In our example Role Activity Diagram above, a design might be expected to contain information such as name of the designer, total estimated cost, etc.

This can be handled, but we need to appreciate two things. First, interactions know very little about the data they pass. In a Human Interaction Management System, an interaction knows who the sender and recipient Roles are, and the names of the objects to be passed, but no details at all of what makes up those objects. It simply takes the object of a specified name from the sender (if it exists), and places it in the recipient under another specified name.[19]

Second, it is up to the process definer—and the process users—to set things up so that the objects within the process are valid. For example, suppose a text document is passed from one Role to another. It may or may not be sensible to replace this with a spreadsheet—it just depends on whether at the recipient's end, the Web browser (or other user interface framework recipients use to operate their Role) knows how to open this type of document. Similarly, if the original text document had file properties that recorded important process information, these properties should also be available in the spreadsheet. Human-driven processes can be configured and operated safely despite the use of different kinds of document at different times—after all, we do this all the time, without thinking of our work in process terms—but some care is required.

If the information resource is not a document as such, but a piece of structured or semi-structured data—XML text, for example—the same principles apply. In a Human Interaction Management System, it is often the case that certain tasks within a Role expect particular data items to exist within particular resources, and will fail if they are missing. However, in general the tasks will not fail—or care at all—if additional fields are present.

This approach permits very flexible behavior. It is only necessary to be aware of, and to allow for, the inevitable complications introduced by the human tendency to change the data they work with.

These complications become greater when multiple versions of a document are kept, something that often happens as a result of interactions. Suppose an interaction passes an object with a particular name into a recipient Role, "Project Plan," for example. What if there already exists a resource with that name in the recipient? It is an issue for the process definer: whether to replace the original, or to keep it and add the new Project Plan to a list of versions. If the latter approach is taken, over time a number of Project Plans will accumulate, and these may be of different formats. This is not necessarily a problem, just something to be aware of.

A further issue with regard to interactions is that of *offline entities*. As discussed, these are resources within a Role that are atoms rather than bits: physical objects rather than just information (keys, printed documents, and so on). Such objects are frequently passed from one Role to another via an interaction, but the nature of what happens is different.

In particular, in certain situations there is a fundamental issue affecting computerized process support. Suppose that there is a Role with an *offline User*, one who does not log onto the process support system. The User may work for another company, for example, and does not have access to the process support system via an extranet. In order to model the process correctly, the process support system still needs to contain a representation of the Role in question—but this Role is not independently active, since no one is able to operate it from within the process support system. Despite this, the Role with an offline User will still have interactions with other Roles—or it wouldn't be a part of the process in the first place.

Some of these interactions may be electronic—in which case they can be simulated by the process support system. For instance, an email message from the offline User can be intercepted by the process support system, and automatically redirected to the recipient Role as an interaction message from the appropriate sender Role, just as if the sender was also using the system. However, if the interaction is to transfer a physical object, such as a signed contract handed over during a meeting, there is no way for the system to know that this has taken place.

Hence it is up to the recipient to say when they have received the object—before the process system is aware that it has been sent. This is the only time when the receiver can be *proactive* within an interaction—to inform the process system of the sender's actions before the system itself becomes aware of them. It is an important case to be aware of when developing a Human Interaction Management System, since it occurs frequently in practice—the situation is not the problem of a process modeler or process participant, but must be understood, and supported appropriately, by the system itself.

Putting it all together

To summarize this chapter, we have introduced the Role Activity Diagram notation for use as building blocks in our approach to modeling human-driven processes. In the next section we will complete the framework itself by introducing higher-level notions of process, and relating them to the understanding of work developed previously.

Our use of Role Activity Diagrams has involved making several changes to the traditional use of the notation. We retain the six standard object types:

- *Roles* that users play within processes

- *Resources* private to Roles—information and other items required to participate in the process

- *Activities* carried out by Roles to manipulate resources

- *Users*—the humans, organizations or machines that take on Roles

- *States of a process*, defined in terms of logical conditions that control the execution and validation of activities.

- *Interactions* between Roles to transfer resources and synchronize behavior.

However, we remove the basis in Petri nets (though we will add this back later, in a different way), and alter the interpretation of many standard symbols. In particular:

- *Process participation.* To model human-driven processes effectively enough to support improvement, we need to understand better the nature of people, organizations, and machines as process participants. In particular, we must be able to characterize the Roles in a process, and the Users that play them, by adding various attributes not found in the standard notation. We also require a better technique for modeling relationships—both on a personal basis as Users, and within a process context as Roles. This understanding must support such typical human behaviors as learning, adaptation and conflict resolution, and such typical process features as goals, responsibilities and delegation of authority.

- *Process management under process control.* You must be able to use a Role to define, start, stop, monitor, and generally manage processes and their associated users. This requires that we support the definition of process objects of all forms as information resources within Roles, and allow them to be passed from one Role to another via interactions.

- *Activity enablement and validation.* Humans typically jump from one activity to another, repeating and interleaving activities as they see fit. If we are to facilitate people's work rather than constrain it unnaturally—and if we expect to gain acceptance for any process support system we attempt to implement—we must support this behavior, while simultaneously permitting appropriate controls to be placed on the process. This leads us toward an approach to process definition based on the use of logical conditions that enable and validate both activities and Roles—and this leads us away from process modeling based on sequencing of tasks (as is usual).

- *Tasks.* Activities are not atomic, but composed of multiple lower-level tasks. It is a modeling issue whether or not to expose a particular task on a Role Activity Diagram as a fully-fledged activity, but there are some simple principles that can be applied. For example, tasks are often unpredictably repeated and interleaved, to the point where it would be hard to find a typical order to draw them in if shown separately. Unless some logical and standardized dependencies can be found for the tasks, they may as well be simply grouped together inside a single activity.

- *Interactions* are not generally synchronous. A closer match to real life is to view them as formed of multiple *channels* for sending and receiving resources, where each channel has a sender and one or more recipients. A sender may donate an item into a channel when they are ready—and recipients may then take it out in their own time. This approach to modeling interaction leads to some specific conclusions. For instance, when it comes to computerized process support, the recipient may be the one to signal that something has been given, not the senders themselves.

In the next chapter, we will take these building blocks, and show how they can be used to construct a complete framework for modeling human-driven processes.

References.

[1] Coplien, J., Harrison, N., 2004, "Organizational Patterns of Agile Software Development"

[2] Holt A. W., Ramsey H. R., Grimes J. D., 1983, "Coordination system technology

as the basis for a programming environment," Electrical Communication, Vol. 57(4)

[3] Snowdon R.A. , 1988, "A Brief Overview of the IPSE 2.5 Project," Ada User, Volume 9, No. 4

[4] This argument is elaborated in Harrison-Broninski, K., 2004, "A Role-Based Approach To Business Process Management," http://www.rolemodellers.com/abstracts/A Role-Based Approach To Business Process Management.pdf. The paper compares and contrasts the mainstream *process modeling languages* BPML, BPEL, XPDL and ebXML, showing how they provide little support for human collaboration, and goes on to describe how this deficiency is remedied by the Playwright process modeling language underpinning RADRunner. The main *graphical notations* currently in use by analysts are Business Process Modeling Notation (BPMN), which is based on BPML and BPEL and hence suffers from their own proclivities in this respect, and the Unified Modeling Language (UML), which was created specifically for use in software design rather than process description. The Role Activity Diagram (RAD) graphical notation, on the other hand, is equivalent to a subset of Playwright and shares its main strengths.

[5] Ould, M.A., 1995, "Business Processes—Modeling and Analysis for Re-engineering and Improvement," Wiley & Sons

[6] Warboys, B., Kawalek, P., Robertson, I., Greenwood, M., 1999, "Business Information Systems—a Process Approach," McGraw-Hill

[7] We adopt this flexible notation for the depiction of multiple Role instances in a process since it is not generally necessary to specify in a process depiction exactly how many Roles of a specific type exist—they are often created and dispensed with during the process itself. However, a process support system may choose to show how many Roles *actually exist at a point in time* as a number above the topmost Role rectangle.
The use of a number above the Role rectangle is similar to the approach advocated by Ould:
"To mark a role with a single pre-existing instance we place a tick next to its name. If the role has exactly four pre-existing instances then we place the number 4 after the tick. If it has an indeterminate number of instances we mark it with "n" after the tick. If a role has no tick against its name we know immediately that, when the process starts, there are no instances of it and we can therefore expect to find it being instantiated by another role somewhere on the RAD."
Ould M. A.,, 2005, "Business Process Management: A Rigorous Approach", Meghan-Kiffer Press

However, Ould's use of a numeric annotation is tailored to the description of processes prior to their being put into practice, rather than to the ongoing description of changing behavior as a process evolves. Moreover, our general approach to showing multiple Roles, using layered rectangles, has the advantage that a process support system can permit the user to select a specific rectangle and examine the properties of the Role concerned.

[8] Michael Jackson, 1983, "System Development," Prentice-Hall

[9] Taken from Wil van der Aalst's Web tutorial on Petri nets, http://psim.tm.tue.nl/staff/wvdaalst/Petri_nets/pn_tutorial.htm

[10] As well as van der Aalst's Web tutorial referenced above, there is an in-depth guide at http://viking.gmu.edu/http/syst511/vg511/AppC.html

[11] Ould M. A., 1995, ibid., p.69

[12] Milner, R., 1999, "Communicating and mobile systems: the pi calculus," Cambridge University Press

[13] It is actually the oval shape which represents the *transition*—the vertical lines are *arcs*.

[14] In formal terms, a *guard* condition for the activity.

[15] The Unified Modeling Language, http://www.uml.org/

[16] Business Process Modeling Language, http://www.bpmi.org/bpml-spec.htm

[17] XLANG, http://www.gotdotnet.com/team/xml_wsspecs/xlang-c/default.htm

[18] Ould M. A., 1995, ibid., p.39

[19] In other words, RADRunner interactions are *polymorphic*.

Four

Modeling Human Interactions

KEY POINTS: We develop a new concept of process management—the principle of *separation of control*. Authority over a process is assigned to a Sponsor Role separate from it (*executive control*), while daily supervision of a process is assigned to key Roles within it (*management control*). We show how the *REACT* and *AIM patterns* can be implemented in terms of this principle, and depicted graphically using a Role Activity Diagram.

We move on to deal with process evolution, and see how *agreement depictions* based on Role Activity Diagrams can be used initially to support executive control of a process, then successively refined to allow day-to-day management control of (and shared commitment among process participants to) process changes made on-the-fly.

As part of this discussion, we see the AIM pattern start to come into its own, and discuss how, in many complex processes, a valuable modeling technique is to break the deliverables down into distinct yet interdependent components, and base a *collaborative transaction* on each component.

We look at how you can determine a *process architecture* for your organization—a breakdown of what distinct processes exist—and discuss the new Riva methodology. Riva is recommended with reservations about its modeling of management, which is different from our own, and perhaps applicable mainly to highly standardized industries and mechanistic processes.

We conclude with a proposal for a new formal foundation for business processes that unites two theories of computation, Petri nets and pi-calculus, and shows how both together with a third approach are necessary to capture everything that is going on for purposes of analysis. In the case of the first two approaches, the suggestion is to change the basis used for abstraction, from modeling work activities to modeling management activities. We show how management control can be described using Petri nets, and executive control using the pi-calculus. We argue that work activities are better modeled via a declarative specification language, and propose use of Z for this purpose.

Reasonable people adapt themselves to the world. Unreasonable people attempt to adapt the world to themselves. All progress, therefore, depends on unreasonable people.
— George Bernard Shaw.

Adapting the world

It is generally recognized that the fundamental problem facing business is that of *change*. There is just too much of it for convenience. Like it or not, change happens—all the time, all over the place.

Strategies and policies change, and such high-level change is expensive to implement—however, it happens relatively infrequently. *Structural changes* to the organization are more frequent, but can be anticipated, prepared for, budgeted and planned. *Staff movement* occurs even more often, but we like to think we can manage this kind of change—even if it is not generally handled as well as we intend, and problems occur all the way down the line as a result, sometimes not manifesting themselves until quite some time after the event. But *process change*—this is the real nightmare. Not only does it happen all the time, for any number of reasons, but it happens on a case by case basis, as well in general. And there are no generally accepted methods for dealing with it.

In other words, we may spend large amounts of time and money preparing a set of process descriptions, and even use these as the basis for computerized process support systems, only to find that the reality of working life has changed, and is now a poor match to the processes thus expressed. There are two fundamental reasons that the processes change.

First, a particular process description is no longer right at all—since the time at which it was drawn up, the business has moved on and now does things differently. For example, the process model describing how purchases over a certain amount require approval from a senior manager, but this has been holding up projects, so in practice all project managers just assume approval will be given, and the requisition forms are signed retroactively.

Second, people may carry out a particular process in different ways, only some of which match the process description. For example, the process model describing how purchases over a certain amount require approval from a senior manager, but this has been holding up large projects, so in practice certain project managers just assume approval will be given, and the requisition forms are signed retroactively.

Note the slight difference in wording! In the second case, it is only for *large* projects, and *certain* project managers, that retrospective approval will be given. The change is on a case-by-case basis, rather than across the board. This latter practice, in particular, may never have been officially enshrined in company procedures, just adopted by all concerned as the best and quickest way to get the work done. It is quite possible that the business analysts who did the process modeling were never even informed that such things happen.

Some executives may see the removal of such workarounds as a benefit of computerized process support. Whether or not this view has merit, it just doesn't work. People will always find a way to beat the system. Particularly if a group of staff members are frustrated with a process support system that doesn't let them work in the way they wish, they will just work round it—exchanging login details, paying for project supplies as out-of-pocket expenses, ordering on account from suppliers, and so on.

The only people who believe that process systems have the ability to control people effectively are those who never use them. There is usually an implicit conspiracy of silence among the users of such enterprise software, developed in order to protect their hard-won ability to make the systems do what they want. However, anyone who has implemented enterprise systems, and taken the trouble to look at how they are actually used, knows that users see the constraints enforced by computers as at best an annoyance, and at worst a challenge. Either way, they will bypass or misuse the system in order to get their work done as efficiently as possible—because what matters to individuals is not the unalloyed purity of the systems they use, but the results they achieve in their daily work, that have a direct effect on their appraisal outcomes, promotion chances, and salary levels.

Hence, if we are to find an effective way of understanding, modeling, managing and supporting human-driven processes, we need to work with people, not impose structures on them that are viewed as hindering the best way to get on with things. Even if you are prepared to ignore basic human psychology, to do anything else aside from accommodating how people actually get work done is just a waste of time.

At this point, some readers with executive responsibilities may feel like putting this book down in disgust! Is anarchy being advocated? Power to the people? A Bolshevik revolution of interaction workers? How are organizations to be controlled if their staff are able to do whatever they feel like?

The response to this lies in understanding *what needs to remain constant about a process*, for purposes of control, and *what needs to change in operation*, in order to empower people to do their jobs properly. What we are saying is that existing enterprise systems, techniques, and tools have focused to date on the wrong level of process, and attempted to constrain human activities at too detailed a level.

To paraphrase Coplien and Harrison, task ordering can't be counted on as a stable component of process structure—in *any* process centered on humans and their interaction. We go further, and say that not even the individual tasks themselves are stable—they are dispensed with or added to based on what people perceive to be necessary. In fact, a person's ability to make these kinds of judgments is a major reason that the person was chosen for his or her position in the first place—it stems from an individual's deep understanding of the work, and a commitment to getting it done properly and on time.

However, this is different from saying that people should be entitled to decide for themselves what the *nature and purpose* of their work is. It is one thing to decide for yourself how to go about doing your work, and quite another to define the work itself. Defining the work itself involves determining the *responsibilities* of the workers—the duties they must uphold—and the *goals* they must achieve—their aims and targets. Giving responsibilities and setting goals are executive activities, carried out at a more senior level of authority.

Goals and responsibilities are the fundamental aspects of a Role, and effectively are what defines the Role. Hence, our claim here boils down to the following:

- It is an executive matter to determine the Roles in a process, and assign them to appropriate people; but

- It is for the Users of each Role to decide how best to carry out the work involved—something that may vary from person to person, and from case to case.

For example, we've already discussed a hypothetical investigation by a government agency into cost reduction that featured Roles including *Project Manager, Business Analyst* and *Accountant*. The executive responsible for the process as a whole—the person who instigated it and funded it, a senior civil servant perhaps—sees his or her self as *in charge* of the process, as opposed to *managing* it on a day-to-day basis. The executive neither needs nor wishes day-to-day involvement with every operational detail. What the executive needs is to know that the work will be carried out in a certain way— e.g., according to an approved project management methodology such as PRINCE 2[1]—or that the work will deliver results in a specific format requested by, let's say, a politician.

In particular, the executive needs to ensure certain specific things. They will engage some, if not all, of the people who will work on the process—almost certainly the project manager, and perhaps others such as analysts and accountants—and be concerned that:

1. *The people involved will perform certain Roles, each with its own goals and responsibilities.* In order to feel confident of the outcome of the process, an executive sponsor needs to know that people of the right caliber, with the right skills, will be involved, and have agreed to carry out specific duties.

2. *The eventual deliverables will meet certain preconditions.* It is unlikely that every detail of the deliverable will be specified at an executive level, although executives may need to know that the deliverable will be in a certain format, or contain specific key sections. However, until the process itself has been carried out, it is not appropriate to specify in precise detail the structure of the documents or other deliverables concerned— defining the scope of the problem is a major part of the work of the process itself, and the eventual deliverables will only mirror the understanding developed along the way.

3. *The process participants will interact in a way to ensure that their individual contributions combine to produce overall deliverables of the highest possible quality.* Although project managers can act to *facilitate* these interactions, they will not necessarily be empowered to *specify* how often each person will attend meetings, and what exactly each participant will bring to the table. Such details are often determined by existing, wider-reaching agreements, with, for example, external consultancy organizations. Project management is often concerned more with negotiation and support than with the authority necessary to ensure that the participants in a process are willing to work together in appropriate ways.

In other words, the executive responsible for a process does need to ensure certain things about a process, but none of these concerns are directly task-related. They concern Roles, deliverables and interactions: who will do the work, the general nature of what the workers will produce, and how they will co-operate in doing so. Joining the process as a participant amounts to agreeing that you will contribute specific parts of the overall work.

This way of thinking about work provides a more reassuring approach to human-driven process implementation, because it leaves executives with a form of control that they seek—and removes from them a level of detail they shouldn't have to worry about.

We will develop a more comprehensive model of process management, and show how the approach enables not only managers, but also workers to *focus on the work that is rightly their own province*. If you are micro-managing your workers down to the level of monitoring each task they carry out, and asking why they have done everything the way they have, you may as well do the work yourself—saving everyone time in the long run, and certainly causing less annoyance. Executives should be concerned with a higher level of process, one that remains more or less constant because it is part of a wider organizational picture. The opportunity—and the challenge—for Human Interaction Management is to support this *separation of control* approach to human activity.

In this section we'll discuss the constant aspects of a human-driven process that we will see can be expressed in terms of *separation of control* between the parties in a process, and captured graphically using Role Activity Diagram notation. We will then look at how the lower-level changes in a process can be managed from within—by the workers themselves—when we come to discuss *agreements*. After these discussions, we will have rounded out our understanding of human activity, and will see how we may proceed to provide both management and software support for human-driven processes:

- We have seen how *a new interpretation of Role Activity Theory* can be used to provide the tool support essential for human activity, in a manner that is suggestive rather than prescriptive, yet still permits necessary business controls to be enforced.

- The concept of *separation of control* we'll now elaborate provides the higher-level modeling constructs needed to go beyond Role Activity Theory, and integrate the REACT pattern and its sub-pattern AIM into a fully-fledged modeling framework for human processes. Our discussion will lead us also to a clearer understanding of what is involved in *managing* human-driven processes.

▪ Finally, the *agreements* principle will give us the means we need to safely control the dynamism that we have seen is fundamental to human activity, and that is permitted by our building blocks. We will show how speech acts, together with a specific use of the Role Activity Diagram notation, give us what we need to ensure that processes run smoothly despite the inevitable changes made along the way by the participants themselves.

We will then move on to take a brief look at how processes fit together at a high level—how to work out what processes *exist* inside an organization—and conclude the chapter by proposing a new *formal foundation* for the analysis of human-driven processes.

Some readers may choose to skip the latter discussion, and move on to the following chapter of the book, where we analyze the benefits to be gained from proper understanding and support of human-driven processes. We will see in that chapter that everyday aspects of corporate life, such as quality and confidentiality, can be revisited from a human perspective, and new avenues thus opened up for improvement.

Separation of control

We have seen that the division of a process into Roles is a fundamental aspect of placing it under executive control, and hence something that should not be changed at the whim of those carrying out the work. In a sense, the process participants sign up for their Role when they take it on: they commit to playing their allotted part, however they achieve it in practice. The executive responsible for a process:

▪ *Determines the key Roles* within the overall process in order to ensure that specific goals and responsibilities will be met

▪ *Assigns certain key Roles to appropriate people* who commit to meeting the corresponding goals and responsibilities to the best of their ability.

Returning to our hypothetical investigation into cost reduction by a government agency, the Roles include *Project Manager, Business Analyst* and *Accountant.* In actual practice there might be several other Roles associated with the project—administration staff, statisticians, researchers, and so on. However, the executive who sponsors the project—a senior civil servant, let's say—is likely to be unconcerned with these others. Their interest lies only in ensuring that the three key Roles exist within the project, and that their players are suitably qualified. The executive may even be concerned only with the Project Manager, if he or she has confidence that this person will decide on and engage the other Roles appropriately.

Note, however, that in either case the *Project Manager* is considered to be "just another" Role in this work—not a higher-level management Role, but a worker like the others, quite likely appointed by the same person as other Role players were, whose responsibility happens to concern planning and resourcing rather than analysis or calculation.

A particular claim of this book is that better understanding of human-driven processes will lead to more effective means of managing process participants. To achieve this, we need to consider how to represent the general activities of management in process terms. What is actually involved in creating a human-driven process, and then facilitating it?

It is conventional in business process analysis to consider each business process as having a corresponding *management process* associated with it. The planning and resourcing activities of the Project Manager, for example, would usually be viewed as belonging not to the same process as the other Roles, but to a different process—one defined at a "higher level," that in principle is also concerned with managing other processes as well. Applying this approach to our example, the Project Manager Role may also be expected to support other current projects apart from the cost reduction investigation. A typical view is the following description by Martyn Ould:

"… the moment we find more than one case potentially in progress, we can expect to find another, connected process that is concerned with managing the flow of cases through the case process. This case management process is responsible for scheduling, allocating work to people, monitoring flows, prioritizing, accepting new cases, negotiating in the event of priority problems, in short: management activities."[2]

This view corresponds directly to a traditional organization chart. For every level below the CEO (or board of directors in some cases), there is someone, or some group of people, to supervise, monitor, and resource the work of people. As a result, it seems like common sense to divide processes into "case work" and "managing case work." But does this match the reality of management, particularly for human-driven processes?

In practice, the traditional approach to organization mapping—showing line management—is nearly always used in conjunction with a separate chart, perhaps overlaid on the first as dotted lines, showing who reports to whom on a daily basis. This second chart is based not directly on organizational seniority, but on the actual work being carried out. Sometimes this work may be project-based. At other times it will span the organization, such as when a skilled person lends his or her abilities to various groups at different times—e.g., to produce custom reports, help with the use of equipment, or consult on an area in which he or she has specialized knowledge.

In other words, the second chart is a more realistic picture of what is actually going on. And in this second chart, the lines of authority are much more complex. In fact, often they do not strictly represent authority at all, merely reporting—delivery of information—and this may have no relation to where power lies.

Moreover, even such a combination of charts—known as *matrix management*—may fail to capture the full picture. It is common to have "true" reporting lines that are not shown on any chart. For example, in a construction project, information from all sources generally flows to the chief architect, surveyor or engineer, regardless of their actual authority over those working on the site (and if doesn't, there are problems in store). Such a person may not be 'officially in charge,' but is acknowledged as the most expert, and hence the appropriate person to monitor and guide the work in progress. Sometimes the person who takes this role of information focus, may not even be the 'chief of anything,' just recognized by all as having the necessary skills to keep things on the right track—an external consultant, for example, who has no authority, yet has a high level of skill and experience, employed for his or her ability to keep things on the straight and narrow.

A 10-year study of software development practices by Coplien and Harrison shows how such information flow—to the main architect(s) of a development project, rather than to the nominal project manager(s)—can be the differentiating factor between ordinary and extraordinary performance. In their discussion of the pattern they call "Work Flows Inward," they write:

"Some centralized control and direction are necessary. During software production, the work bottleneck of a system should be at the center of its communication and control structure ...

You should not put managers at the center of the communication grid: they will become overloaded and make decisions that are less well-considered, and they will make decisions that don't take day-to-day dynamics into account ...

Organizations run by professional managers tend to have repeatable business processes, but don't seem to reach the same productivity plateaus of organizations run by engineers. [3]

We can see from this that it is not always possible to divide human-driven processes neatly into "work" and "management of that work." The activities typically ascribed to management may well come from within a process, and can potentially be carried out by someone who has no authority over proceedings.

In other words, *in human-driven processes, the activities of management cannot be separated from the activities of the process itself.* Management of human activity is an integral part of the work itself, not a higher form of activity, peering down from a position of superior knowledge and authority to provide godlike assistance as and when required.

In one way, this makes intuitive sense, since it is becoming the norm for managers to be involved on a day-to-day basis with their staff, not distant and unaware, in a remote corner office on a higher floor of the building with the door closed. However, in another way, this is a counter-intuitive notion—are we trying to dispense altogether with the authority innate to management?

Certainly, the conventional idea of "case processes" and corresponding "case management processes" is a very persistent one in business analysis. It is necessary to fully justify taking an alternative approach for human-driven processes, and present a way forward that permits work to be properly supervised. What we are talking about is not removing high-level responsibility or authority from organizational life, but understanding better the way in which managers and workers interact to get things done—finding a better *model* for getting work done than the traditional hierarchical, command-and-control representation, which is too simplistic to match reality.

To develop such a model of management, we must, in fact, go even further in our abandonment of traditional process modeling approaches.

Just as the day-to-day management of a human-driven process cannot be separated from its operation, the division between *process design* and *process enactment* can be very hard to draw for human activity. We will go into this in detail when we discuss process improvement, but illustrate the point initially here by taking a specific example—that of user interface design.

In the general case, *user interface design* goes far beyond the design computer screens. Anything prepared by one person for the use of others has a user interface—even a letter. When we choose a template for a document, or decide it should be sent to someone as paper in the post rather than by email, we are making user interface design choices. Any form of communication between people, whether those people are management, process participants, or both, has a user interface. To see in a general way how the user interface impacts the communication concerned, let's consider some examples unconnected with computerized process support:

- A chatty email memo to a supplier "tells a different story" from a formal letter on headed notepaper, whatever the text therein—it says something about the nature of the relationship considered to exist between the sender and recipients.

- An informal conference call called by the project manager to find out how everyone is getting on, is a different matter from a multi-page form with many fields that everyone must fill in categorizing their progress so far, and may well reveal different aspects of what is going on.

- New health and safety regulations may in some cases find more understanding and acceptance from staff if presented via cartoon-style posters around the workplace as opposed to text documents on an intranet.

Turning to Human Interaction Management Systems, the user interfaces available during computer supported process enactment should reflect the diversity we find in normal business life—if they don't, they offer less functionality than we have without them. Moreover, they should allow change during the life of the process—just as we change the nature and tenor of communications among ourselves from time to time, according to circumstances.

Suppose you are team lead on a construction project, and it is nearing a milestone date. An effective means both of monitoring progress and of reminding people that time is short is to request status reports more frequently, and to ask for additional information such as precise forecasts of delivery dates and anticipated problems meeting deadlines. Hence, if you are using a process support system, it should allow corresponding change to the screen(s) used for status reporting. If we were working without the aid of process support we would be likely to adopt such techniques—so computers should enhance this ability, not reduce it.

What we are seeing here is that user interface design is not separated from the runtime activity of the process itself, but an integral part of that activity. Just as with process management in general, there are complex feedback loops between process design and process enactment. Circumstances within an unfolding human-driven process can, and will, require changes to the user interfaces available within it.

However, current enterprise systems do not, in general, allow this. For example, when implementing a new human-driven process, creating the user interfaces to be presented by those activities intended to have computer support is generally seen as something to be completed before starting production use of the process—after this point, the user interfaces will be left well alone. In other words, design of the user interfaces available to process participants is usually seen as a one-off activity, the very last thing to be addressed during the process development stage. The design of a screen is generally viewed as derived directly from the function of that screen—so the screen is handed off to, let's say, a Web designer to implement once the general nature of the activity concerned has been determined by analysts—to enter customer details, perhaps, or approve a purchase order. This approach does not expect, or permit, ongoing changes to the screen to be made during process enactment.

Such rigid interface design may be appropriate for mechanistic processes—the kind of repetitive task sequences found in typical workflow systems. However, to adopt such an approach for processes of the kind we discuss in this book—human-driven, innovative, dynamic processes—is to waste a major opportunity for communication among participants. The *user interface presented for an activity* by a computer can itself be used as a flexible, dynamic and powerful tool for communication from one person to many others.

In a Human Interaction Management System, the screen used to present a task to the user can itself be treated as an object within the process—it can then be altered at any time by another process participant with the necessary access and authority, or even by automated means, should that be appropriate. In other words, a process participant can be empowered to change, while a process is running, the design of a screen used by other participants.

This means that the screens available within the process themselves become an effective and immediate means of communication without needing to send any direct, overt, messages at all. The change might be as simple as to inform people that a new person has joined a project, implying that a new capability has been added to the project. Alternatively, it might be functionally significant—to require that new information be submitted, to show details not previously made available, or to remove the display of information now deemed inappropriate. In any of these cases, suitable explanation can be made where it is needed—on the screen itself, rather than (as is typically done) in an email that people either don't read carefully or have forgotten by the time they next use the screen.

We saw above that one of the deficiencies of speech acts as a model of communication was that they allow only for *direct* communication. Very often indirect communication is not only as common, but more effective. Information communicated via alteration of the user interfaces people encounter every day in their work is likely to be absorbed more immediately, and taken more seriously, than another email cluttering up their inbox, or notification in a workflow task list.

In fact, such change to user interfaces is often necessary at ground level, in order to support the *dynamic nature of information* within a human-driven process. Screens presented by a process support system reflect, and may allow certain forms of maintenance to, the data available to the user. We argued above in *Resources* that this data can be *different in structure and format* from user to user, and from time to time. Hence the screens available to each person for access to that data must be capable of corresponding change, as and when necessary.

A common case is that you need to capture some piece of data that was never predicted by the original process designers. For example, an insurance investigator may wish to qualify a piece of evidence, link it to some other aspect of the case, or add subsidiary items. If you are one of a team of engineering designers, you might wish to add links to parts of your design specifying materials requirements, or potential safety issues.

Such examples arise in any field in which people are doing adaptive, innovative, *human* work—and the resultant changes to data structure may come from any process participant. In particular, you may choose to change your own data to add new and unexpected forms of information that have come to light, or need to be recorded for the benefit of others. The structural changes cannot be predicted, but they must be supported—and they have an effect on user interface design. If you've added (or removed) elements from a data item, your screens will need to change accordingly.

We emphasize again that these changes take place in all sorts of ways, whether or not computerized Human Interaction Management is involved. Without process support, we tend to create free-form documents of the format we require, and this format cannot in general be predicted in advance by those who designed the process in which we are engaged. Once process support systems are brought into the picture, the requirement remains—so we must enhance this ability, not remove it, by allowing process participants to change the data structures within a process, and hence making corresponding changes to the screens that present that data.

We discussed above in *Activities* how processes naturally evolve as they unfold in operation. Just like data structures and their user interfaces, the activities within a process (and their enabling/validating conditions) are likely to change during the life of the process, as a result of unforeseen events, or even just the normal operation of the process—and the changes are not necessarily introduced by management, but by the process participants themselves. A responsible worker knows intuitively that having to make such continual changes to process design is just another aspect of his or her job.

This discussion—of how process design naturally changes during the life of a particular human-driven process instance, as a result of actions by process participants (even if some current process support systems do not permit this)—gives us the clue to an innate feature of human-driven processes that is not generally true for mechanistic processes. We are seeing how a basic responsibility of both participating in and managing a human-driven process is to *redesign it on an ongoing basis*. Without this capability, it will be hard for a support system to deal appropriately with situations encountered as the process takes its course.

In the end, this is an inevitable corollary of the dynamic nature of human-driven processes. Any process developer, like any builder of anything, knows that you never think of everything at the start. You adapt to new requirements, and better understanding of the requirements, as you go along—and this generally means adding in activities you did not intend at the start to carry out. These activities must be added by management—or even by process workers—in order to carry out their work to the satisfaction of the customer.

However, the implementation of current enterprise systems assumes that process management is mainly a matter of resourcing and monitoring, with only occasional need to alter the behavior of the process itself. In general, to *alter the design of a running process* (a feature sometimes known as *adaptive workflow*) is not usually possible at all. Where it is possible, such alteration requires specialized skills and access permissions generally available only among IT staff. In other words, to make it happen, you must add a request to the service desk queue and wait your turn—and by the time the change is made, it is probably too late to be useful.

Our assertion is that adaptive workflow may or may not be necessary for processes that are largely automated (or automatable), but in human-driven processes, it is a fundamental enabler. Management of human activity frequently involves change to process design—so frequently that it is a basic and routine part of managing. Moreover, making design changes in this way means being integrated so deeply into the activities of the process that the manager's own activities cannot realistically be considered as outside the process itself. Hence those who are managing a process, and thus changing it as they go along, are *process participants*—not higher level beings, whether executives or IT staff.

Have we thrown the baby out with the bathwater? The assertion made here—that process management and design must be handled as part of the process itself, not separate from it—represents a significant departure from conventional approaches to business process analysis, and raises deep questions of control. Can processes be guaranteed to operate properly as part of the organization if modeled and implemented in this way? How can anything be supervised properly in such a world, where managers are workers like any other, and an agreed processes may change at any time?

There are two answers to this. First, as discussed throughout this book, for the most part we are not proposing a new way of going about business—we are describing what people all over the world, in all sectors and types of organization, *do now*. This is the way that things are, and if we are to have any chance of improving the way we manage human activities, we must first recognize the way people really carry out their daily work. It's no good burying your head in the sand. Modern enterprise systems need to deal with human-driven processes by supporting the way people really go about their jobs, and recognize the need for on-the-fly change to running processes.

Second, there are ways and means of safely providing management and redesign capability from within the context of a process itself. Returning to my very first assignment in the IT industry, IPSE2.5, I was tasked with developing a conceptual model for project management (see *Preface*). Acting on a suggestion from a more experienced colleague, this work eventually resulted in a framework called Process Model for Management Support (PMMS) that included Roles such as People, Logistics, Quality, and Technology.[4] The PMMS framework was skeletal, but gave rise over time to more sophisticated models, for management of more generic processes.

For example, Brian Warboys and his team at the Informatics Process Group, University of Manchester, published a book in 1999 that describes a process model termed The Process for Process Evolution (P2E), shown in Figure 15.

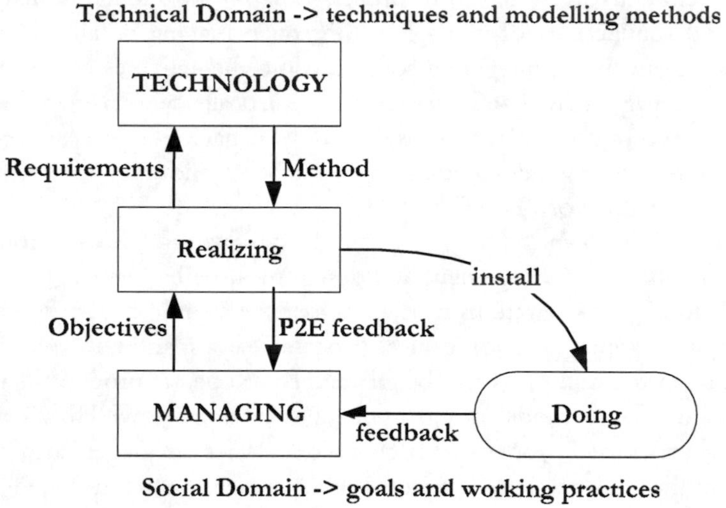

Technical Domain -> techniques and modelling methods

Social Domain -> goals and working practices

Figure 15: The Process for Process Evolution (P2E)

The P2E process model is described by Warboys et al as follows. "The model consists of four components. Each of these can be thought of as a set of activities that are carried out in an organization. .... Each of the components is described below:

▪ Managing—this is concerned with perceiving the state of the process, deciding upon desired goals ('Objectives'), assessing progress toward the achievement of these objectives, and then reassessing progress and objectives according to feedback.

- Realizing—this is concerned with moving toward the fulfillment of the objectives by the provision of a process model. This process model is specialized both for these objectives and for the organizational context, and the implementation of this model in the environment.

- Technology—this is concerned with furnishing the method for achieving the set goal. In other words, it acts as a library so that existing methods can be reused in different contexts. Where no suitable method is available, a new one is created and then specialized by Realizing.

- Doing—this represents the real-world performance of the methods (i.e. the real-world process). It constitutes both the activities themselves and the feedback from the activities to Managing."

It follows that by moving through the P2E, from Managing through to Doing, the organization is navigating toward the set of objectives that it has defined for itself. The organization's identity becomes embodied in the set of behaviors that it can carry out through the P2E structure. Hence, it is autopoietic. The maintenance of this identity is then preserved through feedback. The loop from Doing to Managing enables the organization to keep this navigation on course toward these objectives, or else to set new objectives."[5]

P2E provides a more natural approach to process modeling, and one more attuned to the reality of organizational life, than notions based on a separation of process operation from process management or process design. It incorporates a fundamental feedback loop from work to management and design—not via separate process models, but integrated into the one process.

We extend the principles outlined in P2E with the notion that there are *two fundamentally different forms of management*. We have seen how *executive control* of a process is concerned with determining the primary Roles, inter-actions and deliverables of a process. We distinguish this aspect of man-agement from the day-to-day facilitation of human activity—ongoing re-sourcing, monitoring and process re-design. We term this latter form of supervisory activity *management control*. In essence:

- .*Executive control* is about setting the framework for a process, and comes from above.

- *Management control* is part of operating the process, and comes from within.

Executive control is closer to the standard notion of a "case management process," although it does not include much of the day-to-day resourcing and monitoring inherent in the standard notion. We define executive control as being a genuinely higher level activity—having authority over more than one process, and being unconcerned with the details of everyday process operation.

Management control, on the other hand, is intimately tied to process operation—so much so that it may be devolved among several participants. Even if there is a nominal *Project Manager* Role, the true ability to support participants and authority to change process behavior may be shared, or largely lie elsewhere. In contrast to accepted approaches to modeling management in process terms, the understanding of human-driven processes developed in this book leads to the conclusion that ongoing process redefinition cannot be separated from the work of the process itself. Hence, day-to-day management activity is truly *part* of a process—i.e., it should not be modeled in terms of a separate process, as is conventionally done by business process analysts.

We will call this division into executive and management authority the principle of *separation of control*. It provides us with various ways forward—in particular, a means to implement the REACT and AIM patterns described earlier in this book using the Role Activity Diagram building blocks introduced previously. Once we have shown this, we will show how changes to process design that form a natural part of human-driven processes can be managed as a co-operative activity, and appropriate management controls applied. What we will need is a specific concept of *agreements* among the participants in a process.

An aspect of management that we do not deal with directly in this book is what might be called *strategic control*—a yet higher level of management activity, concerned with the general direction of the organization, as expressed in vision and mission statements, corporate policies, corporate roadmaps, and so on. This level of activity has *indirect* rather than *direct* impact on processes—the content of a security policy, for example, or a refocusing of sales direction, may well affect many different processes, and in a way that is hard to generalize about. Strategic control acts to establish the overall framework in which individual business processes are defined and carried out. It *is* possible to define the human-driven processes via which strategic control is effected—the board-level activity, committee meetings, legislation enactment, and so on—but the manner in which the outputs of these processes affect other processes does not proceed according to a fixed pattern, since the nature of those outputs may vary so enormously. Executive and management control, on the other hand, are implemented via certain universal mechanisms—as we shall see.

Returning then to the notion of separation of control, we have isolated two distinct forms of control within a process. First, *executive control* is typically located in a single person, body (such as a committee), or organization—it is therefore natural to identify this entity with a particular Role. We will call this the *Sponsor* of a process. The Sponsor wishes to know that things will get done, and that they will get done within certain constraints.

Second, *management control,* on the other hand, is typically diversified—even if there is a project manager or line manager nominally in charge of activity, in practice, the authority over process operation may be spread among several parties. In other words, several Roles are often involved in the day-to-day implementation of the work commissioned by the Sponsor Role, as well as having responsibilities for reporting on the work and delivering its outputs.

Is there a natural map for these concepts onto the REACT pattern that we claim captures the universal essence of human-driven processes?

Let's return again to our hypothetical cost reduction investigation, and see how we can represent it on a Role Activity Diagram.

Executive control is embodied in a *Sponsor* Role, whose User is perhaps a senior civil servant responsible for commissioning the study.

Management control is embodied in two Roles, *Project Manager* and *Business Analyst,* who share responsibility for the organization of the work. It is the *Project Manager* who prepares the plan, engages the *Accountant,* and reports to the *Sponsor.* However, it is the *Business Analyst* who determines the nature of the study: what it will focus on, how it will be carried out, and (eventually) whether or not it is ready for submission to the Sponsor. This division is shown by:

- The Research, Evaluate and Analyze activities being assigned to the *Business Analyst* (with help from the Project Manager when it comes to the Access part of Research);

- The Constrain activity, start Role activity for the Accountant, and reporting interaction with the Sponsor Role being assigned to the *Project Manager.*

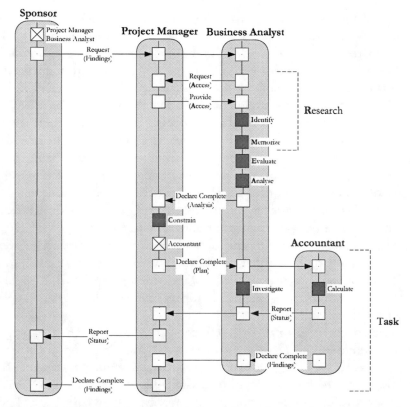

Figure 16: Role Activity Diagram for an investigation into cost reduction

Let's dwell on the Constrain activity for a moment. In our example process, the Project Manager starts an Accountant Role as part of the Constrain stage. Whether or not we are using computerized process support, this means appointing a specific person (or organization) to take on the Role—and the particular qualities of this person (or organization) will significantly affect the way they carry it out.

We discussed, in the description of a *Complex Sales* process in *A New Theory Of Roles*, how both Roles and User have aspects that are not captured by conventional analysis methods, but are important for the effective management of human activity. In particular, we identified the following attributes:

Role:

- Goals
- Responsibilities
- Interests
- Agreements
- Private information resources
- References to other Roles
- Capabilities
- Process authority

User:

- Identity
- Physical location
- Virtual location
- Relationships
- Behavioral tendencies
- Capabilities
- Organizational authority

For a Role, these properties are part of conventional Role Activity Diagram approach. We have seen how the goals and responsibilities of a Role can be expressed as a *terminating condition* and *always condition* respectively. Interests and agreements are *information about process* that can be stored in a Role along with other private information resources (we will deal further with agreements later). Similarly, references to other Roles can be maintained within a Role. Capabilities and process authority are implicit from the activities belonging to the Role.

For a User, however, the situation is not so simple. Role Activity Diagrams make no allowance for the people who are to carry out the tasks. When processes are largely mechanistic, this may not matter—one server may be as good as another for running a specific program (although some people with enterprise IT experience would question this assertion). But when it comes to human-driven processes, one person definitely does not equate to another. *Two people will not carry out the same Role in the same way—*

basically, people are not fungible.

Hence, it is important to somehow capture the properties of a User in our modeling framework, in order that we can manage the process better, and facilitate it better with computers. A Role Activity Diagram cannot do this in its current form. And as previously described, we chose not to extend the graphical notation when developing our building blocks for process depiction. Role Activity Diagrams get complex enough already, so we make the trade off for clarity against expressive power, and choose to avoid cluttering up diagrams with too much detail.

Moreover, in practice, much of the information we need to capture for a User will already be held in a enterprise human resource system. All companies have some form of employee database, and usually it will store most of the information we need. Certainly, identity, physical location and virtual location will be there, as well as organizational authority. Possibly capabilities in terms of knowledge and experience will be stored information. Almost certainly *not stored* are behavioral tendencies and relationships with other people—although these are among the most important qualities of an individual, they are sensitive points and thus hard to capture in a formal way inside a database.

We take what we can get, do the best we can, and deal with any remaining problems as they surface. The critical point at which knowledge of User properties affects the process is when they are invited to join it. After this point, it's a done deal—whatever their strengths and weaknesses, it is hard to remove a process participant, and doing so is an unwelcome decision for a manager to have to make. Hence the type of activity most affected by knowledge of User properties is one that involves starting one or more Roles—and, therefore, the assignment of people or organizations to those Roles.

So we require that implementation of any *Start Role* activity includes:

- Provision of access to such repositories of User information as are available in the organization concerned
- Transfer of information about the User(s) chosen as process participants into the Role making the assignment.

In day-to-day corporate life, this is of course a natural part of human resourcing by a manager—but it is done *informally*. The information concerned is gathered in conversation, requested via email, looked up in a database, and so on. Our whole drive is to expose the stages that are necessary in a human-driven process, and capture the information *in a formal way within the process*, which means making it part of the process support system if one is being used.

In the case of capturing User properties, there are various immediate reasons for doing so. One is as justification of the assignment, should things go wrong later. Another is to allow for personnel change—should the manager making an assignment hand over their own Role to another person, this person will need access to the same User information that the original manager possessed. A more long-term reason is for purposes of process analysis—why did certain processes succeed and others fail? If it was because of the Users concerned, this will remain hidden unless the corresponding information has been captured as part of the process.

In a Human Interaction Management System, Users can be treated as private information resources of a Role—like any other resource, User properties can be extended in any way that captures as wide a range of properties as possible. Moreover, the data object representing a User can be populated automatically, via a Web service call, for instance—so the information can be taken from existing repositories. Updates made to User information, as part of a process, can similarly be fed back to the appropriate repository, so that information gathered is held in the natural place and not lost. Such an approach to management of process participation is crucial if the assignment of Users to Roles is to be handled as efficiently as possible, and any problems encountered tracked for purposes of future improvement.

Let's continue our journey through this example process. With regard to the Task work, it is split across activities in multiple Roles—the Investigate activity in *Business Analyst* and Calculate activity in *Accountant*. As the process unfolds in practice, this breakdown of work across Roles will be refined, into more detailed activities, perhaps divided differently between process participants. In many common cases the Task stage naturally breaks down further into recursively nested REACT cycles, a refinement necessary both to manage change and to deal with complexity. We will see below when we come to discuss *agreements* how such change can be managed, while preserving the essential executive and management controls built into the process from the start.

For now, however, it is enough to note how the REACT sequence of human activity allows us to model, in a generic way, the *response to a request*.

Something has been commissioned, and REACT describes, in the most generic way, how a human-driven process is established to get things done, as requested.

Moreover, the essence of the response is to *organize work*. In effect, REACT is the embodiment of *management control*. The main part of the pattern (Research, Evaluate, Analyze, Constrain) is concerned only with activities prior to doing the job. And since REACT is not so much a process as a repeating, overlapping, nested pattern, this focus on organization will continue, even once the final stage (Task) has commenced.

Our focus on a pattern that is 80% groundwork and 20% work itself reflects what everyone knows, whether their profession is software engineer, entrepreneur, sales person or house painter. The secret is in the preparation. More haste, less speed. In a way, the argument of this book is that, since human-driven processes are fundamentally collaborative, they are fundamentally about management.

In particular, if we are to support such processes properly with software, we must manage not only the visible parts, but also the part of the iceberg that is under the water—the mental activities that are the true skill sets of interaction workers. These must be exposed as part of a process, given the necessary resources (in particular, time), and acknowledged for their crucial value—not ignored or brushed under the carpet as is done in conventional approaches both to management and to mechanistic process modeling.

Moreover, we live in a world that is moving faster and faster toward globalization, not just of supply chain goods but of services. Hence organizations of all sizes are looking to cut costs by locating their human activity where it is cheapest to resource. The current popularity of outsourcing, for example, is driven partly by the belief that *work can be commoditized*.

For example, a major current trend is for Business Process Outsourcing, via which entire activity streams within an organization are spun off to external suppliers. This is not really anything new. For many years, companies such as Marks & Spencer have operated a "relational arrangement" with key suppliers—providing them with much (and sometimes all) of their business, in exchange for close control over how the work is managed. In effect, such activity often amounts to process outsourcing, whether of an entire process in one go (for example, a fast food chain contracting all its logistics to a single courier, who has no other revenue stream) or broken up among fixed suppliers (for example, certain types of clothing might be provided by a small number of manufacturers, who have few other clients).

In order to manage this separation, companies often treat the arrangement as amounting to a partnership—staff from customer and supplier work in each other's offices, for example, and participate in each other's key meetings. This informal approach allows companies to build up a long-term working arrangement that provides the basis for processes to be successfully split across organizational boundaries—a basis not only of knowledge about each other's working practices, but also of trust and mutual commitment.

This may work well for companies that are located nearby geographically (e.g., a glass bottle manufacturer located in the same town as a brewery) and who are willing to establish such relationships over the long term. However, such proximity relationships are simply not practical for an American company that is considering outsourcing new product development to a consortium based in China, or IT support to an Indian software house. In such cases, the parties can only gain mutual agreement and understanding on working practices by sharing a common definition of the processes involved—which, in such cases, are largely human-driven processes. How can this possibly be managed if most of the work is beneath the corporate executive management radar?

Just to take the most basic example, the customer (the company doing the outsourcing) will seek justification for time spent by the supplier (who is doing the outsourced work). A new product development process, for example, will consist in large part of the first stages of REACT—as we have seen, the mental preparation for design work is probably the most important part of the job. If the customer company does not recognize the value of the necessary early-stage REACT activities, which may have little in the way of conventional output, they will tend to be unhappy with the service provided and reluctant to pay for it. Moreover, the supplier will find the time spent equally hard to justify, since it is likely to share the same outlook as its customer. Hence, the supplier may have to resort to covering up the true activity of its staff with smokescreens—hardly a healthy approach for either party.

There are other, deeper issues, concerned with the organization of outsourcing activity itself. For example, we saw in the discussion of Users above that it is critical to recognize, use, and record for later analysis information about the people who engage in human-driven processes. Unless there is a means of doing this, the supplier will be unable to provide visibility to the customer of key factors affecting the operation of the processes that they have taken on. Hence it will be impossible for the two parties to establish a neutral basis for discussion on how to do things better, or just differently—how to improve service desk response by assigning a different type of person to specific calls, for example.

There are compelling arguments that current approaches to outsourcing are failing, and new approaches emerging. For example, Francis Hayden identifies problems in various different areas, as shown in Table 1: Old Problems and New Solutions in Outsourcing.[6] Hayden describes the general situation with respect to outsourcing as follows:

"Outsourcing of IT services has the potential to cut costs, improve services, promote innovation and reduce the burden on senior managers. But our years of research for one of the biggest suppliers in the world have convinced us that this potential too often goes unrealized. There are signs that a new framework for the management and governance of outsourcing deals is emerging as customers and suppliers begin to realize what is going wrong."[7]

Table 1: Old Problems and New Solutions in Outsourcing

OLD PROBLEMS	NEW SOLUTIONS
The contract is awarded to the supplier who makes the most unrealistic promises. The contract fixes the scope, the objectives and the priorities of the supplier even though everyone knows they need to be changing all the time. The contract focuses on cost cutting without regard for whether the supplier can make money. The supplier immediately begins to argue that work is out of scope and focuses its attention on winning new work on which a higher margin can be charged. The attitude, behavior and priorities of the supplier begin to undermine trust. The two sides begin the mutual blame game that results in a spiral of worsening relationships, closer policing, higher	Contracts are fine for defining static relationships and services but the partners to an outsourcing deal are involved in an active and dynamic process. It is the health of that dynamic, not the completeness of the contract, that will determine the success of the deal. The partners are involved together in the ongoing management of change—changing technologies, changing markets and changing business priorities. Specific objectives and priorities have to be under constant review and renegotiation. Incentives need to be positive, clear and related to current objectives, providing good margins in return for good performance and better margins in return for great performance.

OLD PROBLEMS	NEW SOLUTIONS
costs and, ultimately, a clear lose-lose.	The supplier also needs to be confident that they will always be rewarded for customer-focused behavior and the development of innovative ideas, esp. ideas that reduce costs to the customer.

In essence, outsourcing of human activity cannot be managed properly unless *people's work is understood in process terms*, not simply as an exchange of deliverables for money. Further, the processes concerned must be founded on basic human motivations—such as trust—if change is to be dealt with to the satisfaction of all parties.

We will see below how the principles described so far in this book can be applied to ensure that processes change as and when needed, without sacrificing the executive and management controls essential to safe management of an organization. This applies whether or not the processes are internal, or shared across organizations as is done when they are outsourced in whole or in part.

Agreements

Tied deeply to the division of a process into Roles is the organization of those Roles into a communicating, co-operating whole. In fact, one is pointless without the other. Consider the investigation into government cost reduction mentioned earlier. Unless the *Project Manager, Business Analyst,* and *Accountant* have some idea of how they are to interact, they are going to have a hard time working together, and crucial information flows may well be left out entirely, however well-intentioned the participants.

As previously discussed, it is an aspect of executive control to ensure that the people concerned are willing, in principle, to co-operate along broadly agreed lines. It is then an aspect of day-to-day management control to ensure that these communication channels are kept open, that process participants know how and when to use them, and that the right things are being sent from one person to another.

With regard to modeling these information flows, we have seen how the Role Activity Diagram notation allows Roles to be specified for the process participants. Role Activity Diagrams can be annotated to describe the information resources within each Role, some of which will form the deliverables of the process. We have also seen how the Role Activity Diagram interaction mechanism, for transfer of resources between Roles, provides a basic form of co-operation. Is this enough for our needs?

It might be enough for the executive in charge, who is concerned with the process only at a broad-brush level. However, for the individuals on the ground there are further issues. People can only work together if the relationship is based, at some level, on mutual commitment. *Trust* among the parties that they all wish to co-operate in order to achieve a specific set of goals, and that everyone knows what is necessary in order to do so. Without this, things break down as soon as any kind of unforeseen event occurs, and a change to the original plan is required—which, as we have seen, is not an exception but the norm in human-driven processes.

Hence we need to understand how such commitment can be expressed in practice, and incorporate that into our description of co-operation. We will see that this gives us a simple way to manage change to a process, and that this can be done from within the process itself.

To drive out this understanding, let's take a simple case. Some people agree to work on a specific item together—a document, a design, a new business model, whatever. They meet to brainstorm ideas, and come up with some possible approaches. How are they likely to leave matters at the end of the meeting?

Unless the process has broken down in discussion, the final few minutes of each discussion in the meeting will consist of a consensus—not just on deliverables, but also on the next steps that each party will take. Some people will go away and work on specific approaches, for instance, while others may investigate availability of resources such as funding or office space.

Such consensus is conventionally expressed in terms of actions in meeting minutes. However, meeting actions are a weak means of description, since they only say who is to do what—not when they will do it, what resources they require, what the dependencies are on other actions, and so on. At best these details are referenced in the main text of the minutes, quite separate from the description of the actions themselves—at worst, action details are left implicit and unstated. The weakness of actions in meeting minutes as a means of agreement on next steps are a common cause of upset later on—for example, people fail to realize that their own actions were holding up others, and thus unwarranted delays get introduced—along with a culture of blame.

What meeting actions attempt, and generally fail at, is to describe a *process*—the process that the meeting is part of, as it continues after the meeting itself. The rest of the process, in other words—the activities that still lie in the future.

It is possible that after a meeting, the actions will be enshrined in a plan, in which the resources and dependencies will be clarified. However, for a start people do not typically base their daily work directly on a plan— charts such as GANTT[8] and PERT,[9] for instance, are intended as a means of management monitoring and support, not as a means to facilitate or explain the work itself to those who must carry it out. Moreover, most projects have very complex plans, in which individual people find it hard to locate and place in context their own activities, let alone those of the others they are working with. A simpler, more immediate way of representing agreement on the rest of the process is required.

Only if a clear way of expressing agreement is available will people have what they need most in order to make collaboration successful—to know, as described above, that the commitment to working together still exists on all sides, and that everyone agrees how this is to be accomplished. Each player needs to know that all other players have signed up to the same process that they have.

We saw, in *How people communicate*, how speech acts are a valuable device for structuring the interactions between process participants—giving each interaction a *label* that describes its intent, for better mutual understanding among the participants. Such mutual understanding gets us part of the way toward a formal description of commitment to the next stage of process.

For example, each action from a meeting could be better described as an interaction between Roles, labeled with a speech act. Let us suppose that we have just held a meeting to discuss the development of new reports against a corporate database, and now wish to document the agreements made. Actions that might be noted as "Business Analyst to check calculations in report specifications" and "Report Developer to write reports" would be better described in terms of three separate interactions:

- An interaction between the Report Designer and the Business Analyst, in which the designer passes a set of specification documents to the analyst. This would be labeled with the speech act "Declare Complete."
- An interaction between these two and the Project Manager, in which the

documents are either signed off or not. This interaction would be labeled either "Accept" or "Reject," depending on the contents of the message.

- An interaction between the Project Manager and the Report Developer, passing across the design documents as a basis for starting development. This would be labeled "Request," to indicate that programming work is being commissioned.

We have applied conventional speech acts, taken from the classic *Conversation for Action* (CfA) pattern, for example, to enhance our interaction list. It is immediately clear that, for instance, the Project Manager will be included in the Accept/Reject notification, and also that it is the Project Manager's duty—not the Report Designer's—to initiate report development.

However, even with speech acts added as labels, a list of interactions on its own does not tell us enough. The CfA pattern in its standard form, for example, leaves it open for either party to withdraw at any time—hardly a reassuring basis for anyone on which to start their work. With our list of required interactions above, it is unclear what the consequences are, if any, of the Business Analyst declaring the calculations incorrect—or that *some of them* are incorrect.

For instance, the Report Designer may believe that if most are okay, the reports will have to be issued with a warning, but development can go ahead as is, at least for now. The Business Analyst, on the other hand, may not feel it sensible to allow the reports to be released at all until every single calculation is 100% accurate. It is quite possible that this difference of opinion was never discussed in the meeting, or if it was, that it was never resolved properly.

The point is that successful co-operation requires more than a list of actions. The need is for:

1. All parties to reach a shared understanding; and
2. Each person to be satisfied all other parties are committed to this understanding.

This does happen sometimes, of course, but the means is generally informal. People talk to one another at sufficient length that they hope things have become clear. If certain things have to be left vague for the moment, people are only happy to do so if they have first established *trust*—made a gentleman's agreement, concluded a deal with a handshake, built a personal relationship. However, you cannot guarantee that informal means will work, and often they don't.

For a start, collaboration between many people is much harder to synchronize than collaboration between few. Further, we all express ourselves in different ways—even between two people who know each other well, simple misunderstandings can arise.

Suppose two colleagues are working on a document together, and meet to discuss changes that one of them has just made. The person who has made the changes comes away from the meeting with the impression that the other will immediately start reviewing their work—but the other person comes away with the intention only of doing so at some unspecified time in the future. As discussed, this is a particular weakness of speech acts. It can be hard to distinguish between "I'll do X straight away" and "I agree that X should be done, and I'm probably the best person to do it."

In fact, what we need is *not* to know exactly when and how the other parties will go about their assigned tasks. This is up to them, and depends on factors we neither need to know about—nor wish to know about. What we do need is to know is that they will deliver something to the rest of us, what sort of thing will be delivered, and that *the person responsible is aware of how this affects the rest of us*. In the example, the person who has made the changes might be hoping to show the revised document to a third party, and waiting anxiously for their colleague's feedback. When it doesn't come, it's no one's fault—but the relationship may end up breaking down.

This is the missing element from the "list of interactions" approach to documenting meeting actions. Even with speech acts added, there is no implied understanding by each party of the impact that their activities have on other people, or commitment on all sides to resolving any problems that arise.

In order to make everyone aware of this context, we not only need to set and agree upon the expectations of each party—the documents they will supply, the sign-off they will make, the funding they will provide, and so on—but also to show how these expectations are part of a wider process.

In other words, we must make a clear, unambiguous depiction of the rest of the process in neutral terms—and this depiction must be easier to understand than a GANTT or PERT chart. We have the basis for such a depiction in interactions between Roles together with speech acts as labels, but these must be used in a way that gives us more detail on when things are to take place, what the dependencies are, and so on.

We can achieve this by a specific use of the Role Activity Diagram notation. A fully-fledged process diagram typically includes multiple activities within each Role, as well as the interactions between them. All we have to do is:

- Leave out most of the activities contained within each Role;

- Label the interactions with speech acts; and

- Draw this up on a Role Activity Diagram to show how the interactions form part of a process.

Then we have a simple picture that can be used to represent the agreement reached in a meeting, between the participants of a process, on what is to happen from now on.

Returning to the report development example, we can draw the list of interactions plus speech acts on a small Role Activity Diagram, shown in Figure 17: Example actions agreed in a meeting, for report development. For simplicity, we leave out what is to happen if the calculations are not correct in the specifications. In practice, this kind of alternative is often left out of meeting actions anyway—an immediate benefit of the graphical depiction is that this becomes obvious.

Now that we have the Role Activity Diagram, it is absolutely clear that no development work will start until the calculations have been checked and the reports completely signed off by the Business Analyst.

This not only resolves the implicit difference of understanding about the basis on which report development can start, but may have a more subtle impact on the process. As with our example of the two colleagues working on a document together, without the Role Activity Diagram it is quite possible that the Business Analyst will leave the meeting with the understanding that the calculations should be checked—sometime. Report development is not the main interest, so the two colleagues don't give much thought to it, and fail to realize that report development is waiting for them. Even if they do think about it, they are quite likely to assume that the developer can at least get started, and only needs their feedback at some point during the programming work.

This kind of scenario is a very common cause of delays, and of frustration among colleagues. To the report developer, it is obvious that there is no point starting development until the specifications have been signed off. Days or weeks go by without draft reports being prepared for testing, with all sorts of concomitant delays arising in other areas, and by the time it's all sorted out tempers are frayed and deadlines slipping.

Moreover, it is not simple enough to say in such a case, "the Project Manager is obviously at fault here, since co-ordination of activity is their job." The example is about as simple as possible—for in a small project containing only a few such activities, no doubt the Project Manager would be able to stay on top of things. Most projects, however, and most team-work generally, is a lot more complex. Interactions and consequent dependencies arise all over the place—it is hard, if not impossible, for any one person to ensure that all of the dependencies are well understood by everyone, and that all concerned are doing their bit.

Moreover, teams in which one person takes all the responsibility for everything are not really teams at all, in the true sense of the word. A successful team is one in which the members each understand, accept and live up to their individual obligations. It is preferable for everybody if people are self-motivated, rather than having to be continually prodded by a manager. Much as people may *wish* to act responsibly, they are *unable to* unless they have a simple means of understanding exactly what their obligations consist of.

This is almost impossible to do unless all concerned have a clear and up-to-date understanding of the *process* that they and their colleagues are engaged in. As we discussed in *How people communicate*, much of the awareness that people have about the actions of others, and much of the information they exchange, is effected via indirect means—gossip and hearsay, interpretation of observed actions, written material, changed workplace layout, even the discovery that work has been passed on from one person to another. Sometimes confusion can be cleared up in these ways, but often as not, relying on such means of communication just creates more confusion.

Take the case of journalists who normally fact-check every column they submit to a Webzine, and suppose they stop doing so for a particular period. This might be due to an instruction from their manager, a change in their terms of employment, the belief that someone else has been delegated to do it instead—or simply due to a misunderstanding of what their duties entail. How is the company that is ultimately responsible for the Webzine to know that the fact-checking has ceased, and take steps to ensure they do not publish material that may be factually incorrect?

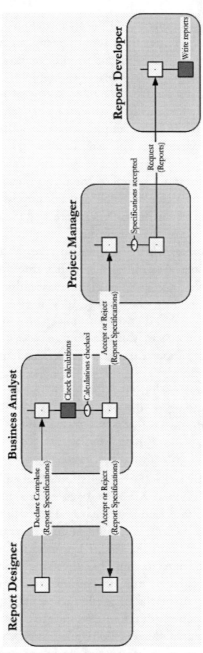

Figure 17: Example actions agreed in a meeting, for report development

It is quite possible that the matter will not come to light until someone reports the errors, which could be days or weeks after the fact-checking ceases. By then, material may have been published on the Web that damages the magazine's reputation, perhaps permanently. If such cases are to be avoided, it is critical for all concerned to have some means of understanding very clearly what they are personally responsible for, and what their colleagues are responsible for—and this understanding must be accurate now, not at some time in the past.

Stopping for a moment to take stock, we have developed a clearer way of sharing among process participants the consensus reached in meetings. The use of *interactions plus speech acts plus graphical depiction* is a simple replacement for meeting actions that is far more effective as a means of documenting *agreements*. Our agreement model provides process participants with a neutral, unambiguous and expressive means of sharing with each other the decisions made on the next stages of a process. As an approach to coordination of behavior, our approach to documenting agreements is much more likely to ensure that consensus reached is genuinely acted on.

Furthermore, this gives us the promised means of safely managing change from within a process. The consensus reached during a meeting, and documented as we've described, is an agreement not on deliverables, but on behavior—what will happen next in the process. In other words, the parties concerned have redesigned the process, documented that redesign as an agreement, and shared it among themselves so as to ensure that everyone is singing from the same hymn sheet. If a computerized Human Interaction Management System is being used, the process change can then be implemented automatically, simply by entering the agreement depiction into the system—but even if process management is manual, the existence of an agreement understood by all parties is enough in itself to facilitate the smooth running of the revised process.

Moreover, the development of such agreements falls naturally under the appropriate management control. Whether this control lies in a project manager, is shared between such a person and several others, or is devolved entirely, the agreement mechanism is *an integral part of that control*—since those with an interest in management control will either be party to such decisions, or made aware of them once the agreements have been circulated. Even if there has been a mutiny in the ranks, and people are deliberately deciding what to do without officially consulting the proper authorities, a working environment in which agreements must be documented, as described, will at least expose the fact that such is the case.

Our example of report development is a very simple case, in which the true complexity of process change is disguised. To see how the agreements mechanism allows us to handle a more problematic situation, we will choose another example, this time drawn from engineering design— although we will see that the modeling approach taken has applicability in all sorts of areas. The discussion builds on work originally carried out jointly in the engineering field with Francis Hayden.[10]

Concurrent engineering is one response by the manufacturing sector to demands for increased productivity and shorter times-to-market. Different parts of a complex product are developed in parallel and then integrated, shortening project schedules. Typical interactions in this type of business process are activities such as agreeing on sub-contract terms, signing off a specification, concluding a project stage, and so on.[11] Each of these may involve several parties, contain processing spread over varied systems on different platforms owned by different organizations, and require a number of steps to complete successfully. Further, although efficiency gains can be achieved via this approach, it carries risks of rework, which arises when concurrently performed work turns out to be incompatible, and an impact of one interaction is that others need to be repeated.

In other words, concurrent engineering is a typical human-driven process—fraught with instability, since engineering managers are dealing with activities that are only partly predictable when the process commences. It is a fundamental characteristic of the whole environment that it is organic and dynamic, so hard coded process descriptions are unsuitable. Even if they are supported by tools that make modification of that process possible, the participants are innovative, creative people who need the flexibility to put their skills and experience to use in what seems like the most appropriate way at the time.

There is a parallel situation in the structure of the product itself. A complex product like an aircraft or a ship may appear to decompose neatly into systems, assemblies, sub-assemblies and parts but in fact it is a densely tangled set of solutions to a huge and varied set of requirements and constraints. A single requirement may be met by a combination of structure, systems and software, for example, while a single part such as a wing rib may be constrained by structural, aerodynamic, fuel, electrical and manufacturing requirements.

Later modifications only increase the complexity. New connections and dependencies are introduced by tracing the impact of modifications, defining and implementing consequent changes, testing the whole package and restoring the integrity of the product.

So, in order to see how agreements might let us manage the changes inherent in such a project, let us take a typical scenario. A design team is in the middle of a concurrent engineering project, and an unexpected issue has arisen—sufficiently serious to warrant specific management attention, and potentially impacting several design domains.

Meeting to discuss the problem, team members realize that a new sub-project is required to manage the issue. Initially they have no plan or structure for this new sub-project. The input to the sub-project is itself a problem definition that may require further investigation and development. However, there are a number of significant things that they can say. They may have none of the detailed elements of a *process*, but what they can talk about is a *pattern*. They know how collaborative problem solving generally takes place in their field.

The pattern they recognize for collaborative problem solution has specific aspects that allow us to model it, at a high-level, as a process. These correspond directly to the areas of interest for purposes of executive control, described above in *Adapting the world*:

1. *The people involved will perform certain Roles, each with their own goals and responsibilities.* There will be a number of participants in the solution process, with skills in different domains—systems engineering, structural engineering, safety engineering, and so on. For each type of contributor, there may well be distinct phases of activity: problem definition, concept design, detailed design and testing, integration and testing, and so on. Hence, the sub-project is in fact composed of multiple distinct streams of activity, one for each domain. The contributions of all these have to be coordinated.

2. *The eventual deliverables will meet certain preconditions.* If successful, the output of the sub-project will be a solution, probably consisting of a set of solution components in different domains. The solution components in each domain will include models and tests that demonstrate that the solution solves the defined problem. There may well be interface specifications and other supporting documentation. Among all these objects there will be varied dependency relationships. Hence, the components of the solution both at domain level and overall are an interdependent set that must be protected from further change unless the whole solu-

tion is revisited and retested. The set of solution components can be viewed as a *transaction*—somewhat like a database transaction, although subject to quite different rules[12]—in which all sub-project participants commit jointly to the resolution of the issue.

3.   *The process participants will interact in a way to ensure that their individual contributions combine to produce overall deliverables of the highest possible quality.* The components of each domain solution must be made available to an appropriate person for integration into a unified domain solution. Similarly, the domain solutions must be made available to an appropriate person for integration into a unified overall solution. The individual domain solutions and the overall solution must all be validated and certified by an appropriate authority, and this activity must be linked to the aforementioned integration.

With this analysis in mind, we can use a Role Activity Diagram to represent the sub-project as a whole. This is shown in Figure 18: Role Activity Diagram for a concurrent design sub-project.

We will interpret this diagram from three different perspectives:

1.   Management

2.   Participant

3.   Solution

The first way to interpret the diagram is *from a management perspective*. In terms of the separation of control principle previously described:

■   At the overall level, the *Overall Sponsor* is the Sponsor Role embodying executive control, while the *Domain Sponsor* and *Overall Design Authority* together embody management control. The *Overall Design Authority* has the Research, Evaluate and Analyze activities, while the Domain Sponsor has the Constrain activity. The Task work is not shown as a single activity, but split between *Domain Sponsor* and *Overall Design Authority*, and consists of work assignment and work validation respectively.

■   At the domain level, the *Domain Sponsor* is the Sponsor Role embodying executive control, while the *Domain Manager* and *Domain Design Authority* together embody management control. The *Domain Design Authority* has the Research, Evaluate and Analyze activities, while the *Domain Manager* has the Constrain activity. As above, the Task work is not shown as a single activity. In this case it is split between all three Roles *Domain Manager*, *Designer* and *Domain Design Authority*, and consists of work assignment, design work itself, and validation of that design work respectively.

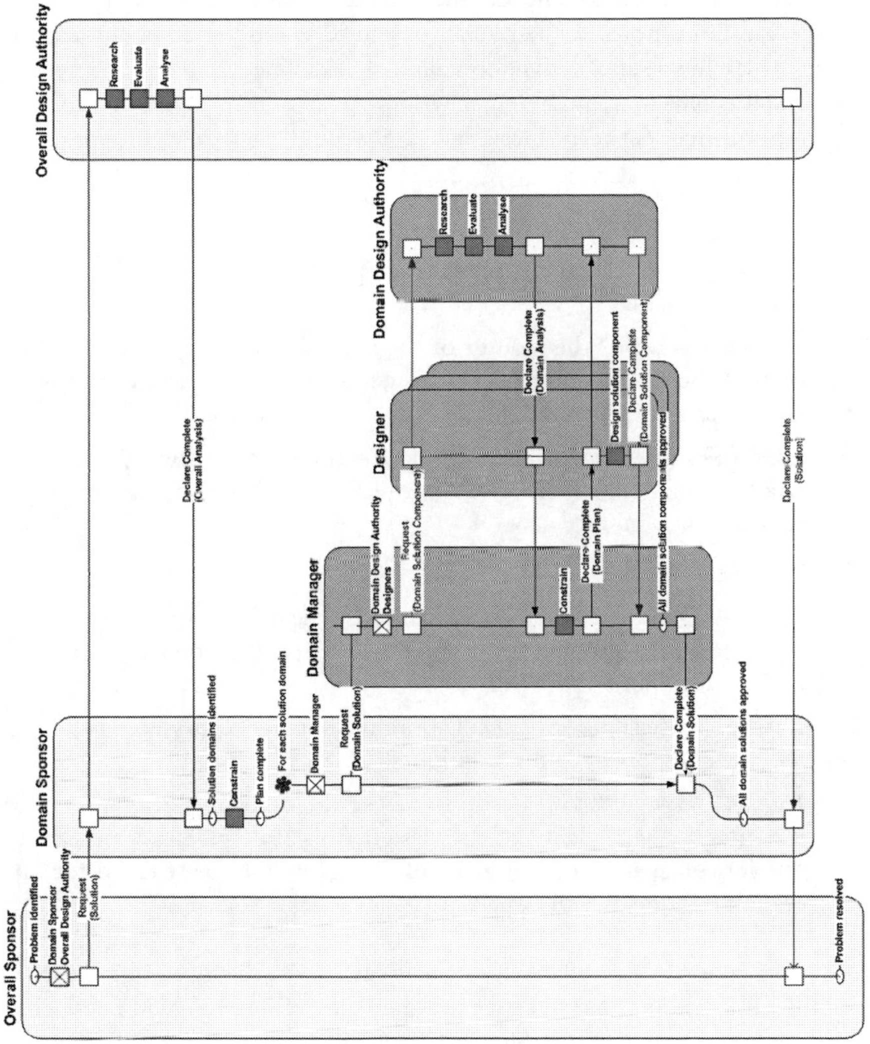

Figure 18: Role Activity Diagram for a concurrent design sub-project

The breakdown of Research into the AIM pattern is omitted from this Role Activity Diagram. At this initial stage, such detail is not necessary. We will see how, as the process unfolds, the Role Activity Diagram will be refined to include the components of each high-level activity depicted at the initial stage, and how this can be done without contravening the controls established at the start.

The second way to interpret the diagram is *from a participant's perspective.*
There are three Roles at the overall design level, and another three at the
level of each specific design domain or discipline (systems engineering,
structural engineering, safety engineering, and so on). There is a degree of
correspondence between these levels that indicates that the model is
natural:

Overall design level:

1. *Overall Sponsor.* Acknowledges that the problem is real and kicks off the
   solution process

2. *Domain Sponsor.* At the request of the Overall Sponsor, initiates work in
   each of the design domains, co-ordinates the separate streams of work,
   and reports on progress

3. *Overall Design Authority.* Responsible for the integrity and quality of the
   whole design (this Role gives permission for the integration of the
   specific solution)

Domain design level:

1. *Domain Manager.* At the request of the Domain Sponsor, assigns expert
   resource to the problem as it applies to a specific domain, then facilitates and supports this work

2. *Designer.* Participates in the collaborative activity to develop a domain-
   specific component of the solution

3. *Domain Design Authority.* Responsible for the domain-specific aspects of
   the integrity and quality of the design (this Role gives permission for
   the domain-specific components of the solution to be released for integration into the overall design)

Different Roles, such as 1 and 3 at each level, may well be performed
by the same person. However, since Role Activity Diagrams do not include
Users, this is not shown explicitly. What we gain from the Role Activity
Diagram with respect to process participants is an overall context for each
person's work. This is done in a simple and effective way by the Role Activity Diagram. It is immediately obvious how each person's work relates to
that of the others, who communicates with whom, and who is dependent
on whom. For instance, it is clear that a domain solution cannot be submitted until each component of that solution has not only been prepared, but

has also been "Declared Complete" by the corresponding Domain Design Authority. Further, it is not even possible to submit a domain solution component that has not been approved. Submission can only be done in tandem with the Domain Design Authority, as part of a single interaction that also involves approval—a review meeting, perhaps.

The third and final way to read the Role Activity Diagram is *from a solution perspective*. It is divided into two *collaborative transactions*—one at overall design level, and one at domain design level. Each transaction is bounded above and below by a 3-way interaction. In each case, the interaction at the top represents an exchange of requirements while the interaction below represents an exchange of solutions.

Both the requirements exchanged in the top interaction and the solutions exchanged in the bottom interaction will involve complex, compound objects. A solution interaction, for example, may pass across:

- The final *problem statement*, now fully developed
- The objects that form the *solution*, contributed by different Roles
- The *models and tests* that justify the solution
- A *map of the dependencies* between all these objects (for use in tracking the impact of changes) and a related *approval chart*, showing who has approved what. (Both these can be maintained automatically. Whenever a participating Role submits a new version of one of their deliverables, all the approvals that are dependent on the new deliverable are removed and new approval activities are triggered. Processes and object relationships interact—as long as they are both represented.)

In between the upper and lower interactions, each participating Role will carry out various different activities, in order to provide its own part of the solution. The Role Activity Diagram shown here is simplified and omits these activities, as well as the phases into which the activities will be broken during the sub-project. Why?

All we need at this stage is to *represent a consensus from the initial meeting on how to proceed with the sub-project*. We are not seeking to prescribe exactly what everyone will do to meet the requirements placed on them—just to establish a common ground on how the issue as a whole will be dealt with. What we are interested in initially is to make it clear to all parties what their responsibilities are to the process as a whole. We need to show only who is to do what, how they will deliver their outputs, and what impact each person's work has on the rest of the process.

As described, the diagram effectively models the *executive and management controls* required over the sub-project at its instigation.

Once the work gets going, it is inevitable that changes will occur to the process shown in the Role Activity Diagram. In particular, the activities in the sub-project will be extended, and broken into distinct phases, and during the course of the sub-project the elements of the diagram will be extended further as required. The project participants will make agreement depictions at overview or detailed levels that not only refine the process, but also allow all concerned to share the consensus reached about next steps.

It is here that day-to-day *management control* can be applied, in order to ensure that the process as it unfolds in operation takes place safely, in accordance with any applicable regulations, and with all parties committed to the same manner of proceeding.

Moreover, it will be possible to do this at either level without contravening the *executive control* applied from above, since it is clear from the diagram how this control is applied—via the application of the REACT pattern. Should the process participants at any time decide that this application was inappropriate, this change can be described in a simple way via a new Role Activity Diagram, and submitted to the appropriate Role for approval.

For instance, suppose that in a particular domain—safety engineering, say—that the *Domain Design Authority* feels it sensible to share some of his or her Research activity with the *Designers* of their part of the solution. After discussion with the Domain Sponsor and Designer(s) in question, the Role Activity Diagram can be altered to show the proposed process change, and sent to the *Domain Sponsor* for official approval. The revised process is shown in Figure 19: Role Activity Diagram for a concurrent design sub-project, altered to share Research responsibility in the safety domain with all Designer Roles.

There are a number of interesting things that we can say about this new Role Activity Diagram. First, it makes the new way in which the process is proposed to proceed from now on completely clear (to the *Safety Domain Manager* and everyone else concerned) The agreement reached in discussion has been documented in a simple pictorial way that allows all concerned to understand what will happen, and to know that this understanding is mutual.

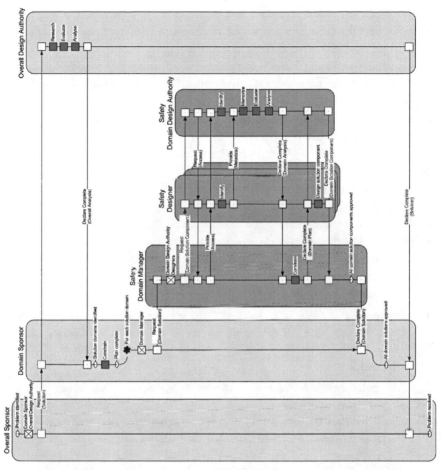

Figure 19: Role Activity Diagram for a concurrent design sub-project,
altered to share Research responsibility in the safety domain with all
Designer Roles

Moreover, *the diagram took only a few minutes to update.* It was probably
quicker to make changes to the Role Activity Diagram than to write an
email or memo to all parties confirming how things would operate differently—certainly it was quicker than updating the GANTT or PERT charts
within a project plan. More to the point, the diagram is a simpler, clearer
and more effective means of communication than any of these approaches.
Not only can you see at a glance how the new process is expected to operate, but the specific changes made can be highlighted in any way desired—

for example, via use of italicized text or, even more effectively, color.

Second, the diagram shows new activities added to the *Safety Designer* Roles—all of them. The implicit assumption is that these new activities will be available in all such Roles. However, if they were only required in certain ones, (*Safety Senior Designers*, say) that could be easily shown as well. This is depicted in Figure 20: Role Activity Diagram for a concurrent design sub-project, altered to share Research responsibility in the safety domain with Senior Designers only.

The Role Activity Diagram has been altered to show a new Role, *Safety Senior Designer*, who unlike a normal *Safety Designer* is empowered to perform additional activities that are part of Research. If a process support system is in use, the existing *Safety Designer* Role can be copied and altered—*specialized*—to create a new Role that is based on the Senior Designer, but includes additional activities. How is this new *Safety Senior Designer* Role to be implemented in practice—in particular, how is the Role to be assigned to Users?

There are two cases:

1. *The people who are to play these new Roles may not yet have been assigned to the project.* In this case, all that is necessary is for the *Safety Domain Manager* to revisit the Start Role activity and assign the new Role to Users as required.

2. Alternatively, *the people who are to play these new Roles may already have been assigned to standard Safety Designer Roles*. In this case, the *Safety Domain Manager* needs to revisit the Start Role activity, assign the new Role to Users as required, and also deassign them from their old Roles.

Either way, the activity to be used already exists in the *Safety Domain Manager* Role, and can be revisited as and when required—because as de-scribed above, we do not restrict the Role from traversing its activities in strict sequence, and we allow repetition and interleaving of different work as required at the time.

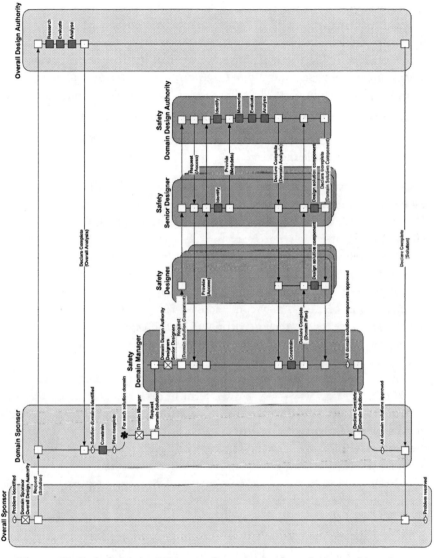

Figure 20: Role Activity Diagram for a concurrent design sub-project, altered to share Research responsibility in the safety domain with Senior Designers only

Third, this example shows us the AIM pattern (Access, Identify, Memorize, that we described in *How people find things out*) starting to come into its own. Appreciating that the Research activity is compound, with separate stages, not only permits us to allocate specific stages to specific process participants, but allows co-ordination of those stages via the use of human-readable metadata.

Considering the diagram above, we see that the Research activity is not *entirely* shared between the *Safety Domain Design Authority* and other team members, but only in part. The Safety Senior Designer's responsibility is to:

- Identify key information of relevance to the work in hand; and

- *Provide* this information to the *Safety Domain Design Authority* in the form of human-readable metadata.

In other words, the third and final stage of AIM—Memorize—is only allocated to the *Safety Domain Design Authority*. Because the *Safety Domain Design Authority* alone has the responsibility for creating a solution in the safety domain, it is only necessary for the *Safety Domain Design Authority* to absorb the relevant information, in order to Evaluate and Analyze it.

Some immediate advantages accrue from this breakdown. It is clear to all that the Senior Designers are not expected to take on board all details of the relevant information they come across. They do not have to read every report, article or book; they need only note the ones that may have direct bearing on the work in hand. This saves them time, and makes sure that the right work is being done by the right people.

Moreover, since they supply their findings to the *Safety Domain Design Authority* in a *formal* way—as what we term human-readable metadata—this information is preserved within the process for future use. It can be lodged in a knowledge management system, used as part of debrief to understand the factors behind the project's success or failure, and shared with other Roles (*Safety Designers*, for example) as and when necessary.

In an environment where computerized process support is available, even more powerful techniques can be brought into play. We discussed in *How people find things out*, how metadata that is readable by machines as well as by humans can be used as a basis for *searching, alerting* and *harvesting*. Here, for instance, searching could be used by any of the Roles involved in Research to identify references of potential interest. Alerting (which often has a basis in harvesting) could then be used to ensure that the *Safety Domain Design Authority* is kept up-to-date with any changes to the material discovered, or to change the appearance of relevant new material.

This use of metadata, whether human- or machine-readable, allows us to replace informal, around-the-water-cooler exchanges of skills and experience, with an approach that *not only* provides the benefits of existing knowledge management systems that support Communities of Practice, *but also* does so within a process context—with all the varied advantages that thereby accrue to process management in the organization.

Returning to the first of these points, and the main subject of this part of the book, we have seen how the updated Role Activity Diagram is not only a basis on which to start the process of the sub-project, but also a means to ensure that changes to the process made on-the-fly can be handled without disruption to either management or executive control mechanisms. In fact, such changes *form a normal part* of those mechanisms—the feedback received by managers and executives can be based from the start on new agreement depictions. Hence change is directly supported, not as an exception to the norm, but as a natural part of it.

We have focused on this example because the use of *collaborative transactions* as a modeling technique is applicable outside concurrent engineering design. In fact, it is applicable in any situation where a problem can be broken into separate but interdependent pieces. Designing a car, for instance, can be broken down, not only by domain as above, but also according to the components of the car—chassis, engine, transmission, and so on—and the same principles would apply. Developing a marketing promotion for a new foodstuff could be broken down into poster production, television advertising, public relations, co-marketing, and so on. Expanding a business into a new region could be broken down geographically.

This particular approach to process description—based on upper and lower interactions, that bound nested sub-processes—is a solution to modeling human-driven activity that not only has wide applicability, but varied advantages for both *process change limitation and effective management control.*

To see this, consider first how the use of collaborative transactions as a basis for agreement in our example allows the impact of process changes to be limited:

- Changes at domain design level need not impact the overall design level. Each lower-level transaction is in effect a separate process, and its participants can make their own agreement depictions without necessarily affecting the higher-level transaction.

- The use of dependency maps and approval charts means that the process even at detailed design level may not have to change. Because the Role Activity Diagram does not specify in detail how each person is to carry out his or her work, it may be that a particular designer can make changes to his or her individual Role definition without impacting the agreement at all, instead impacting only the information resources that are created and used in the process.

- Any of the interactions shown on the Role Activity Diagram may repeat ad infinitum, as requirements evolve and the solution shapes up. Iterations and loops of rework are not shown explicitly on the diagram, since the modeling technique allows for them from the start. If a domain solution component design is rejected in review, for example, it cannot be submitted and further design work is automatically enabled.

Then consider the benefits that collaborative transactions provide for management control of the design process:

- *Visibility of design progress.* The split into domain-level transactions provides a convenient mechanism for monitoring progress as a whole—in particular, deadlocks and bottlenecks can be isolated and remedied as soon as they manifest themselves.

- *The ability to track key decisions and approvals for audit purposes.* All necessary information can be stored explicitly in the compound object passed via the lower bound interaction. Moreover, this object can be exported to an external system such as a database or spreadsheet for further analysis as desired.

- *The ability to manage transactions.* In particular, transactions can be combined or split them into sub-transactions. This may be especially useful when some parts of a solution can be created much faster than others, and it is desirable to free up some people to move on before the entire transaction is complete.

- *Partial sign-off of deliverables can be managed.* This can be done by completing the original transaction and creating a new one to produce just the missing piece (like canceling a part-paid invoice and issuing a new invoice for the balance). The new transaction can then manage a simpler dependency relationship, between the missing piece and the overall solution.

- *The ability to manage dependencies.* The dependency map can be used to identify mutual dependencies that always cause process problems. Interface contracts can then be introduced to make design activities more independent.

Similar advantages would likely accrue in any area to which the collaborative transaction pattern is applied. The Role Activity Diagram technique allows complex situations to be made simple, with varied benefits both to process participants and to their management.

Let's take stock. We saw above how the *REACT* and *AIM* patterns can be implemented in terms of the relationship between the sponsor Role of, and the primary Roles within, a process. These represent *executive control* and *management control* respectively.

We have now seen how *agreement depictions* based on Role Activity Diagrams can be used initially to support executive control of a process, then successively refined to allow day-to-day management control of process changes made on-the-fly, as well as shared *commitment* to these changes among process participants.

We then saw how, in many complex processes, that a valuable modeling technique is to break the deliverables down into distinct yet interdependent components, and then base a *collaborative transaction* on each component.

Having established a framework for the general depiction of human-driven processes, we now need to ask: where do we start? If we seek to support human-driven processes in our organization, how can we work out what the separate processes that exist actually are?

The helicopter view

We looked at organizational theory for what it can tell us about human collaboration (see *How people communicate*). However, the understanding gained from autopoeitic theory does not give us a way of understanding or modeling the enterprise as a whole in terms of distinct processes. For a representative modern approach to depicting an enterprise, see Figure 21: The BPTrends Pyramid—A complete enterprise architecture[13].

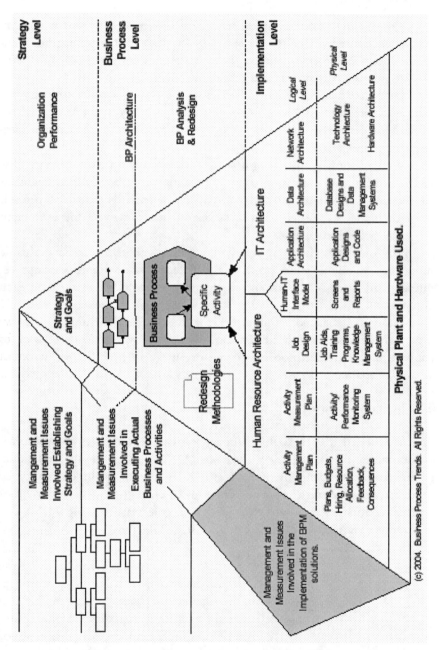

Figure 21: The BPTrends Pyramid—A complete enterprise architecture

This diagram provides an overview of how both mechanistic and human-driven processes can fit into the wider goals and structure of an organization, and how measurement and control can be applied at every level. Once such a model has been prepared, it could well be used as a starting point for a detailed analysis of human activity based on the ideas in this book.

It is interesting to note the equal emphasis the diagram places on human processes and machine processes. In other words, the subject matter of this book, when considered from an enterprise viewpoint, is important—as important as the automated, machine-like processes that are the mainstay of the IT industry today. Many business people and research organizations would argue from experience that more organizational activity is human-driven than machine-driven—some would say a lot more.

Such a diagram is valuable once it has been drawn up. However, a diagramming technique by itself does not provide what we are seeking—a means of breaking the organization down into chunks, in which each chunk constitutes a separate high-level process. Once we have carried out a *chunking* effort, we can represent the results as above, or any other way, but we need a way formulate the breakdown in the first place. A new contender for a methodology to achieve this chunking is Riva, the subject of a recent book by Martyn Ould,[14] whose previous work on Role Activity Diagrams is the original textbook on the subject, and has been referred to throughout this book. Riva represents the summation of Ould's work on Role Activity Diagrams in the decade since the publication of his original book.

The Riva approach is to isolate *Essential Business Entities* (EBEs)—the high-level information objects with which the organization is concerned—and to identify certain of these with high-level *Units Of Work* (UOWs), termed *essential UOWs*. The EBEs and UOWs are the starting point for a more detailed analysis of constituent processes.

For instance, in a pharmaceutical organization, a Clinical Trial would be an EBE, with a corresponding essential UOW to run the trial. The organization then invents *designed* entities (for example, an Invoice) that arise from decisions about how to do business around the EBEs—from processes that are created to carry out the essential UOWs.

For purposes of process design, and implementation of computer support, both types of UOW (essential and designed) are treated as types of data object, and a generic *process type* is constructed around each one.

When it comes to process enactment, each object of a particular type is identified with an actual process of the corresponding type. More precisely, Riva identifies an enacted process with the "lead Role" of the process. It is not so much processes that are created, but lead Roles that then carry the responsibility for a particular stream of activity associated with the corresponding data objects.

Riva also has the concept that there are three levels of process associated with each essential and designed business entity:

- A *case process*, which handles the work associated with a specific entity—the operation of a particular Clinical Trial, or settlement of a specific Invoice within such a Clinical Trial.

- A *case management process*, which deals with the concurrent operation of case processes—in particular, allocating access to shared resources. Riva associates with case management process actions to do with planning, reporting, monitoring, scheduling, resourcing, prioritizing, negotiating, reconciling and so on. There is assumed to be a case management process for all Clinical Trials, another within a particular Clinical Trial for all Invoices, and so on.

- A *case strategy process*, which takes a longer-term view of management and deals with overall improvement to both forms of process, taking into account business and industry trends as well as operational issues. The case strategy process for Clinical Trials might look at how they can be re-engineered to cut cycle time dramatically, or how quality measures can be applied to improve efficiency.

Riva is attractive in its formality and simplicity—it sets out specifically to give process modeling both a rigorous underpinning and a methodology that can be applied to any form of organization. Moreover, Riva, like the approach of this book and its conception of Human Interaction Management software, is based on Role Activity Diagrams. The RADRunner documentation, for example, assumes that the starting point for process definition is modeling of the information resources within key Roles. A process identified and designed using Riva can be implemented in a straightforward way using a Human Interaction Management System such as we specify.

However, the approach outlined in this book is in some ways inconsistent with Riva. While we would agree that entities are fundamental to process analysis, and that runtime processes can often be identified with their lead Roles, our interpretation of Role Activity Diagrams is different, being more flexible and attuned to human behavior patterns. Such common practices as the making of provisional decisions, or negotiations of indefinite length and nature, are very hard to capture using Riva.

Moreover, our analysis of *management* is rather different. Our approach leads to a different understanding of the activities in a case process and a case management process, and hence to a different division of work between them. In fact, the principles developed in this book make it hard, in many cases, to justify the existence of a case management process at all.

This is because the principle of separation of control (as discussed in this book) allows us to distinguish the different Roles inherent in sponsorship of a process (*executive control*) and day-to-day supervision of its activity (*management control*). This is in direct contrast to the Riva notion of case management processes. Not only does a Riva case management process combine elements of both our forms of control, but it is distinct from the case work itself, a viewpoint that we argue does not reflect the reality of human activity. In general, support, facilitation and resourcing of human work is intimately tied to its execution—and if not, there are problems in store.

The Riva case management process concept is closer to our notion of *executive control* than to *management control*. However, executive control is not really concerned with a flow of individual cases in the manner of a Riva case management process. Where an executive has authority over more than one process, those processes may be entirely unrelated. In the example of a government cost reduction study, the civil servant who sponsors the process is unlikely to sponsor similar studies simultaneously, but to be in charge of other entirely different projects that happen currently to be underway.

The idea of multiple similar processes under the authority of a single individual is more closely tied to what we call management control—a project manager who is running many projects at once, for example, or a line manager with many staff members doing the same job—and we argue that this activity is *part of the process itself*. Hence, it is hard to justify the existence of a separate case management process. We would prefer to model this in terms of multiple "instances" of the same type of management Role.

The process that starts off these management instances is typically higher-level in terms of *authority*, but this process does not have the features of a Riva case management process—planning, reporting, monitoring, scheduling, resourcing, prioritizing, negotiating, reconciling and so on. Its nature is in fact no different from that of the process it starts—it is the same kind of thing, just at a more senior level in the organization. We see no justification for distinguishing this kind of process from a low-level case process. The same sort of activity happens from the lowest to the highest level in the organization, and you can model it all using the principles we've described.

The approach to modeling of both work activities and management in Riva may stem from its use to date in industries, such as pharmaceuticals and utility supply, that are highly regulated, and in some ways the most straightforward domains to model. We would suggest that Riva applies particularly well to processes that are either:

- *Mechanistic*, such as supply chain automation and factory control; or

- *In an industry with standardized processes*—for example, pharmaceuticals, financial services, telecommunications and utilities.

It is to these areas that an approach such as Riva is most naturally suited—areas in which rules can be applied across-the-board to companies of different kinds, and assumed to remain fairly constant during process operation.

In fact, a particular assertion of Riva is that the process architecture of an organization can be derived *solely from an understanding of what business the organization is in.* In other words, two organizations in the same business will have the same high-level breakdown of processes.

This is a dramatic claim, a Big Idea. Like all Big Ideas, it is contentious, and may be both true and not true.

The claim seems particularly applicable to companies in industries such as those described above—a view borne out by the emergence of standardized process definitions in such sectors. These standards are drawn up by industry bodies, and intended for use by all companies in the sector without variation. Examples are the Supply Chain Council's SCOR (Supply Chain Operations Reference) and the TeleManagement Forum's eTOM (e-business Telecom Operations Model). In due course it is likely that sector-specific business standards currently focused on *transactions*—such as ORIGO and ACORD in the insurance marketplace—will follow suit and evolve into fully-fledged *process* standards.

However, there are no signs that such standards will emerge in more diversified sectors: IT, entertainment, retail, agriculture, construction, and so on. In these areas it may be harder to argue that different companies have the same process architecture. Could Microsoft and IBM operate according to a common set of high-level process descriptions? CNN and the BBC? Wal-Mart and Marks & Spencer?

Perhaps. It is hard to say—the proof of the pudding will be in the eating. If process architectures are truly the same for all companies in a particular business, there is no competitive advantage in keeping yours private—in fact, you can cut costs by using any competitor's, getting together with them to prepare a shared standard process architecture, or looking to an industry body to draw one up for all concerned. So in due course process architectures may become publicly available, and the issue will then become clearer.

However, our interest here is not to question this aspect of Riva—process invariance for a type of business—which has no direct relevance to human-driven process analysis. The discussion above is given in order to suggest that there may be a fundamental difference between organizations, analogous to the fundamental differences we see between mechanistic and human-driven processes. On the one hand, there is constant pressure from outside, and drivers from within, toward regulation and automation. On the other hand, business processes should provide a foundation for ongoing innovation and flexibility.

Therefore, with regard to construction of a process architecture, and drawing up of a diagram such as shown above, we would suggest that the *base* techniques of Riva should be adopted—that is, the derivation of Essential Business Entities and their corresponding Units of Work—together with refinement of these into designed objects and processes. In particular, Riva includes a number of practical techniques drawn from experience that will help in the identification of distinct processes within an organization—these processes can then be depicted in a diagram such as Figure 21 above.

However, where the organization or the processes concerned are of the creative, dynamic type, an eye should always be kept on the aspects of process elucidated in this book. In particular, the use of Role Activity Diagrams should be guided by the more flexible interpretation given in this book. Moreover, the modeling of *management* should be treated differently from the division of work into *case process* and *case management process*, advocated by Riva. Instead, these processes should be handled according to the principle of *separation of control,* by which authority over and daily supervision of a process are divided between a *Sponsor Role above the process* and *key Roles within the process* respectively. Without this enhanced approach, the constant evolution of processes innate to human activity cannot be safely controlled or even monitored.

Reasoning about processes

We conclude this chapter—and the setting out of our theory of human-driven processes—with a discussion of a business problem that may seem rather abstract, but whose resolution is recognized by practitioners of process orientation as essential. How can we underpin business processes in a *formal* way?

Of course, the entire theory of work presented in this book is formal, in the sense that it describes the methodical application of principles. However, in this section we mean something very specific by "formal"—how can we apply the principles of *mathematics* and *logic* to the complex, multi-faceted, ever-changing flow of activity inside an organization? Solving this problem is important for practical reasons, not just theoretically.

Work support technologies have traditionally suffered from being complex and expensive to implement. Maintenance is even worse. Moreover, and just as importantly, how can you really know whether the systems you have put in place do what you think they do? Do they implement the diagrams you drew up at the start to represent processes? Even if they did at the start, what happens when processes change— as those processes centered on human activity, that we call *human-driven*, inevitably and constantly do?

These issues are not just of concern to IT staff, but are visible at the board level—concerns such as feasibility, cost, resourcing, and operational quality, are fundamental to proper management of the enterprise. Moreover, with the wave of recent corporate scandals and consequent appearance of new regulations, *transparency* is a major concern for senior executives. For example, in the USA the Sarbanes-Oxley Act of 2002[15] places responsibility for financial accounting squarely on the shoulders of company board members, who may even face a custodial sentence if they don't get it right. Similar statutes are likely to appear in other parts of the world.

As a result, there has been increasing interest in the provision of a *formal foundation* for process analysis. In fact, the nature of this foundation—in particular, whether it should be graphical *Petri nets*, or a more recent, algebraic approach to process description known as the *pi-calculus*—has been the topic of much study among leading process practitioners.[16]

But why would such a foundation solve the problem of change in human-driven processes? How is this kind of stuff genuinely relevant? Surely it's just something for those with brains the size of a planet to discuss at conferences and to write highbrow papers about.

To justify the importance of such theoretical work, and locate it with respect to industry initiatives, Robin Milner (inventor of the pi-calculus) and Ole Høgh Jensen write of the latest effort to provide a formal underpinning for computation (a graphical approach called *bigraphs*, that deals with the relationship between "locality" and "connectivity"—between *where you are* and *what you can access*):

> "The long-term aim of this work is to provide a model of computation on a global scale, as represented by the Internet and the World Wide Web. The aim is not just to build a mathematical model in which we can analyze systems that already exist. Beyond that, we seek a theory to guide the specification, design and programming of these systems, to guide future adaptations of them, and not to deteriorate when these adaptations are implemented. There is much talk of the vanishing ubiquitous computer of the future that will obtrude less and less visibly in our lives, but will pervade them more and more. Technology will enable us to create this. To speak crudely, we must make sure that we understand it before it vanishes.
>
> This will only be achieved if we can reverse the typical order of events, in which design and implementation come first, modeling later (or never). For example, a programming language is rarely based thoroughly upon a theoretical model. This has inevitably meant that our initial understanding of designed systems is brittle, and deteriorates seriously as they are adapted. We believe that the only acceptable solution, in the long run, is for system designs to be expressed with the concepts and notations of a theory rich enough to admit all that the designers wish.
>
> The arrival of ubiquitous mobile computing provides an opportunity for this, simply because it is new enough for its languages and implementation techniques not to be entrenched. Another reason is that concurrency theorists have anticipated mobility and have some structures to offer for new languages. Thus designers and analysts may come to speak the same tongue."*[17]*

The reference to *mobility* at the end of this passage is crucial. Many people involved in the development of process support systems focus on the importance of allowing processes to change their definition *during their enactment*, via the exchange among participants of information about the process itself. In particular, the participants can use this information to change the connections within the process—the parties to an interaction, for example, or the systems that co-operate to supply a service.

The provision of mobility is a complex technical matter, bringing with it potential problems that are hard to predict. Hence, giving process support systems a formal mathematical basis makes sense—such a basis can then be used to deduce properties of the system's behavior, and help ensure not only that they will operate as intended, but also that no unforeseen security risks will be introduced. Just as importantly, if we do it right, a formal basis will help clarify how such advanced features as mobility can be *managed*— not only *permitted*, but also *monitored* and *controlled* simply and effectively.

However, supplying such a formal basis is harder than it seems. Milner and Jensen are saying above that, if computer systems are to be successfully provided with a formal basis, this basis must be introduced *during development of the systems*—not applied afterwards, papering over the cracks where the systems do not quite match the theory. Deductions made from theory about a system that only partially matches it are going to be misleading, not reassuring. This means that you need to understand all the relevant mathematics before you can even start building a new form of process support system—you can't just hire an academic to sort it out afterwards.

In many ways, the poster child for providing a mathematical foundation to computing is the relational database, now the main and ubiquitous storage method for enterprise data.

In the early days of data processing during the 1960s, data was stored in "flat-file" format: each piece of information was kept as a single record in a file. A file of customer orders, for instance, would contain customer information such as address and phone number *in every record*—no matter how many times the customer had previously dealt with the company, the information was repeated for every order record in the file.

This made for files that were unnecessarily large, and therefore took up lots of disk space (which was expensive at the time). Worse, such data was hard to maintain—what do you do if a customer changes his or her address? Data management was costly, complex and time-consuming.

The problem was solved by the "relational model" for data—which appeared *before* the software to implement it. In 1970, Dr. E. F. Codd published a paper entitled "A Relational Model of Data for Large Shared Data Banks," introducing a set of rules that eliminated the need to store redundant data. These rules were the starting point for relational database theory, that not only made money for companies such as Oracle and IBM, but saved money for the rest of the world.

Many people feel that process support in the early 21st century is in a parallel situation to data processing in the 1960s—it is too costly, complex and time-consuming. As a result, they feel that a similar formal underpinning is necessary to sort out the problems. Where should we look for such an underpinning?

As described above, the two main contenders to date are Petri nets and the pi-calculus:

- We have given a brief introduction to Petri nets above. It is a graphical technique based on the movement of *tokens* from one *place* to another in a network. The connections between places, known as *transitions*, control the movement of the tokens. An example Petri net is shown below:

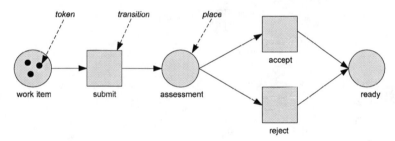

Figure 22: An example Petri net

- The pi-calculus is based on the notion that a computing system is composed of independent, communicating objects, known as *automata*. Things that happen inside these automata are termed *actions*, which move an automaton as a whole from one *state* to another. An automaton can send messages to another automaton via a channel connecting them. Each end of such a channel is known as a *port*—one end is considered to be for output (labeled with an overbar) and the other for input. A port can itself be sent from one automaton to another, which enables the connections in the system to change during execution. The pi-calculus is an algebraic theory, but it is possible to depict automata graphically, as shown in Figure 23: Example pi-calculus automata. Here we essentially see the same situation as depicted in Figure 22, but the upper automaton represents work *performance*, and the lower automaton work *assessment*:

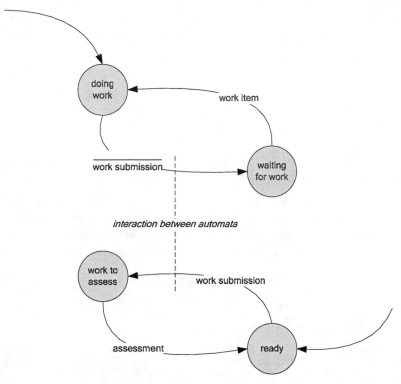

Figure 23: Example pi-calculus automata

Both Petri nets and the pi-calculus have inspired several variants that extend the original theories to add functionality or cater to specialized situations. Hence, one approach taken to date is to seek specific variants of one or both that meet the needs of a process support system in terms of its formal underpinning.

These pages are not the place to take up this discussion in depth. However, it is possible that the theory of human-driven activity offers a new approach to formal description of processes, one that allows the two competing formalisms to be combined—perhaps in conjunction with a specialization of one or both theories. The essence of this approach is to:

- Reconsider the basis on which formal theory has been applied to processes; and

- Recognize that, for such a complex problem, we may need not one formal technique, but several—and more than one way of applying them.

When a formal theory is used to describe a computer system, or any other real world activity, it is done so by creating an *abstraction*. This simply means that each object in the formal theory is identified with a specific sort of object in the real world. There will always be more objects in the real world than in the formal theory, so some real world objects will have to be left out. However, if you choose your abstraction wisely, this doesn't matter. In fact, this is the *strength* of abstraction. By simplifying the world, you can see more clearly what is going on and deduce things that weren't obvious beforehand—see the forest for the trees, in a way.

So, what abstractions have been used when applying formal theories to business processes? In general, it is always the same one. An activity in the theory (a Petri net *transition*, or pi-calculus *action*) is mapped straight onto a work activity in the real world. The real world activity may be a simple, atomic task (a calculation, for example) or something very complex (such as assembling a car from component parts), but either way, the principle is to identify something that takes place in the abstraction with some work that takes place in the real world.

What if we were to change this, and try a new abstraction? In particular, the principle of *separation of control* proposed for human-driven processes allows us to distinguish *management control* (day-to-day facilitation of human activity, carried out as part of the process itself—ongoing resourcing, monitoring and process re-design) from *executive control* (exercise of authority over the process, via determination of its primary Roles, interactions and deliverables).

Process evolution can be implemented under management control via the establishment of consensus among certain participants, based on *how they would proceed from now on*—we term such a consensus an *agreement*. People decide to do things a certain way in the future (which we suggest is best documented and shared via a Role Activity Diagram), then go away and do some work. After a while, the same cycle repeats—a group of current participants meet, decide how to evolve the process further, depict and share this agreement, then go away and do some more work.

We propose that a way forward for the provisioning of human-driven process support with a formal basis is to map theoretical activities (Petri net transitions and pi-calculus actions) *not* onto real world work items, at least when the processes concerned are human-driven rather than machine-driven, but onto the means by which such processes are instantiated and changed. The process moves forward not in terms of tasks executed, but in terms of *how the organization of work evolves*.

This approach places mobility at the very heart of process theory. Process evolution is the building block, not a by-product, of formal process description.

In addition, it seems eminently possible to support this approach to formal description of processes with either Petri nets or the pi-calculus. More importantly, we need both, since one allows us to reason about *management control* and the other about *executive control*.

- Petri nets can be interpreted as not modeling the flow of activity, but modeling instead the activities of *management control*. A Petri net place represents a stable process definition. A Petri net transition depicts the distribution for approval or implementation of an agreement made by process participants on future process change, which potentially moves the running process from one definition to another, either to refine it or alter it. This is depicted below in Figure 24: A Petri net showing management control:

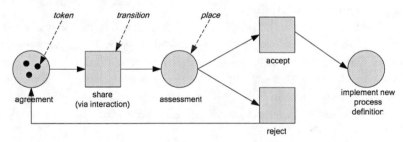

Figure 24: A Petri net showing management control

- A pi-calculus automaton can be taken to represent a self-contained process network—a group of Roles, co-operating via interactions, and responsible both for management control and for the work itself. Pi-calculus actions equate to process changes—in a sense, a pi-calculus action summarizes the impact of the individual Petri net transitions described above (distribution, approval, and implementation of an agreement on change). This gives us a higher-level view of process change, abstracted away from the individual agreements made, in which ports show the fundamental mechanisms of *executive control*—how communication is effected between the executive sponsor who initiated a process and the lead Role of the process itself. Mobility in pi-calculus terms then equates to the implementation of executive control, and its transfer from one Role to another—for instance, when authority over a process is granted or delegated. Example automata are shown below in Figure 25: Executive control depicted via the pi-calculus:

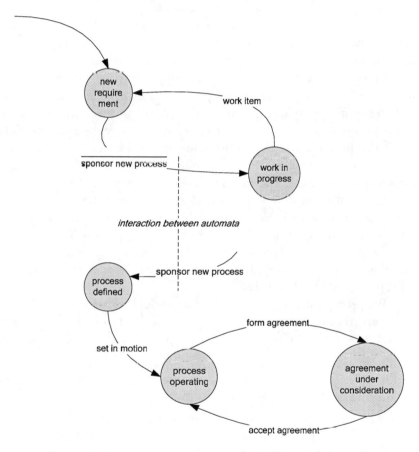

Figure 25: Executive control depicted via the pi-calculus

These abstractions are fundamentally different from any applied to date, and offer the chance to grab the bull by the horns—the ongoing management of processes that inevitably change. Change may be necessary on a frequent basis, under management control, or made more occasionally via intervention from above, under executive control. In both cases, we need a way of reasoning about change, if we are to deal with it properly.

This change of abstraction—from work activity to management activity—may offer a way forward that deals with critical issues, and in so doing resolve a dilemma by uniting two powerful forms of reasoning. But it also leaves a gap. How, with this approach, can we reason about the work activities themselves? Surely this is important too. After all, a process is only there in the first place in order to *get things done.*

The problem to date has been one of terminology. Computer scientists have a tendency to think about human work activities as if they were steps carried out by a computer program. This leads to process descriptions that are framed in terms of *sequences of tasks.* Both Petri nets and the pi-calculus, for example, allow the history of a process to be examined in such a way. However appropriate this may be to automated or mechanistic processes, this is unfortunate when it comes to human processes, because the end result is that powerful and elegant mathematics are devoted to analyzing work in a way that is ultimately of little meaning. We do not think or act like machines, so what value is there in analyzing our behavior as if we were?

We need an approach to modeling work activities that is closer to the true basis on which we decide how, when and what to do. It may not be possible to capture all this in a mathematical formalism—but that doesn't necessarily matter. As discussed, the virtue of an *abstraction* is that, by leaving some things out, general truths become clear. So what abstraction is the most useful for human activities?

We propose that such an abstraction should be based on *business rules.* In general, humans do something if and when it seems necessary, or just sensible—regardless of what they just did previously, or originally intended to do:

- On an ongoing basis, we re-evaluate the world around us, and make a judgment about what we should do next.

- Having done something, we and our supervisors then look at the results and make a decision about whether the work has value. If it does, we keep it—otherwise we discard it.

These aspects of human behavior correspond closely to the use of *preconditions* and *postconditions* that we propose for the application of Role Activity Diagrams to human-driven process modeling. A precondition *enables* an activity. If the precondition is true, the work can be carried out whenever desired. A postcondition *validates* an activity. If the postcondition is false on completion, all the work must be undone. Is there a similar mathematical formalism available?

A particularly appropriate approach is the language Z.[18] Z was originally intended for formal descriptions of computer systems—it is based on set theory and mathematical logic, and generally used to help prove that high-integrity, safety-critical systems conform to their original specification. However, Z happens to provide exactly the foundation we need for the description of human activity.

In particular, while Z has the ability to describe task sequences, there is no need to *constrain* activities to follow one another in a particular order, using techniques of control flow (if-then-else tests, loops, and so on). Rather, you can use Z to describe for particular activities the specific conditions under which they may be executed, and how the state of a system is changed on their completion—*when you may do things, and what effect they will have.*

In Z, schemas are used to describe both static and dynamic aspects of a system. The static aspects include:

- the states it can occupy; and
- the invariant relationships that are maintained as the system moves from state to state.

The dynamic aspects include:

- the operations that are possible;
- the relationship between inputs and outputs; and
- the changes of state that happen. [19]

An example of Z notation is given below. The "schema" shown in Figure 26 is the formal description of an activity that submits a new white paper for publication on a Web site.

```
  SubmitPaper _____
 ┌──────────────────────────────────────────────────────┐
 │ ΔWhitePapers                                           │
 │ content? : TEXT                                        │
 │ topic? : KEYWORD                                       │
 ├──────────────────────────────────────────────────────┤
 │                                                        │
 │ topic? ∈ keywords                                      │
 │ whitePapers' = whitePapers U {content? → topic?}       │
 └──────────────────────────────────────────────────────┘
```

Figure 26: Z schema showing submission of a white paper

The declaration, Δ*WhitePapers,* indicates that the activity is describing a state change to the "domain" of white papers. The declaration implicitly makes several variables available for use:

- *whitePapers*—the current list of white papers
- *whitePapers'*—the list of white papers after the activity has completed
- *keywords*—the current list of subject areas with which the Web site is concerned
- *keywords'*—the list of subject areas after the activity has completed (not used above).

After the declaration of a domain come the declarations of the two inputs to the activity: *content?* (a document containing the new white paper) and *topic?* (the subject area of the white paper). Input names conventionally end in a question mark.

The part of the schema below the line starts with a *precondition,* stating that the subject area of the new paper must be one with that the Web site is in general concerned. This must be true in order for the activity to take place. Otherwise it cannot proceed.

The schema concludes with a *postcondition,* stating that the new list of white papers must include the submitted paper, mapped onto its subject area.

Due to its background in the most rigorous aspects of computer system development, Z has not traditionally been viewed as a process modeling technique. It is ironic that, in moving to an understanding of how human-driven processes are deeply unlike machine processes, we find that the most suitable formal basis for describing human work activities is one originally conceived specifically for the most highly constrained computer systems.

However, used in an appropriate way—e.g., as a "declarative" technique based on pre- and postconditions—Z allows us to describe human work activities in precisely the manner that people conceive of them.

Moreover, we can use Role Activity Diagrams to visualize processes described with Z. We need to interpret the diagrams appropriately in order to incorporate Z constructs—to remove the original basis in Petri nets, and impose instead a stronger approach, more suited to processes that involve human activity. The elaboration of a suitable Role Activity Diagram based approach to the graphical depiction of processes was presented in *A New Theory Of Roles*. Role Activity Diagram activities used in the sense described above correspond naturally to Z schemas. Interactions can be modelled similarly, using a separate domain to describe the body of each Role concerned, and showing, via pre- and postconditions, how data flows between Roles.

To conclude, we have seen how a full description of human-driven business processes can be made in formal terms, as a basis both for analysis and for system development. The proposed approach uses Petri nets and pi-calculus in conjunction for the description of process evolution and its management, together with Z for the modelling of detailed process activity.

Our focus in presenting this set of abstractions is on the management of ongoing process design change. Such change is a natural part of human interaction, and we therefore propose the formal basis described here for application to *human-driven* processes. By contrast, *machine-driven* processes change in more limited and tightly controlled ways. Hence it may be more appropriate to apply different formal bases to machine-driven processes— we do not make an assertion either way. Our specific proposal is that, when it comes to the analysis of business activity that is centered on humans, the three techniques of Petri nets, pi-calculus and Z notation can all be used in conjunction to provide a sound formal basis—a basis that deals not only with behavior, but with how that behavior changes over time. Such a basis is essential for process management in order to permit an enterprise to *guarantee how its operations are being carried out*—for instance, to provide financial transparency of the kind now required by statute in some jurisdictions.

The further elaboration of these principles, and investigation of their ramifications, is beyond the scope of this book. We encourage those interested in pursuing the necessary research to join the Web forum *Role Based Process Support* (www.smartgroups.com/groups/roles), which serves as a focal point for collaboration on relevant work.

Putting it all together

To summarize this chapter, we developed a new concept of process management—the principle of *separation of control*. Authority over a process is assigned to a Sponsor Role separate from it (*executive control*), while daily supervision of a process is assigned to key Roles within it (*management control*). We showed how the *REACT* and *AIM patterns* can be implemented in terms of this principle, and depicted graphically using a Role Activity Diagram.

We moved on to deal with process evolution, and saw how *agreement depictions* based on Role Activity Diagrams can be used initially to support executive control of a process, then successively refined to allow day-to-day management control of (and shared commitment among process participants to) process changes made on-the-fly.

As part of this discussion, we saw the AIM pattern start to come into its own, and discussed how, in many complex processes, a valuable modeling technique is to break the deliverables down into distinct yet interdependent components, and base a *collaborative transaction* on each component.

We looked at how you can determine a *process architecture* for your organization—a breakdown of what distinct processes exist—and discussed the new Riva methodology. Riva is recommended with reservations about its modeling of management, which is different from our own, and perhaps applicable mainly to highly standardized industries and mechanistic processes.

We concluded the chapter by showing how a full description of human-driven business processes can be made in formal terms, as a basis both for analysis and for system development. Our approach uses Petri nets and pi-calculus in conjunction for the description of process evolution and its management, together with the Z notation for the modeling of detailed process activity.

However, our concern in this book goes further than theoretical discussion. It is now time for companies to incorporate an understanding of human-driven processes into management techniques, and insist that their software vendors produce a roadmap for incorporating Human Interaction Management into their systems and offerings. In the next chapters we will show why this is important, and how it can be done.

References.

[1] A project management methodology originally developed by UK government, which has also been found useful in the commercial world—see the official PRINCE 2 Web site http://www.ogc.gov.uk/prince/

[2] Ould, M.A., 1997, "Designing A Re-engineering-proof Process Architecture"

[3] Coplien, J., Harrison, N., 2004, "Organizational Patterns of Agile Software Development"

[4] See, for example, Warboys, B., 1991, "The Practical Application of Process Modeling—some early reflections," http://www.cs.man.ac.uk/ipg/Docs/bw91.html

[5] Warboys, B., Kawalek, P., Robertson, I., Greenwood, M., 1999, "Business Information Systems—a Process Approach," McGraw-Hill, p.82-83

[6] http://www.dynamic-outsourcing.com

[7] http://www.dynamic-outsourcing.com

[8] A GANTT chart is a horizontal bar chart developed as a production control tool in 1917 by Henry L. Gantt, an American engineer and social scientist. Frequently used in project management, a GANTT chart provides a graphical illustration of a schedule that helps to plan, coordinate, and track specific tasks in a project. GANTT charts may be simple versions created on graph paper or more complex automated versions created using project management applications ... GANTT charts give a clear illustration of project status, but one problem with them is that they don't indicate task dependencies—you cannot tell how one task falling behind schedule affects other tasks. The PERT chart, another popular project management charting method, is designed to do this. http://searchcio.techtarget.com/sDefinition/0,,sid19_gci331397,00.html

[9] A PERT chart is a project management tool used to schedule, organize, and coordinate tasks within a project. PERT stands for Program Evaluation Review Technique, a methodology developed by the US Navy in the 1950s to manage the Polaris submarine missile program. A similar methodology, the Critical Path Method (CPM), which was developed for project management in the private sector at about the same time, has become synonymous with PERT, so that the technique is known by any variation on the names: PERT, CPM, or PERT/CPM ... The PERT chart is sometimes preferred over the GANTT chart, another

popular project management charting method, because it clearly illustrates task dependencies. On the other hand, the PERT chart can be much more difficult to interpret, especially on complex projects. Frequently, project managers use both techniques.
http://whatis.techtarget.com/definition/0,,sid9_gci331391,00.html

[10] The example process shown develops and extends an earlier version of the collaborative transaction pattern presented in Harrison-Broninski, K., Hayden, F., 2004, "Role-Based Transaction Management In Collaborative Systems," http://www.rolemodellers.com/abstracts/Role-Based Transaction Management In Collaborative Systems.pdf

[11] Murdoch, J., et al., 1999, "Modeling Complex Design Processes with Role Activity Diagrams," Journal of Integrated Design and Process Science.

[12] Harrison-Broninski, K., Hayden, F., 2004, ibid.

[13] Harmon, P., 2004, "The Human Side of a Business Process Architecture," http://www.bptrends.com/deliver_file.cfm?fileType=publication&fileName=11 -04 NL Human Perf and Ent Architecture.pdf

[14] Ould, M.A., 2005, "Business Process Management: A Rigorous Approach," Meghan-Kiffer Press

[15] The Sarbanes-Oxley Act was signed into law on 30th July 2002, and introduced highly significant legislative changes to financial practice and corporate governance regulation. It introduced stringent new rules with the stated objective: "to protect investors by improving the accuracy and reliability of corporate disclosures made pursuant to the securities laws."
It also introduced a number of deadlines, the prime ones being:
- Most public companies must meet the financial reporting and certification mandates for any end of year financial statements filed after November 15th 2004 (amended from June 15th).
- smaller companies and foreign companies must meet these mandates for any statements filed after 15th July 2005 (amended from April 15th).
The act is actually named after its main architects, Senator Paul Sarbanes and Representative Michael Oxley, and of course followed a series of very high profile scandals, such as Enron. It is also intended to "deter and punish corporate and accounting fraud and corruption, ensure justice for wrongdoers, and protect the interests of workers and shareholders" (Quote: President Bush).
The Sarbanes-Oxley Act itself is organized into eleven titles, although sections 302, 404, 401, 409, 802 and 906 are the most significant with respect to compliance (Sarbanes Oxley section 404 seems to cause most concern) and internal

control. In addition, the Act also created a public company accounting board. Perhaps one of the most remarkable aspects of this legislation however relates to its profile. It is very much in the public and media arena. The focus is certainly intense in this respect, creating yet another clear motivation for compliance. There is simply no escaping it!
(http://www.sarbanes-oxley-forum.com/)
A more detailed overview of the Act is available at:
http://www.aicpa.org/info/sarbanes_oxley_summary.htm
The Act itself can be downloaded in PDF form from:
http://frwebgate.access.gpo.gov/cgi-bin/getdoc.cgi?dbname=107_cong_reports&docid=f:hr610.107.pdf

[16] An article in October 2003 extolling the virtues of Robin Milner's pi-calculus as the way forward (Smith, H., and Fingar, P., 2003, "Workflow is just a Pi process," http://www.fairdene.com/picalculus/workflow-is-just-a-pi-process.pdf) was closely followed by two responses (van der Aalst, W., "Pi calculus versus Petri nets: Let us eat 'humble pie' rather than further inflate the 'Pi hype'," http://tmitwww.tm.tue.nl/staff/wvdaalst/pi-hype.pdf, and Pyke, J., Whitehead, R., 2003, "Does Better Math Lead to Better Business Processes?," http://www.wfmc.org/standards/docs/better_maths_better_processes.pdf). The debate then spread across the Business Process Management industry generally, via many other articles as well as Weblogs and mailing lists.

[17] Jensen, O., Milner, R., 2003, "Bigraphs and mobile processes," University of Cambridge Computer Laboratory

[18] Spivey, M., 1988, "The Z Notation: A Reference Manual," Prentice Hall

[19] Spivey, M., 1988, ibid.

Five

Improving Human Interactions

KEY POINTS: We look at several areas in which a better understanding of human-driven processes can improve organizational performance. Not only is such an understanding the basis for improved people management, support of vital mental activity, and enablement of creativity in the workplace, but it also enables key business processes to be made transparent and amenable to control. In particular:

- *Better human relations* are possible between colleagues.
- *Quality management* can be revitalized with a new and powerful sets of process measurement techniques.
- *Human work processes can be improved* via the use of standard patterns.
- *Assignment of process participants* can be better controlled.
- *Confidentiality* can be preserved more easily.

Talk to me, so you can see
Oh, what's going on
What's going on
—Marvin Gaye, 1971.

Why we need Human Interaction Management

Before setting out our theory of human-driven processes, we described how amplifying human processes will bring benefits to executives, middle management and interaction workers themselves. Since then we have covered a lot of ground, so you may wish to pause and review the benefits of Human Interaction Management outlined in the first chapter. We hope that the basis for the claims made earlier is now clear.

In this chapter we go into more detail about some of these assertions. We discuss particular ways in which the proper understanding and support of human-driven processes can lead to large-scale benefit for the enterprise, and show how improvement can be achieved simply by understanding better *what is actually going on*, whether or not computerized support for human-driven processes is implemented. Such an understanding leads to a re-evaluation of fundamental aspects of organizational management including human relations, quality, task assignment, and confidentiality.

Better human relations

Human-driven processes are, of course, all about humans. Moreover, they are about *humans collaborating*, not individuals working in isolation—because an entirely solitary activity can, for management purposes, simply be treated as a task. Hence, if we are to genuinely improve human-driven processes—and deliver competitive advantage from the activities of interaction workers—it is necessary to put in place an environment in which each participant is able to *understand the actions of the others*.

This means understanding the *interactions* in the process—since, by definition, these are the only points of contact between participants. Hence, interactions are the only time at which one participant can gain knowledge about the other participants.

Focusing on interactions and their content, rather than on task sequences (as in conventional process modeling) or data recorded about activity (as in Customer Relationship Management), instantly suggests all sort of ways in which human relations can be improved:

- *Cultural clashes can be minimized, as can clashes of personality.* Both these manifest themselves in a variety of ways ranging from the order in which actions are carried out, to the way in which documents are written, to "token" gestures that may carry great significance.

- *Incentivization can be re-engineered.* In many organizations, it is only sales staff and their managers who are given additional compensation on an ongoing basis in accordance with the results of their work. This can lead to resentment among other staff, (for example, the technical support team who were the critical enabler of a sale), but even if no one minds, how much better would all concerned perform if they too were compensated fairly? Taking a process view of human relations even permits the fair allocation of reward to third parties such as suppliers, if that is desired.

- *Meetings can be streamlined.* Whether a meeting is a physical get-together or an electronic (audio, video or Web) conference, all too often many of those involved are not really required, at least not all of the time. Or the meeting accomplishes less than intended because someone who is not there should be. And who hasn't attended a meeting that had no clearly defined aim? Better meeting planning can only be achieved via better understanding of the interaction(s) represented by each meeting.

- *Communication within a team can be improved.* In many collaborative efforts, a number of those involved feel they should be privy to information that others alone possess. Sometimes this is inevitable, but often it is just an oversight, because there is no way to see "who knows what." Feeling that you are out of the loop is disempowering, and can cause not only discontent but also resentment. Moreover, a very common cause of problems is that someone wasn't informed of something they needed to know.

- And so on.

Any good manager sees it as their duty to resolve these sorts of issues. But without a way of managing interactions that caters to Roles, Users, and the information that each of them owns, achieving this is at best a black art, and in general unlikely to happen.

Some of the areas suggested for improvement come down to clarifying intentions—cultural clashes, for example, are usually the result of one party misunderstanding what was meant by the other. The use of *speech acts* for interaction description is not enough on its own to reduce this—we discussed in *How people communicate,* how a speech act can often leave more unsaid than said. For example, it can be hard to distinguish between "I will do such-and-such if I can, when I find the time" and "I promise faithfully to do such-and-such"—yet both might be expressed as a speech act "Promise." Such confusion is typical of the misunderstandings that arise from a cultural difference, and speech acts only make it worse.

What we need in order to resolve the cultural clashes, as well as to aid in the other areas mentioned (incentivization, meeting planning, and information distribution), is a better general understanding of *what is going on* in team interactions. This requires not only a process context, but one founded on an understanding by all parties of their individual *Roles*—and consequently both the contribution expected of them and the resources they require.

Further, the understanding of what is going on must change as the process changes. It will only make matters worse if you *feel* you have such an understanding, but, unbeknown to you, the ground has shifted under your feet—and no one thought to request your acceptance of the change or even let you know that it took place.

Hence, better human relations can be achieved, but only if:

- Processes are described to those participating in them in terms of *Roles, resources,* and *interactions,* and

- Process changes are made under *management control,* by consensus among the appropriate process participants. Then these *agreements* are depicted as Role Activity Diagrams and circulated to all interested parties to keep them in the loop.

Quality revitalized

In the 1980s, I worked for a forward-thinking software house, Praxis Systems. Praxis was so committed to a modern approach that it became the first UK software house to achieve BS5750 certification (and later ISO 9000). At the time, this meant that each staff member, on commencing any task at all, had to consult a printed Quality Manual, bound in several large volumes, in order to look up and follow the appropriate procedure. Procedure descriptions were lengthy. There were lots of printed forms to fill in and file before, during and after carrying out the work itself. And every few months the company would enter a state of barely concealed panic when the man from the BSI (British Standards Institution—the National Standards Body of the UK) came to call.

Nevertheless, the system worked. By and large, staff members subscribed to the view that by working in this cumbersome way we were delivering products and services of *quality*—that to us, back then, had a plain and simple definition. It meant that what we supplied was *fit for purpose.* Our products and services did what we claimed they would, and what the customer expected. This was unquestionable, because we had stated what our procedures were, and proved that we stuck to them.

Fifteen years down the line, things have changed—almost beyond recognition. In part this is because computer support for business operations has helped to automate procedures, and to alleviate the burden of paperwork—so we don't have to look up "what to do" the whole time in order to be sure we're getting things right. More fundamentally, our understanding of quality *management* has also progressed, to the point where some organizations hardly need a Quality Manual at all, since quality assurance and control are built directly into core operational procedures. Yet this is not all. Even deeper changes have taken place in the quality world, to the point that most people working in the field, if pressed to define quality now, would say that the old definition in terms of *fitness for purpose* no longer has much practical relevance.

Unless you are fortunate enough to be a monopoly supplier in some way, it is not enough that your product or service does what it says on the box. If you are to stay in business, in some way at least, you must provide something better (or at least cheaper) than anyone else. Since your competitors are in the same boat, the target is always moving, and you must either continuously get better, or drop out of the race for good.

The only way to achieve this ideal of continuous improvement is to measure as many as possible of the factors that impact delivery of your products and services. This means getting to grips with your business processes. The International Organization for Standardization (ISO) recognizes this in the latest revision of their quality standards (ISO 9001:2000, *Quality Management System Requirements*). ISO 9001:2000 requires an organization to:

- Identify the various processes needed to consistently and systematically deliver high-quality products and services to its customers, that meet or exceed customer expectations

- Document and implement a quality system that ensures these processes are not only maintained but can be continuously improved.

In other words, ISO 9001:2000 insists not only that key processes are properly documented and adhered to, but also that they are *measurable for improvement*. When implemented effectively, the standard enables an organization to both deliver a quality service/product and to create a mechanism for continuous improvement of the organization. ISO 9001:2000 is broken into the following five clauses, which address the major process areas within an organization:

- *Quality Management Systems*—an organization must establish, document, implement, and maintain a Quality Management System and continuously improve its effectiveness. Such a system must include defined quality policies and procedures to meet the organization's established quality objectives.

- *Management Responsibility*—Top management must provide evidence of its commitment to Quality Management System development, implementation, and continual improvement.

- *Resource Management*—The organization must determine and provide the resources necessary to effectively implement its Quality Management System.

- *Product Realization*—An organization must address all the functions and processes necessary to design, develop, and deliver products or services to its customers.

- *Measurement, Analysis, and Improvement*—The organization shall plan and implement the necessary monitoring, measurement, analysis, and improvement processes to support the consistent and reliable delivery of quality products and services to its customers. Such measurements and data must be identified and continuously monitored for effectiveness.

So, a term (*quality*) that originally represented adherence to a fixed set of procedures has come to represent something almost the opposite—continual process improvement. Effective management of process change is now at the heart of any modern quality system.

So, what techniques are currently applied to manage this new approach to quality management? Perhaps the most popular at the moment is Six Sigma—a methodology for incremental process improvement. Six Sigma uses statistical analysis of process data to measure and improve a company's operational performance by identifying and eliminating defects in manufacturing and service-related processes.

Six Sigma is all about consistency. To achieve Six Sigma quality, a process must produce no more than 3.4 defects per million *opportunities*, where an opportunity is defined as a chance for nonconformance, or not meeting the required specifications. The ultimate aim is flawless performance—*every time*. While you can use Six Sigma to improve processes in a more general way, this is not the emphasis. Rather, primary importance is placed on reducing operational error.

"Often, our inside-out view of the business is based on average or mean-based measures of our recent past. Customers don't judge us on averages, they feel the variance in each transaction, each product we ship. Six Sigma focuses first on reducing process variation and then on improving the process capability.

Customers value consistent, predictable business processes that deliver world-class levels of quality. This is what Six Sigma strives to produce."[1]

Six Sigma is typical of a general movement in the quality world, away from the radical techniques advocated by the Business Process Reengineering movement of the 1990s that were not, in general, successful. Despite the power of the ideas set out by Hammer and Champy,[2] and the success stories described in the original literature, many companies' experience with Business Process Reengineering was nothing short of disastrous. True figures are hard to come by for commercial reasons, but the standard view is that between 50% and 80% of reengineering projects failed in their original objectives—and many of the others may have achieved their original aims but caused lasting harm to the organization. This dealt the world of business process analysis and support a blow from which it is only now starting to recover. Unfortunately, Business Process Management still suffers from the association with reengineering.

Hence, the current trend is toward a safer, incremental approach. Six Sigma, in particular, is seen by some as the modern approach to Total Quality Management (TQM), with a more structured description of management that provides a greater chance of success.

So, why did business process reengineering fail? The underlying principle was to look first and only at current customer requirements. Once these had been determined, you could create new processes specifically to support them, automated as far as possible, and dispense with everything else—including as many unnecessary *people* as possible (downsizing). What you ended up with, if you were lucky, were some very efficient processes— that were almost impossible to change. How could you adapt to new market conditions, or grow your business, if you had dispensed with all your staff except the bare minimum required to keep things ticking along in one inflexible way?

Not only did none of the remaining people have the time available to make changes, but the industry knowledge and business skills picked up over the years were all gone. Most people at a senior level—middle management in particular—had been judged extraneous to day-to-day requirements and made redundant. Hence it was impossible to do anything differently, since no one left around had much idea how to go about making changes. Many companies downsized only to end up having to take on their old staff all over again, but this time on a freelance basis, as highly paid consultants who understandably now felt little or no loyalty to their old employers.

The problems were all to do with people. Reengineering made no allowance for the varied contributions that staff with different knowledge and abilities make to a company—simply by being there. At the time, there was little understanding of what are now called *intangibles*. As Verna Allee writes:

"Mastering value creation in the knowledge economy requires appreciating the pivotal role of intangibles in the business model and a thorough understanding of network dynamics. ...

Intangibles are at the heart of all human activity, especially socioeconomic activity ...

[There] are serious attempts to develop new indexes, equations, measures, and analytical approaches for calculating knowledge assets and for understanding intangible value creation."[3]

So, since intangibles are now in focus, is the time right for a reevaluation of reengineering? Well, not really, at least not in its original form. Few people still think that you can shape a company directly around current customer requirements. The lasting contribution of the business process reengineering movement was to show the importance of business processes in and of themselves. Now that most senior executives have a fairly good idea of what their high-level processes are, they are starting to manage their companies in process terms, and they recognize the true nature of *functional silos* (departments or teams that handle a specific function—a type of activity carried out on behalf of multiple simultaneous processes).

However, even if we ditch reengineering itself as a developmental stage that is now past, that is no reason to ditch *radical improvement* as a goal of quality management. Moreover, the approach described in this book provides the means to *deal with intangibles in process terms*. How can we use an understanding of human-driven activity to dramatically improve business processes? And why should we bother?

The key to answering both these questions is to look again at *indicators*—the metrics used to measure a sound process. Methodologies such as Six Sigma typically pay constant attention to traditional process metrics such as:

- Is the error rate as low as possible?
- Is the process efficient in resource usage?
- Is the cycle time as short as possible?
- And so on.

Such *hard* factors are undoubtedly vital, because they have a direct and measurable effect on an organization's bottom line. However, many quality-driven organizations have now reached the point where there is little improvement to be made in these areas—or little improvement that affects the price or customer perception of their products and services.

So, where does such an organization look for the continual process improvement necessary for business competitiveness, and mandated by ISO 9001:2000? Are there *soft* factors too—subtler aspects of quality, that turn out also to impact the bottom line? And since we cannot improve anything without measuring it, what sort of metrics should we be gathering in order to understand these soft factors?

General models do exist by which an organization as a whole can be measured, and some of these include a process aspect. For example, two widely used approaches are:

- *European Excellence Model.* The *EFQM Excellence Model,* a non-prescriptive framework based on nine criteria, can be used to assess an organization's progress toward excellence. "The Model recognizes there are many approaches to achieving sustainable excellence in all aspects of performance. It is based on the premise that Excellent results with respect to Performance, Customers, People and Society are achieved through Leadership driving Policy and Strategy, that is delivered through People, Partnerships and Resources and Processes."[4]

- *Capability Maturity Model Integration.* This is a staged approach to institutionalizing best practices that extends the original *Capability Maturity Model for Software* to domains including systems engineering, software engineering, Integrated Product and Process Development, and supplier sourcing.[5]

Both these methodologies allow some features of organizational performance to be quantified in process terms. What they do not supply is a rounded and generic set of criteria that we can use to *judge an individual process in terms of the humans who operate it.* For instance, the European Excellence Model analyses the process aspect of an organization in the following terms:

"Excellent organizations design, manage and improve processes in order to fully satisfy, and generate increasing value for, customers and other stakeholders.

- Processes are systematically designed and managed
- Processes are improved, as needed, using innovation in order to fully satisfy and generate increasing value for customers and other stakeholders
- Products and Services are designed and developed based on customer needs and expectations
- Products and Services are produced, delivered and serviced
- Customer relationships are managed and enhanced"[6]

Just as with reengineering, the focus is all on the *immediate deliverables* of the process, whether these are products, services, or a better relationship with the customer. If we are to move beyond the limitation that caused reengineering to fail, we must take a wider view of process, and assess it in more general terms. In particular, we need a set of criteria by which an individual process can be judged according to *how it makes best use of the people involved.*

This broader approach will give us an idea of whether or not a particular process is implemented so as to have lasting value, as well as immediate benefit. If a process is designed to capitalize on what enterprises conventionally state is their chief asset—their employees—then it is more likely stay afloat throughout the storms of continual business change, and to deliver its cargo come what may.

A set of criteria for measuring processes in terms of how people are used is presented in Table 2: Human-Driven Process Metrics. Some of the criteria are related to the hard factors mentioned above, while others are softer—which simply means that the impact on the bottom line is indirect. However, the impact on the bottom line is always there, in every case.[7]

Moreover, each criterion is generic—applying to both the public and the private sector, profit and non-profit organizations, SMEs and large enterprises, and all industry sectors. Hence all the criteria are relevant to any organization.

For each criterion, we give example indicators that can be tracked, in order to provide metrics that permit process improvement against the criterion. In some cases, there is the risk that tracking will itself influence the process metrics—for instance, monitoring creative activity can inhibit it, or render it artificial. We are careful to provide indicators that minimize this risk.

Other indicators are possible, and those shown are for illustration purposes only. There may also be other metrics appropriate for measuring the effectiveness of human involvement in a process.

Table 2: Human-Driven Process Metrics

Process Metric	Discussion	Example Indicators
Cross-cutting	Processes should be designed to allow maximum sharing of human resources. This applies not only to direct process participation, but also to indirect re-use of information gathered, lessons learned, customer and market contacts, mechanisms of management, and so on.	Are product development and service skills reused between value streams? Are different products and services being cross-sold to the same customers? How streamlined is process design activity in terms of skill levels and tool usage?
Agility	Process design changes should be made as often as necessary, and implemented as quickly as possible.	Do the same problems recur time after time? How well does a process scale to support increased throughput? What is the decision-to-change time?
Creativity	To foster a learning, innovative culture, it is necessary first to *notice* and then to *act on* individuals' responses to the process they are part of, and the suggestions they put forward about it. Only some ideas will be good— nevertheless, even the poor ones should be rewarded if made in the right spirit. Moreover, in	How many ideas have been submitted? Of those submitted, how many have been discussed properly? When the ideas that were implemented are analyzed retrospectively, how many were done in haste and without due consideration?

Process Metric	Discussion	Example Indicators
	most cases a dialectic can be expected (*thesis* followed by *antithesis* followed by *synthesis*)—the process should permit this to take place.	
Flexibility	A process may need to be operated differently to meet the needs of different customers, or to suit the nature and skills of different participants. It is usually possible to include some flexibility in the design, so as to support some new situations without the process itself having to change. The more generic a particular process is, the less onerous process management becomes. It is something of a trade-off, however, since more customized processes may be more efficient and make better use of specialized skills—a balance must be struck.	Can we identify precisely the inputs, outputs and internal dependencies, in order to determine the requirements placed on process participants? Can the process spawn customized sub-processes to deal with specialized situations? Do process participants struggle to cope with the variety of demands placed on them, or customers complain that they are receiving service from unqualified staff? Can the services or products concerned be personalized for individual customers?
Resource Utilization	A good process should capitalize on the human skills present among its participants. For instance, people are often capable of more than is expected of them. Alternatively, people may perform badly simply	Do process participants regularly offer useful advice to those in different Roles? Are people dealing with their work too easily, to the point where they seem not to be putting

Process Metric	Discussion	Example Indicators
	because they are unsuited to the Roles they are playing.	much into it? Are people having continually to consult others about details of the work they are personally charged with?
Empowerment	It is a truism that people perform better, and get on better with their colleagues, if they enjoy their work and feel appreciated. Hence, processes should be designed so that participation is not unduly stressful, and by itself acts to foster increased job satisfaction. A large part of this is the sense that you are learning something as you work, not just repeating the same mundane tasks days after day.	Are tasks carried out in good time, or generally left until the last minute? Are deadlines slipped on a regular basis? Do users find themselves working overtime, and if so, is it because they choose to or because they have to? Are interactions among colleagues strained, and tempers frayed? Do users demonstrate increased competence over time as they participate in a particular type of process?
Embodiment of values	Increasingly people are recognizing that corporate life should represent— even exemplify—the same beliefs and values that are held up by society in general. Not only is this mandated by regulation in various ways (with respect to the environment, wage laws, child exploitation, and so on) but workers	Is a process designed to make good use of natural resources—avoiding pollution, recycling waste products, and so on? Do people working in a process have to cover up aspects of their work in order to comply with company policies or government regulations? Is the balance of

Process Metric	Discussion	Example Indicators
	and management at all levels need to know that the organization to which they devote the best part of their waking hours is acting a manner they consider responsible, and can be proud of.	recompense in a process fair—in particular, is undue favoritism shown to workers in a particular location, or level of the organization? Are there ways in which the process contributes positively to the communities in which it is carried out?

The metrics given above are quite different from those conventionally used to measure processes. However, they are no less important.

It is often the case that these aspects of process—those focused on human involvement—are handled better in small organizations than large ones. This is because people know intuitively that they should pay attention to such issues—and when direct control over the entire workplace is available attention can be paid to them relatively easily. However, as organizations grow in size, other issues start to predominate.

For instance, people who were part of a large company when it was still a small one often bemoan the loss of a culture that they valued. They may declare that as a result their job satisfaction has changed in inverse proportion to their financial status, and say they are only hanging on until they have gained enough stock options to get out.

This benefits no one. Everyone gains more from a job to which they can give their all, wholeheartedly—and the organization gains most of all. Moreover, it *is* possible for large organizations to maintain a personal approach and values more typical of small organizations. They just need a new approach to quality.

Refactoring human processes

We have discussed throughout this book the necessity for continual change to human-driven processes, and presented guidelines for managing that change. In our discussion of quality, we also provide metrics to determine whether such change has been successful. But what are the principles we should use when designing a process in the first place—and when redesigning it?

What would be useful are some general guidelines that we can use to *categorize a process*. Is there a way to analyze what *sort* of process we are looking at—or *sorts*, since a process may fall into many brackets at once?

If we could gain such an understanding, of the different sorts of process that exist, we could start to judge which sorts are best in which situations. Based on enough experience, we should be able to say that a particular approach works well in this situation, but poorly in that one.

Moreover, it should then be possible to go further. If we discover that we have an existing process of an unsuitable sort for the situation it is used in, we can change it appropriately—make it into a different, more suitable, sort of process. We may or may not keep the same Roles, interactions, activities and so on, since some may no longer be required once we've changed the sort of process we have. What we will keep, however, are the *outputs*, since we need these to ensure customer satisfaction—we'll just go about producing them in a better way. Changing the products and services supplied to customers is generally a higher-level matter than the kind of process redesign we are considering here, subject to what we refer to above in the section *Separation of control* as *strategic control*.

The *inputs* of the process may, on the other hand, need to change—depending on the improvements we make in the process, some inputs may become obsolete, or it may be necessary to obtain new items, or obtain existing ones in a new way. The revised process will continue to satisfy the demands that the world made on it originally, but the process may now make different demands on the world around it. It all depends on how the internal operations of the process have been reconfigured to make the process of a more appropriate sort for the situation.

This approach to design—looking at the sorts of object and the contexts to which each one is best suited—is called *pattern-based*. The *sorts* that we have described are termed *patterns*, where:

> "A pattern is an element of design that is most commonly ascribed to the architect Christopher Alexander, who uses a pattern-based approach to the construction of towns, neighborhoods and buildings. Each pattern solves a problem by adding structure to a system. The main tenets of the pattern approach to system construction include incremental repair and piecemeal growth, building on experience, and an attentiveness to quality of life.

...

> [A pattern can be defined as a] recurring structural configuration that solves a problem in a context, contributing to the wholeness of some whole, or system, that reflects some aesthetic or cultural value."[8]

A pattern is some general property, or set of properties, that many objects have in common, whether these objects are buildings or a processes. Each pattern re-occurs since it has been found useful in certain common types of situations.

Pattern-based design has been applied with great success to software systems. The classic textbook, *Design Patterns: Elements of Reusable Object-Oriented Software* was written by the "Gang of Four."[9] Since its publication in 1995, the book has been followed by many other works identifying patterns that can be used to improve software design in various areas. Pattern-based software design has reached the point of ubiquity, in that knowledge of at least the most common patterns is now considered a necessity for the professional software developer. New software design patterns appear daily on the Web, to cater to situations from the most generic problems to those caused by the quirks of a specific programming environment.

Patterns have proven particularly useful in the software world for their ability to *improve software that has already been written*. We've discussed how it should be possible to change a process that is of an unsuitable sort for the situation it is used in, to make it into a different, more suitable, sort of process. The new process operates in a new and more efficient way internally, while providing the same products and services to the world.

It turns out that this applies very well to software—you can change the way a program is written so that it does effectively the same thing, but does it in a way more appropriate for its context. It is so easy to change programs this way, in fact, that the change can be automated. Many software development tools now provide the facility to apply a wide range of patterns to existing software objects, restructuring them to work in a more efficient and more maintainable way. The action of changing a pattern in a software system, to suit its context better, is known to software designers as *refactoring*.

So, can we apply the lessons learned in the software world to the arena of process improvement? Can we refactor processes as we do software objects, to work more suitably for their context?

Of immediate relevance to this question is a recent work by Coplien and Harrison, on patterns that can be applied not to software itself, but to the software development process.[10] Based on 10 years of research, they identify typical organizational patterns found in software development teams, and discuss each in terms of its suitability for specific situations. Moreover, some patterns were found to appear repeatedly in particularly high-performing organizations.

In spite of this work, Coplien and Harrison do not identify a core set of patterns that should be adopted across the board. Instead, they list all their patterns to make up a general purpose *pattern language*, and say:

> "a pattern language is an outline of many ways that patterns may be put together. How they are put together depends on context. When we apply a pattern, the context changes. When someone joins the organization, or when the organization decides to build a new product line, the context may change. Depending on the context at any given time, different patterns might or might not apply." [11]

In other words, there is no set of ultimate, general-purpose patterns for best practice in software development. The choice of suitable patterns to use is always context dependent, and a methodology that works well in one situation is by no means guaranteed to work well in another.

A full exploration of patterns that apply to human-driven processes, and of how to use these patterns in refactoring, is beyond the scope of this book. Coplien and Harrison devote nearly 500 pages just to elaborating the patterns specific to software development. However, there are some things we can say here that relate to the theory of human-driven processes, and that may guide future work in this direction.

1. All the patterns described by Coplien and Harrison are given in terms of *Roles played by the process participants*. Hence there is a direct match to our own Role-based approach to process modeling This suggests that the use of Roles in itself is a fundamental enabler for process improvement, at least if such improvement is carried out via the use of standard patterns.

2. Just as with the Role Activity Diagram notation—which itself arose from a study of collaborative software development—many of the patterns described by Coplien and Harrison are applicable in a more general context. In fact, the patterns could be applied to a situation where something is to be designed or constructed collaboratively by a team.

Hence, much of the groundwork is already there, at least for certain common situations.

3. We have already met several new patterns specific to the theory of human-driven processes: REACT, AIM and the collaborative transaction example introduced in the context of concurrent engineering (see *Agreements* above). REACT and AIM could and should be used in any context, because they are completely general purpose. The collaborative transaction pattern, on the other hand, is specific to processes where the deliverable is some form of composite object that can be constructed piecemeal—the pattern offers a way to derive a corresponding breakdown of the work itself, while resolving interdependencies among the parts. This technique is of emerging importance in the engineering field, but applies equally to collaborative development work in any other field, whether it is developing a marketing campaign, incorporating a new operational unit into the company, developing training material, or any other *composite object*.

4. Some, but not many, of Coplien and Harrison's patterns discuss personal qualities of the individuals who should be assigned to particular Roles. More often, such qualities are implied rather than stated. For instance, a PATRON ROLE is described as *a visible, high-level manager, who champions the cause of the project.*[12] However, if such champions are to be effective, they require certain personal qualities: self-confidence, commitment, persuasiveness, and so on. A more rounded description of patterns requires that such qualities are elucidated, in order that appropriate process participants can be assigned. This aspect of process improvement is critical, and we devote a separate section to it below.

Assignment of process participants

We have seen from the discussion of process patterns that an understanding of the Roles in a process is in itself an underpinning for process improvement. Further, Role-based analysis is a *necessary* underpinning if improvement is to be done via application of process patterns. We concluded the discussion by looking at the importance of assigning to each Role an individual with appropriate personal qualities. So, how can one go about this? How is it possible to categorize the *qualities of individuals*, and match these up with the requirements of specific Roles?

In fact, there are existing systems that attempt to deal with the personal characteristics of team players, in order to assign them work to which they would be particularly well suited. A typical example is Belbin Team

Roles. A team role as defined by Dr. Meredith Belbin is: "A tendency to behave, contribute and interrelate with others in a particular way." Belbin team roles describe a pattern of behavior that characterizes one person's behavior in relationship to another in facilitating the progress of a team.

The value of Belbin team-role theory lies in enabling an individual or team to benefit from self-knowledge and adjust according to the demands being made by the external situation."[13] The nine team roles identified by Belbin are:

- *Action-oriented roles*—Shaper, Implementer, and Completer Finisher
- *People-oriented roles*—Co-ordinator, Teamworker and Resource Investigator
- *Cerebral roles*—Plant, Monitor Evaluator and Specialist

The properties of these roles are summarized below in Table 3: Belbin Team Roles. A person can be "profiled" in terms of these roles, with the aim of helping the individual:

- Understand their own identity in terms of team roles;
- Manage their strengths and weaknesses;
- Learn how to develop their team roles;
- Project themselves in the best possible way;
- Work more effectively in teams.

Table 3: Belbin Team Roles

Team Role Type	Contributions	Allowable Weaknesses
PLANT PL	Creative, imaginative, unorthodox. Solves difficult problems.	Ignores incidentals. Too pre-occupied to communicate effectively.
CO-ORDINATOR CO	Mature, confident, a good chairperson. Clarifies goals, promotes decision-making, delegates well.	Can often be seen as manipulative. Off loads personal work.

Team Role Type	Contributions	Allowable Weaknesses
MONITOR EVALUATOR ME	Sober, strategic and discerning. Sees all options. Judges accurately.	Lacks drive and ability to inspire others.
IMPLEMENTER IMP	Disciplined, reliable, conservative and efficient. Turns ideas into practical actions.	Somewhat inflexible. Slow to respond to new possibilities.
COMPLETER FINISHER CF	Painstaking, conscientious, anxious. Searches out errors and omissions. Delivers on time.	Inclined to worry unduly. Reluctant to delegate.
RESOURCE INVESTIGATOR RI	Extrovert, enthusiastic, communicative. Explores opportunities. Develops contacts.	Overly optimistic. Loses interest once initial enthusiasm has passed.
SHAPER SH	Challenging, dynamic, thrives on pressure. The drive and courage to overcome obstacles.	Prone to provocation. Offends people's feelings.
TEAMWORKER TW	Co-operative, mild, perceptive and diplomatic. Listens, builds, averts friction.	Indecisive in crunch situations.
SPECIALIST SP	Single-minded, self-starting, dedicated. Provides knowledge and skills in rare supply.	Contributes only on a narrow front. Dwells on technicalities.

From the point of view of this book, Belbin's terminology is confusing. Belbin's team roles are not like our Roles, since they have no process context whatsoever. The relationship between the two is roughly as follows. A Belbin team role is a summary of the personal characteristics required to play *a certain type* of process Role—not a specific Role in a specific process, though, since Belbin team roles are very generalized.

For instance, returning to the PATRON ROLE discussed above, certain personal qualities are necessary in order to play the Role well: self-confidence, commitment, persuasiveness, and so on. Together these qualities are close to Belbin's conception of a team role—they describe a certain *kind of person*.

The intention of the Belbin system is to classify people, not to describe what we term Roles, which are fully-fledged process participants. The aim is to help you understand what kind of person you are, so that you are better able to choose what types of Role you should be taking on in a process. In practice, the system is often used by human resources professionals, either when interviewing for a position or when considering assignment of staff to duties within an organization.

Approaches such as the Belbin system are a starting point for process improvement via better assignment of Users to Roles. However, they do not fully meet our needs, for two reasons.

First, we saw from the discussion of PATRON ROLE that you need a certain kind of person to play the part—someone who might be characterized as a *leader*. There is no corresponding Belbin team role. Presumably this is because the purpose of the Belbin system is to support certain kinds of collaboration—the kind that takes place *within* a team—and leadership is assumed to belong outside the team itself.

However, not only have we shown that some forms of leadership are in fact an integral part of a process rather than superior to it (*management control*), but we also analyze leadership from above the process in Role terms (*executive control*). Hence, we need to deal with both forms of leadership, and the omission from the Belbin system of people whose nature is oriented toward one or the other of these functions means that the approach needs to be extended for our purposes.

It is possible that any such system of categorizing personal characteristics will have a corresponding omission. For various reasons, the choice of people to play leadership Roles in an organization is often not conducted in the same manner as the choice of less senior personnel. However, our understanding of process management places leadership at the very heart of it, at every level, either in the form of executive control or management control. Hence the assignment of such Roles is at least as critical as the assignment of the other Roles in a process, if not more so. In particular, management control is often split across more than one Role, so it is necessary to appreciate this and make sure that the people chosen for the Roles concerned have the necessary personal characteristics to play their part appropriately, either singly or in combination.

In terms of the Belbin system, for example, at least two additional team roles are needed to embody the behavioral qualities suited to management control and executive control, respectively. In brief, a MANAGER requires skills such as hands-on support, negotiation and facilitation (with allowable failings such as dilettantism and over-talkativeness), while an EXECUTIVE requires skills such as leadership, strategy and promotion (with allowable failings such as obstinacy and being a prima donna).

Second, a system such as Belbin does not set out to include any *process context* in its description of personal characteristics. Hence, there is no discussion of matters that pertain to a specific assignment—particular personal relationships, industry background, experience with certain customers, relevant skills, and so on. Yet all these and more are critical in the choice of individuals to play Roles in a specific process.

We discussed how any form of personnel information available in corporate repositories can be retrieved and stored in Roles, to assist with informed assignment of Users to new Role instances. In order that the information thus made available captures personal characteristics, it should include any details of personal characteristics such as those in Belbin team roles, or those in any other similar system by which people are categorized in terms of suitability for particular types of work.

This will allow the manager or executive responsible for starting new Roles to make *as informed a judgment as possible* about the right person to play each Role. Judgments on User assignment will then be made, not in isolation from the process, but as part of it, with both Role detail and User characteristics available for reference.

Confidentiality

The safeguarding of confidential commercial information is a headache of such proportions that, the more you think about it, the less you want to think about it. The problem is not related specifically to IT, of course. Nor would we wish to claim that it is essentially to do with processes. Security by nature is a multi-faceted issue, with aspects that range from highly technical questions of cryptography through to ensuring that, when entering a building, people do not hold the door open for the stranger walking behind them.

We do not propose to address every aspect of confidentiality here. What we will do, is to show how the use of Roles as the foundation for process definition offers a way forward for determining *who should be able to access what.*

First we will look again at how a properly defined process puts information where it belongs—inside a Role. Then we will go on to see how computerized process support systems based directly on private information stored within Roles can be used to provide an access control layer superior to that offered by low-level middleware such as operating systems and databases. This layer not only provides a way forward for the protection of confidential company information, but also offers more general advantages with respect to IT system security. Our argument is that adopting Human Interaction Management just as a management principle is enough *in itself* to place some proper control over the distribution of data and documents—but the adoption of a computerized Human Interaction Management System provides further, extremely valuable benefits.

We discussed above (see *Resources* in chapter three) how private data is tied deeply to the nature of a Role as process participant. The tie between Roles and private data is emphasized by the appearance of a new Business Process Management methodology, Riva (see *The helicopter view* in chapter four). Riva asserts that the starting point for identifying processes per se is to look at the information resources they operate on, and associate each of these with an appropriate set of Roles. This approach has been borne out in practice by use of a Human Interaction Management System for Role-based process support, with which the first step in process definition is always to define the data objects that will be used by the Roles in the process. With regard to confidentiality, then, what we can take from this?

Roles tell us how to think properly about confidentiality—something we rarely do. In many cases, writing COMMERCIAL IN CONFIDENCE or CONFIDENTIAL AND PROPRIETARY TO XYZ CORPORATION on a document is almost a meaningless gesture. Confidential to whom, exactly? There may be a copy list in the document, but in practice this is generally just used to determine who gets the document initially. Each recipient may then need to copy it to others in their company, project or team in order to carry out the actions that arise from the document. Excerpts may be taken and sent to suppliers, copied to managers, or used in status reports. Moreover, there are people who see the document not as a result of any direct business need, but as part of processing it on behalf of others—system administration staff, proofreaders, secretaries, and so on.

Executives may not like to admit it publicly, but this spread of information is almost impossible to control. The main reason for this is that the injunction "in confidence" gives you no basis for control. It is an empty phrase, which at best suggests that you shouldn't place the document on a public Web site, or show it to a journalist—suggestions that are often not respected anyway. How can the situation be improved?

A way forward is to appreciate that such information really belongs in Roles, not in operating system files or database records. If people access their private information through the mediation of a specific Role, they have a better chance of keeping it private. In particular, when they decide to share a piece of data with others, the decision will be *conscious*, not accidental, and *tracked*, not invisible.

This is because Roles exchange information via structured interactions. If a process support system is used, these interactions are automatically controlled and monitored. Even if no computerized support is available, simply managing processes in the terms described in this book provides the basis for understanding who sends what to whom, and when they do it. This alone provides management with some kind of handle on what is happening to confidential data.

So, Role-based process management allows some structure to be placed on use and sharing of specific information items. Unfortunately, that is only part of the security headache facing the modern organization. What we really need is not just control over documents; we need control over *systems*.

Most corporate information lives in some form of centralized repository, whether it is a database, a messaging system, or a file system. We've argued that the true home for much process data is inside a Role—yet we do not argue that all centralized data stores should be abolished. Some data will live entirely within a Role; other data will live inside a data store and be accessed from a Role; yet other data will live in both and be synchronized as and when appropriate.

Operating system files, databases, email repositories and the like are not going to vanish any time soon. Hence the confidentiality problem is as much about how these systems are accessed as about how specific documents are shared between process participants. This is particularly true for systems that belong to another organization, as will often be the case, for example with processes that include multiple trading partners.

Having said this, the solution principle is the same for systems as for documents. We have described how Human Interaction Management is an integrating technology that provides a better way to make use of existing information resources. Roles in particular are the best way to structure the access that people make to corporate systems. We claim, therefore, that access to computer systems is, like access to confidential documents, best done via the use of Roles as a mediator.

However, in this case, we cannot argue that you can reap the benefits of a Role-based approach purely from better management. When it comes to providing access control mechanisms for computer systems, you need to do so via a computer system—a computer system for Role-based process support. We need to discuss the technical issues in securing system access via Roles. The non-technical reader should bear with the rest of this section, since it has significant business relevance (and includes no low-level detail).

Looking at security engineering from a technical perspective, we find that the use of Roles as a guiding principle for security policy creation is not only well-established, but seen by experts as the most promising way forward. Ross Anderson, in his authoritative survey of computer system security techniques, wrote in 2001:

"the policy model getting the most attention at present from researchers is role-based access control (RBAC), introduced by David Ferraiolo and Richard Kuhn ... This sets out to provide a more general framework for mandatory access control than [Bell-LaPadula] in which access decisions don't depend on users' names but on the functions they are currently performing within the organization. Transactions that may be performed by holders of a given role are specified, then mechanisms for granting membership of a role (including delegation). Roles, or groups, had for years been the mechanism used in practice in organizations such as banks to manage access control; the RBAC model starts to formalize this. It can deal with integrity issues as well as confidentiality, by allowing role membership (and thus access rights) to be revised when certain programs are invoked. Thus, for example, a process calling untrusted software that had been downloaded from the Net might lose the role membership required to write to sensitive system files."[14]

Anderson's emphasis on role-based access control has been borne out by recent work carried out in both the academic and commercial worlds. The fundamental aim of this work is to allow computer systems that are located in different places, controlled by different organizations, and based on different technologies to be used as if they were all one system—to remove the virtual barrier between systems, even where physical ones exist.

The Web has provided technologies to support the *mechanism* of remote access to diverse systems:

- Web browsing allows a user to request data from, and interact with applications on, systems anywhere to which a network connection is available
- Web services permit messages to be exchanged between any two systems, and operations on one system to be invoked by the other system.

However, there is a security problem that must be solved in order to make safe use of these Web mechanisms. How do you know whether the person or computer trying to access your system via the Web is entitled to do so?

This problem is known as *identity management*. The solution is first to *authenticate* the person or computer (determine exactly who they are), and then to *authorize* their access (decide whether they have the necessary permissions and privileges). This second aspect, authorization, is where Roles come in. If role-based access control is being used, permissions and privileges are based on the Role currently being played by a person or system.

The strength of the Web is that is has provided *standardized* protocols by which systems can communicate. What is required now is a standardized means of authentication and authorization. The two main contenders for such a standard are Liberty Alliance,[15] an alliance of more than 150 companies, non-profit and government organizations from around the globe, and Shibboleth[16] from Internet2,[17] a consortium led by 207 universities working in partnership with industry and government (Internet2's corporate partners include the likes of Cisco, IBM, Microsoft, and Qwest).

Both systems are now converging on a common underlying standard.[18] However, fundamental differences remain. Broadly speaking, the Liberty Alliance is business-focused and Shibboleth is aimed at academia. However, we will see that there are reasons to believe that Shibboleth may offer at least as much as Liberty to the commercial world, if not more.

With respect to *authentication*, the two systems work in much the same way. The principle is to *federate* authentication, which simply means that the system being accessed can get confirmation of the accessor's identity from a trusted third party, rather than having to do it themselves.

However, there are differences between Liberty Alliance and Shibboleth with regard to *authorization*. Liberty Alliance assumes that the permissions and privileges of the accessor may be provided, as user *attributes*, by a variety of systems—in particular, some attributes will typically be stored on each system that is accessed. Shibboleth, on the other hand, assumes that these attributes will be stored only at the accessor's home location, and requested as needed by each system that is accessed.

The Liberty approach has already caused some concern, in that the privacy of user attributes stored all over the place cannot be guaranteed. Effectively, you have to trust that each system you access keeps your personal information secure. The reason Liberty works like this is to support "orchestration" of Web services—the use of several systems as part of a single extended transaction—which generally requires that each participating system remembers personalized information about you and your interactions with it.

Hence, this flaw of Liberty is really just a by-product of what it sets out to achieve. However, from the point of view of providing a basis for role-based access control, it also means Liberty is not ideal. A Role is a unified object—a process participant with its own private data—not a set of attributes scattered about all over the place under no centralized control.

To see how Shibboleth may offer a more promising way forward for role-based access control, and what we need to do in order to make this happen, we need to take a closer look at it. In the process, we will also provide more explanation of identity management.

The Shibboleth system was developed by Internet2/MACE[19] in partnership with IBM:

> "When you want to share secured online services or access restricted digital content, the Shibboleth system offers a powerful, scalable, and easy-to-use solution. It leverages campus identity and access

management infrastructures to authenticate individuals and then sends information about them to the resource site, enabling the resource provider to make an informed authorization decision."[20]

Shibboleth is a scalable approach to "securing distributed resources." What does this mean, exactly, and why is it important to a consortium led mainly by universities? In academia, it is common for researchers or students to require access to systems or databases located at other institutions. To date, this has called for each institution's administration staff to maintain large and complex lists of who is allowed to do what. This was an almost impossible task, since the people and permissions concerned not only belong to other institutions, but chop and change continually: students arrive and leave, researchers change what they are looking into, working groups form and disband in a flexible way, and so on.

Shibboleth sets out to reduce the administration burden, by placing as much control as possible where it belongs: with the staff of the *person's own institution*, not with the staff of those to whom they need to provide access. To achieve this, the person's own institution sets up specific data about the person—in particular, it assigns to each person a set of *attributes* that describe their privileges and responsibilities. Attributes can be of any form: they can describe groups or projects that the person belongs to, for example. When the person tries to access a system at a remote institution, Shibboleth provides a means for that system to securely interrogate their home institution to find out what *sort of person they are*. The remote system uses this information to decide whether or not to grant access.

There is more to Shibboleth—in particular, it also allows someone to choose how much of their personal information should be released to a specific remote site. However, our interest in Shibboleth is that it can be used to support role-based access control. Attributes can be used in such a way that they represent Roles, and various systems have been developed to put a layer on top of Shibboleth that facilitates such usage.[21] These systems aim to cleanly separate *authentication* (enabled via Shibboleth) from *authorization* (defined and implemented via Roles).

If this could be made to work, such a system would be of great value to industry as well as to academia. Most large companies possess a large number of computer systems, and they are generally of varying kinds, spread across geographical locations, with different administrators. It is even becoming common to grant access to certain parts of certain systems to partner companies—suppliers and customers with whom there is a close working relationship. Moreover, the situation changes constantly—systems are introduced and retired, employees are assigned to different jobs or projects, relationships with partner companies alter. Controlling these diversified and dynamic access rights is exactly the same problem faced by university administration staff.

However, none of the role-based access control systems being developed at present will be sufficient for the needs of industry—they may not even satisfy the needs of academia. While they allow a basic representation of Roles to be made in terms of Shibboleth attributes, the "Roles" thus defined have no true process context.

As we have seen throughout this book, the basic nature of a Role is as *process participant*. Hence a Role definition must include essential aspects of collaborative process behavior, such as:

- Goals
- Responsibilities
- Private information resources
- Interactions with other Roles
- Well-defined activities including the ability to start and stop other Roles
- Logical conditions that enable and validate such activities.

Critically, it is necessary to support the dynamic nature of a business process, which means that a Role must not only be able to modify the structure and contents of its own information resources, but also to change its own behavior and that of others.

To do this requires a role-based access control layer above Shibboleth, which treats Roles as the process-based objects that they are. In other words, we need a Role-based process support system that supports the principles outlined in this book—and is able to talk to Shibboleth. This can offer to the commercial world a way of solving one of the knottiest problems in IT: secure access to distributed systems.

Shibboleth is not the only option—Liberty could also be used as an underpinning for role-based access control. It would be necessary, however, to ensure that Liberty was used in such a way that all the attributes that defined a person's or system's Role were stored together, in a centralized location—their home system, for example. It wouldn't matter if different Roles were stored in different places, as long as for each particular Role, all the attributes were maintained as an indivisible unit.

In fact, having different Roles in different places is quite a natural approach, since both people and systems may participate in processes that are hosted on different systems. A consultant, for example, might be taking part in processes on behalf of several clients at once—each of these would be hosted by the client concerned, yet the identity of the consultant would be confirmed by the consultant's own company. The critical thing is to ensure that Roles are implemented as self-contained objects, not as a set of attributes scattered about all over the place. Shibboleth offers a more natural approach to supporting this than Liberty, but either could, in principle, be used, and both offer a secure means of separation of *authentication* from *authorization*.

Moreover, neither system offers all that is required. There are serious security questions related to *delegation of authority* that can only be solved via process support. In real life, it is common for one process participant to offload a particular piece of work to another, perhaps adding a new person to the process specifically for this purpose. In a process support system, this can be done by starting a child Role, and passing across to it a specification for some work, along with the resources necessary to complete the work—an architect working on a skyscraper may commission lobby furniture from another architect, for example, or a graphic designer may request a particular graphic from another designer. For example, suppose that one resource passed across to the child Role is a communication channel with a supplier of construction materials or stock photos.

How does the supplier know that a request received from the delegate is to be trusted in the same way as a request from the original architect or designer? Can the supplier even tell the difference? Once the job is finished, should the supplier still respond to communications from the delegate? How does the supplier even know when the job is finished?

These questions are complex, and the subject of current academic work. We made reference earlier to the graphical theory of *bigraphs* by Robin Milner (inventor of the pi-calculus) and Ole Høgh Jensen, who are attempting to provide a formal underpinning for computation that deals with the relationship between "locality" and "connectivity"—between *where you are* and *what you can access*.[22] In the long-term, such work may provide generic answers. In the short-term, the solution lies in providing process support that addresses delegation specifically, and provides tracking mechanisms to deal with it.

One thing is certain. Sooner or later, you'll have to use process support to deal with distributed access to systems. In the world of the networked supply chain, no company is an island. Eventually, unpalatable as it may seem, particularly to IT staff, you have to open up your systems to the outside world—not just for viewing data, but for others to create, edit and delete information.

Massive security problems are inevitable. In the best case, the problems will simply result in overworked systems administrators. The worst case could put you out of business. A way forward is needed that reduces the maintenance overhead while guaranteeing full control over access. The most promising is to combine the Role-based process support provided by a Human Interaction Management System with an industry-standard authentication system such as Shibboleth or Liberty. The companies that develop and implement such technology will find themselves way out ahead of their competitors. They will be able to open up their systems to partners without strain and with a minimal level of worry. In particular, the problem of *confidentiality*, currently unrecognized due to lack of practical solutions, will be resolved rather than exacerbated. If you want to become a real-time enterprise, this is where to start.

Putting it all together

To summarize this chapter, we have looked at several areas in which a better understanding of human-driven processes can improve organizational performance. Not only is such an understanding the basis for improved people management, support of vital mental activity, and enablement of creativity in the workplace, but it also enables key business processes to be made transparent and amenable to control. In particular:

- *Better human relations* are possible between colleagues.
- *Quality management* can be revitalized with a new and powerful set of process measurement techniques.
- *Human work processes can be improved* via the use of standard patterns.
- *Assignment of process participants* can be better controlled.
- *Confidentiality* can be preserved more easily.

In the next chapter, we will consider what a computer system for supporting human-driven processes looks like, and discuss how to build one.

References.

[1] http://www.ge.com/sixsigma/sixsigstrategy.html

[2] Hammer, M., Champy, J., 1993, "Reengineering the Corporation: A Manifesto for Business Revolution," HarperCollinsBusiness
Hammer, M., 1996, "Beyond Reengineering," HarperCollinsBusiness

[3] Intangibles are at the heart of all human activity, especially socio-economic activity. A number of intangible accounting approaches have been proposed to explain, measure, and manage intangible assets. Intangibles, like other assets, are increased and leveraged through deliberate actions. Among these efforts, one finds the intellectual capital methods of Karl-Erik Sveiby, Leif Edvinsson, Johan and Goran Roos, and Annie Brooking, and Pat Sullivan. Related work from the U.S. is the Balanced Scorecard approach of Norton and Kaplan. There are also a number of other experiments such as Kanavsky and Housel's system for calculating knowledge valued added, a variation of economic value added or EVA.

Recent important work in this area includes the Brookings Institution project in intangible assets spearheaded by Baruch Lev of New York University and Steve Wallman, former Commissioner of the American Securities and Exchange Commission. Virtually every accounting standards body in the U.S. and Canada has special task forces on accounting for intangibles, and the OECD in Europe has also held special hearings. Typical categories of intangible assets include business relationships, human competence, internal structure, and social capital or culture and values.

Other intangibles are being addressed through indicators regarding social responsibility and sustainable business practices. There are a growing number of assessment tools such as the Deloitte & Touche Corporate Environmental Report Score Card, and the Future 500 Performance Tool Kit. One of the most telling examples is the recent shift of focus for Shell. Since 1998, the annual Shell Report for Royal Dutch/Shell Group has emphasized their efforts to support the "triple bottom line." Shell defines this as "integrating the economic, social and environmental aspects of everything we do and balancing short-term wants with long-term needs."

These are serious attempts to develop new indexes, equations, measures, and analytical approaches for calculating knowledge assets and for understanding intangible value creation. All this adds up to a serious attack on traditional accounting and enterprise models that regard only revenue and physical assets as "valuable," and that regard people as liabilities rather than important resources and investments.

Verna Allee, 2002, "A Value Network Approach for Modeling and Measuring Intangibles,"
http://www.vernaallee.com/library%20articles/A%20ValueNetApproach%20white%20paper.pdf

[4] "Introducing Excellence," EFQM, available from http://www.efqm.org/, p.5

[5] http://www.sei.cmu.edu/cmmi/

[6] EFQM, ibid., p.14

[7] The author would like to acknowledge the value of the feedback on this topic provided by participants in an Open Space gathering held at the British Standards Institution on 30 September 2003 to discuss the ISO 9000 standard, which involved members of TC176 (the group responsible for writing ISO 9000), a range of managers (both quality management and line management), consultants, trainers, auditors, certifiers, accreditors, standards writers and members of learned bodies. The event was organized by the Business Improvement Network (http://www.bin.co.uk).

[8] Coplien, J., Harrison, N., 2004, "Organizational Patterns of Agile Software Development," p.13-14

[9] Gamma, E., Helm, R., Johnson, R., Vlissides, J., 1995, "Design Patterns: Elements of Reusable Object-Oriented Software," Addison-Wesley

[10] Coplien, J., Harrison, N., 2004, ibid.

[11] Coplien, J., Harrison, N., 2004, ibid., p.18

[12] Coplien, J., Harrison, N., 2004, ibid., p.172

[13] http://www.belbin.com/belbin-team-roles.htm

[14] Anderson, R., 2001, "Security Engineering: A Guide to Building Dependable Distributed Systems," Wiley Computer Publishing, p.145

[15] http://www.projectliberty.org

[16] http://shibboleth.internet2.edu/

[17] http://www.internet2.edu/about/

[18] *The SAML standard provides the means by which authentication and authorization assertions can exchanged between communicating parties.*
Oasis, 2004, "Security Assertion Markup Language (SAML) 2.0 Technical Overview, Working Draft 01," http://xml.coverpages.org/SAML-TechOverviewV20-Draft7874.pdf
Liberty Alliance and Shibboleth are converging on release 2.0 of SAML.

[19] Middleware Architecture Committee for Education, see http://middleware.internet2.edu/MACE/

[20] http://shibboleth.internet2.edu/

[21] Currently the best known system for providing a role-based access control layer on top of Shibboleth is PERMIS—Privilege and Role Management Infrastructure Standards Validation (http://sec.isi.salford.ac.uk/permis/). Various other approaches are being developed and tested via case studies, including: Zhou, W., Meinel, C., 2004, "Implement role based access control with attribute certificates,,"http://www.informatik.uni-trier.de/~meinel/papers/ Paper_code16.pdf and
Adabala, S., Matsunaga, A., Tsugawa, M., Figueiredo, R., Fortes, J.A.B., 2004, "Single Sign-On in In-VIGO: Role-based Access via Delegation Mechanisms Using Short-lived User Identities,"
http://invigo.acis.ufl.edu/docs/publications/ipdps04_4.pdf

[22] Jensen, O., Milner, R., 2003, "Bigraphs and mobile processes," University of Cambridge Computer Laboratory

Six

Implementing the Human Interaction Management System (HIMS)

KEY POINTS: We show what a Human Interaction Management System (HIMS) looks like, and liken its user interface to a set of helpful elves (Roles) rather than the toolbox approach used by current enterprise systems. We go on to discuss certain aspects of process support implementation in detail:

- *Content management*—how the private information resources of a Role can be implemented via eXtensible Markup Language (XML)

- *Automation*—the interdependent techniques necessary for machines to share the workload with people in carrying out human-driven processes

- *Categorizing collaboration*—criteria against which forms of interaction can be assessed, in order to provide architectural guidelines for their implementation via specific messaging protocols

- *Transactions*—the differences between the database-style transactions required to maintain the integrity of private information within a Role, and collaborative transactions that orchestrate human activities at a higher level

- *Service-oriented architecture*—what Web services really are, and how they can be implemented within the context of a Human Interaction Management System

- *How to build a Human Interaction Management System*—the definition in technical terms of what a HIMS actually *is*, and the sort of technology you need to construct one

---

Does a firm perswasion that a thing is so, make it so?
— William Blake, "The Marriage of Heaven and Hell," 1790.

Why we need Human Interaction Management systems

The history of Business Process Management to date has shown a gradual realization of why computerized process support is valuable. In particular, a main strength has turned out to lie in providing mechanisms for monitoring and analysis. For example, a summary of Business Process Management activity during 2004 predicts that in 2005:

"There will be more emphasis on business process architectures and business performance measurement. Leading companies will want to assure that their core processes are measured and that all of the appropriate data is assembled for senior managers in a timely fashion. Companies are embracing processes, in large part, as a more efficient way of coping with change. To achieve this, companies need a clear map of their existing processes and accurate measures to pinpoint what's working and what needs improvement."[1]

Reading between the lines of this statement, we see that the Business Process Management world is moving away from a justification in terms only of Return On Investment (ROI). This comes as a relief to many Business Process Management system vendors, who have struggled to justify their products in terms of cost reduction.

For instance, based on the 2003 report on supply chain performance from the Grocery Manufacturers of America, Business Process Management consultant and writer Roger Whitehead makes an analysis of the potential cost savings offered by Business Process Management to the food, grocery and consumer product industries, and concludes that:

"We could possibly reduce [the cost of activities in the five areas that might be amenable to business process automation] by an average of a tenth, if we're lucky. That is roughly 0.1 per cent of these companies' total costs. This is not going to cut the mustard. Something that *might* cut less than 0.1 per cent of a company's costs is not going to head anyone's list of favorite cost-reduction programmes."[2]

Business Process Management is fundamentally not about greater operational efficiency in traditional quality management terms, as implemented for instance by a Six Sigma program. It is about doing things better in ways that are harder to quantify—in particular, doing things in a way that can change as and when necessary. Whitehead goes on: "In these consumer product and food companies, Business Process Management is a *busted flush* as a cost cutter. Its promise is as an aid to better response and to customer satisfaction."

This argument is right to focus on less tangible benefits for Business Process Management, but does make it hard for the CIO to justify the expense of a process support implementation at the board level. In fact, it is becoming harder and harder to justify *any* IT expense at the board level. Academic research based on the practical experiences of commercial organizations with implementing computer systems is showing that you don't always need to spend money on IT to derive benefit from it—it is generally more efficient to make the best of what you already have. This viewpoint is gradually filtering through to senior executives, who are only too receptive to it after years of wasting money on the latest Next Big Thing:

> "It is known from extensive research being conducted by the former CIO of the US Department of Defense, Paul A. Strassmann ... that there is no relation between information management per employee and return on shareholder equity. Also there is no relation between profits and annual IT spending. So he shows that there is no direct relation between spending on computers, profits or productivity. Indeed, there are companies--in the same industry--each spending about the same on IT of which the one makes high profits, and the other makes huge losses ... This leads to shotgun patterns showing the absence of correlations between any kind of return and the intensity of IT investments. The only vague correlation that Strassmann ever found was that when from two comparable enterprises one is spending slightly less than the other, the less spending organization is doing slightly better. This loose correlation leads one to suspect that governance of IT investments aids in creating value with IT instead of destroying profits."[3]

So, are Business Process Management vendors caught in a double bind? On the one hand, they cannot argue a case for their products in ROI terms. On the other hand, a board of directors may be quite willing to accept that Business Process Management brings benefits, particularly with regard to process-based measurement and analysis of activity, but be quite unwilling to spend any real money on it.

The way forward is to understand that Business Process Management generally—and human-driven process management is no exception—is an *integrating technology*. It is not about throwing out well-worn systems and replacing them with shiny new ones, but about capitalizing on what you have already—re-organizing their use in accordance with carefully developed process principles. In particular, Business Process Management systems allow you to make better use of existing *middleware*: information repositories, transaction management, messaging systems, and so on. By using such systems from within a process context, rather than directly, it becomes possible to change patterns of use more easily, as well as to monitor and manage what is going on.

Hence, a Human Interaction Management System should be a thin, almost invisible layer of technology—not a vastly expensive revamp of your IT infrastructure, but a *better way in* to existing enterprise systems.

What will such a way in look like? For a start, we can assume it will be browser-based. Nearly all commercial computer programs provide a Web interface these days, and people are becoming more and more accustomed to doing everything via a browser. Hence, for the next few years at least, Human Interaction Management Systems can be visualized as providing a better *personalized Web portal*.

Such a process-based portal not only presents customized business data via the Web (like a conventional portal), but also:

- *Divides up data* according to the processes you are participating in;

- Lets you *carry out process activities* using that data; and

- Allows you to *interact with your colleagues* as part of a process.

So, how will this work in practice? Currently, when you login to the network, you see a choice of databases, reports, application systems, and so on. What will a process-based portal offer instead?

It can only be one thing. We have shown how human participation in a process is always via *taking on a Role*. Hence, a process-based portal will offer you a choice of Roles to use—the Roles that you are currently playing in different processes. If you happen only to be playing one single Role at the moment, it will log you straight into that Role: *Project Manager for Government Cost Reduction*, say, or *Technical Support for the OilCo Bid*.

Once logged into a Role, what will you see next? You will expect to

have various forms of information available—the private information resources of your Role, for example, as well as more general information
about the process you are now part of. In particular, though, you will be
interested to know what activities are currently available for that Role. Of
all the activities you could carry out at some time using a specific Role, at a
particular moment in time only certain ones will be *enabled*—have preconditions that are currently true. So you will see a list of currently enabled activities: *Start Team Members*, say, or *Respond to Support Queries*. As above, if only
one activity is enabled, you would expect to be logged straight into that activity—since it saves time to be taken directly to the only work items currently awaiting your attention. Of course, you may wish to do something
not directly activity-related, for example to inspect the information held
within the current Role or the information held within a different one of
your Roles—the user interface will provide a simple visual means to do
such things, as and when required.

Continuing the theme, what will you then see? An activity is made up
of atomic tasks—the low-level actions that actually get stuff done. It is
these that provide access to existing systems on the network, and do it
transparently—in other words, they conceal for your convenience the tedious
technical details such as usernames and passwords, and just provide you
with the facilities you need. The user interface for a particular task might be
drawn directly from an existing system, or reinvented for use within the
process (we have seen above how such reinvention might be done on an
ongoing basis as part of process enactment). Suppose you are logged into
an activity *Respond to Support Queries*. You might see a choice of tasks such as
*Get Next Support Query, Identify Potential Reference Material for Solution, Document
Solution Ideas,* and so on. In most cases, there will be more than one task
involved in an activity, but again, if there is only one, you will be placed in it
directly.

All this is configurable, naturally. Some people may prefer to manually
navigate through the system, explicitly choosing where to go next even if
only one option is available. However, most people will choose to let the
system guide them, in order to *minimize the time they spend messing about with the
computer program and maximize the time they spend actually working.*

This is the real point, isn't it? By providing a user interface such as the
above, based directly on the true structure of human activity, people can get
on with their work as immediately as possible—without the technicalities of
the computer systems they use getting in their way. To the contrary, the

computerized resources they require are made available to them automatically, as and when they need them. There is no need to track down each system they need on the network, obtain (or look up) the necessary username and password, copy and paste information from one system to another, and so on. The Role paradigm makes it possible for the Human Interaction Management System to do all this on their behalf.

At present, most enterprise systems are like a toolbox. When you log on to the network at the start of the day, you are presented with a set of useful tools—an email program, a knowledge management system, a database, an ERP system, a set of reports, and so on. It is up to you to decide which ones you need and work out how to use them.

Human Interaction Management should transform this rather primitive arrangement. Once the principles of human-driven process management have been applied, enterprise software should work more like a Personal Assistant—a knowledgeable aide, that organizes your data and activities for you, and guides you without being prompted to the items that are currently most important. In fact, each Role is like a separate Personal Assistant—concerned with participation in a specific process, and possessing deep understanding of how to help you carry out your personal responsibilities in this process. The difference between the two approaches is depicted below in Figure 27: Typical enterprise user interfaces.

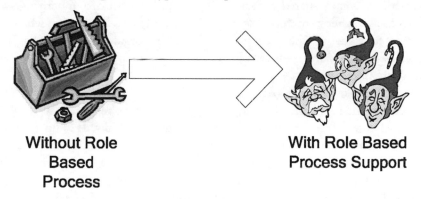

Without Role   **With Role Based**
Based   **Process Support**
Process

Figure 27: Typical enterprise user interfaces

It's the story of the shoemaker and the elves. At first the cobbler is toiling away in the old-fashioned way—it takes him days to make a single pair of shoes, and he lives from hand to mouth, never having enough time or making enough money to turn things round. At the point when he is about to go out of business, the elves turn up. Then all he has to do is the most crucial part of the job, the part that makes the best use of his skills and experience—cut the leather. Once cut into patterns, the elves know what to do with it, and finish each pair of shoes off while he is sleeping. The end result is that he can make several pairs each day, satisfy more and more customers, and get rich.

The elves that we need in an enterprise computing environment are Roles in a Human Interaction Management System. As we've seen, when you first log on to a Role-based human-driven process management system, your browser (which comes up automatically) will just show a list of Roles—or place you in a Role automatically, if you are only playing one at the moment. Once in a Role, you click an activity to carry it out—or again, are just assigned to that activity automatically if only one is currently enabled. The same for tasks—you see immediately *what you need to do*, and when you choose to do it, all the necessary computer resources are provided without you having to know any details whatsoever of what they are, or where they come from.

Roles not only allow a portal to be driven by process, but provide a mechanism for secure and flexible exchange of data between disparate underlying systems. The private information resources of a Role are like a clearing house, where data from one system can be lodged, altered, extended, enhanced, shared with other Roles, and fed back to underlying systems as and when required. It is not only a simple and effective mechanism for co-coordinating the separate systems in an organization, but has the crucial—and essential—advantage of corresponding directly to how we think about our work.

In a sense, the approach described above is, in practice, how we use systems at the moment. The only difference is that we're doing the work of such a Human Interaction Management System manually. It is up to us to decide what Role we are about to play, and what activity to do within it. We then choose the corresponding tasks and systems to use, and carry out the sort of information processing and transferal described above. However, we're doing it all by hand—not only finding and accessing systems individually, but copying information from one place and lodging it in another, using it in a document, sending it to someone by email, posting it on the Web, and so on.

From a human perspective, Human Interaction Management has a very simple purpose: to connect the dots in the organization, and make computers an almost invisible support system—a well-trained helper that is always there when needed. Using current enterprise systems can be like rehearsing a cast of children in a school play. They may each be able to play their part well, but have to be continually rounded up and coaxed into action when needed. Moreover, their interactions are not only unpredictable but can often be downright infuriating, with much time being wasted as a result.

It is one thing to appreciate the value of the approach outlined in this book—and as we have shown in *Improving Human-Driven Processes*, improvements can be made simply by adopting the modeling approach, with or without computer support. Process *management*, in particular, can be transformed without the aid of any process support systems whatsoever. However, to get the maximum benefit from an understanding of human activity, you need to use computers to support and augment it. This does not have to be expensive, and certainly does not require anything you have now to be thrown away. To the contrary, it is all about making the best use of what you have already.

In this chapter we look at various aspects of computer system architecture that are fundamental to the proper implementation of human-driven process support. Based on experience with the development and use of a Human Interaction Management System, we outline principles that an enterprise software architect must take into account if they wish to implement a Human Interaction Management System for themselves. Specific features of a Human Interaction Management System are described below not to assert that this is the best or only way to implement such principles, but to illustrate typical human-driven process support *mechanisms* and the benefits that they provide in practice.

Content Management

We have seen in various places in this book how a fundamental aspect of a Role as process participant is the private data that it owns. The data that a process participant makes use of when carrying out his or her part of the work may be taken from, and ultimately synchronized with, data held in centralized corporate repositories. However, from a process perspective it belongs inside a Role, and most activities in the Role will involve maintenance of data held locally, not externally.

This raises data management issues. Standard solutions exist for control of enterprise data that we need to replicate inside a Role:

- We require the ability to create and use multiple *versions* of a document, and these must be properly separated—as elements of a collection, for example.

- We need to handle *structured data*, so that we can assign certain properties as part of a process activity: enter *author* and *date*, for example, or populate specific fields via a Web service call.

- We need support for *searching*, so that appropriate information can be located when required, however deeply nested it may be inside a data structure.

Hence, in order to manage the content of a Role, we need an approach to data storage that is capable of supporting all such requirements. Today's enterprise computing systems are converging on XML (eXtensible Markup Language)[4] as a multi-faceted solution to content management.

XML is not so much a format for data as a way of creating any standard format that you might need. XML allows you to make a general description of how a particular type of data will be structured. This description is made in such a way that any particular data item can then be automatically validated against it, without manual intervention.

Currently, most XML documents are plain text, which makes them readable by humans as well as by computer programs. This aspect of XML may be about to change, as the use of binary XML data becomes more common. However, for our purposes, the important properties of XML are that it supports the requirements outlined above. XML has built-in provision for collections, can be structured via use of arbitrary levels of nesting, and there are automatable search techniques that can be applied to extract particular parts of an XML document. In particular, the new XML Query Language (*XQuery*) offers the potential for simple creation of searches that span multiple data sources at once (multiple XML documents, for instance), based on a theoretically sound data model that helps to guarantee reliability.[5]

Hence it is advisable for a Human Interaction Management System to store all data inside a Role in XML format. In fact, a Role itself can be stored natively as XML, along with all other process objects (entities, interactions, and so on). This means that a process object can be used and passed about just like any other piece of data, something that is important for enabling process change on-the-fly.

The use of XML for storing Role resources has subtler advantages, as well. For instance, resources can be used directly as parameters to a Web service call, and the results of the call placed directly into the Role as new or replacement resources. Further, user interface screens can be defined not as static pieces of program, but as *dynamic conversions of Role resources into corresponding input and output objects*.

Recall that XML is not so much a data format as a way of defining whatever data format you might want. To make best use of this flexibility, XML has an accompanying standard for the transformation of one such data format into another (eXtensible Stylesheet Language, or XSL).[6] Since screens can themselves be defined via XML, XSL used appropriately, permits information resources held in a Role to be converted automatically into screens suitable for modifying them.

Such facilities arise from the combination of a customizable approach to *data definition* (XML) with a customizable approach to *data use* (process Roles). The combination offers many potential benefits. Tools exist to turn XML directly into PDF files,[7] to return database query results as XML,[8] to use XML as metadata (see *How people find things out*—a promising XML metadata standard achieving widespread take-up is Dublin Core)[9] and there are any number of other possibilities in existence already or just on the horizon.

Some such possibilities have already been explored using an existing Human Interaction Management System. Others remain to be discovered. What is certain is that the use of Roles to store information in XML form provides the opportunity to make in-depth use of this new and powerful technology for information storage.

Automation

Automation of mundane tasks is a traditional benefit of computerized process support. While the focus of this book is on human involvement with processes, we do not argue that automation features should be omitted from a Human Interaction Management System. To the contrary, a proper analysis of human-driven processes will identify new areas in which manual effort can be removed, and thus new time and costs savings made.

Moreover, a Human Interaction Management System permits Web service calls to be made, computations to be performed in the background, and so on. We do not recommend that *all* low-level, machine-oriented transactions be controlled using the Human Interaction Management System (with IT systems it is always horses for courses[10]), but it is possible to do so when required. Moreover, in some ways the flexibility of a Human Interaction Management System offers interesting advantages.

For instance, in a Human Interaction Management System it is possible to select and invoke Web service calls *under user control during process operation*, something that is generally not possible with conventional enterprise systems. However, it can be useful in certain situations, since more and more Web sites now provide a Web service interface. A bibliographic database may offer to the researcher a list of references on a particular topic in this way, or a vendor may offer to the consumer a list of products meeting specified criteria. The lists returned in such cases may be intended for human consumption—so why not access them as part of a Human Interaction Management System? In fact, doing so can be made very easy—with a Human Interaction Management System, all you need to do in such a case is to specify the address of the Web service via a screen.[11] The software is then able to work out for itself how to call the service, and will retrieve and format the results on your behalf in the background.

Moreover, this scenario can be made to work whether the Web service is based on the SOAP protocol[12]—a standard permitting highly structured data to be exchanged and validated—or the simpler and more general purpose architectural style REST,[13] whereby the standard Web browsing protocol HTTP is used to Create, Read, Update and Delete documents of any kind. SOAP and REST are currently competing for mindshare in the Web services world, a discussion we take up briefly later on in this section.

For the moment, however, we need to consider how automation will work in a Human Interaction Management System. It will not work in the same way as in a conventional process support system, since the use of Roles means that automation can be configured more flexibly to better suit human activity. Further, the use of activities dynamically enabled by preconditions (rather than placed in a predefined sequence) means that automation naturally operates on a different basis.

Looking first at how a basis in Roles changes the way that a Human Interaction Management System offers automation, we see that automation can be *decentralized* and *controlled as part of the process itself.*

A process support system based on Roles can be envisaged as a tree. When you first install the software, there is only one Role running—the root Role of the entire system. This Role is capable of both defining and starting other Roles, and it does this in order to get some processes going. Some or all of the Roles it starts may also have the capability to define and start others, so they will kick off other processes. And so it goes on, with Roles all the way down creating new process definitions and spawning other Roles. This is illustrated in Figure 28: A tree of Roles.

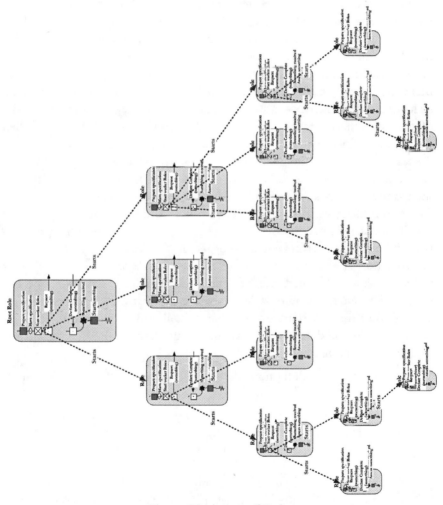

Figure 28: A tree of Roles

In terms of system administration, this naturally gives rise to a decentralized approach, with each Role taking responsibility for those beneath it.

This has massive advantages for large organizations, where all too often control over enterprise systems with huge numbers of users resides with a small number of overworked IT staff in a central location. The Role tree provides the opportunity to divide up administration responsibilities along the same lines as the work itself.

To a certain extent, the fact that a Human Interaction Management System *itself deals with work assignment* means that much of the normal system administration overhead is an in-process activity from the start. This is how it should be—it's just that normal enterprise systems make an artificial division between activities that require IT skills and those that can be carried out by ordinary mortals. As discussed above in *Why we need Human Interaction Management systems*, a Human Interaction Management System is like a group of helpful elves. Each elf—a Role instance—acts to disguise the complexity of dealing with enterprise software and lets you do what you want, when you want to do it, without putting technical barriers in the way. When it comes to work assignments, a Role instance lets you start other Roles and assign Users to them at the click of a button, without needing to grapple with arcane matters such as LDAP directories and database access rights.

When it comes to automation, we can extend the same principle used with work assignment. *Each Role can be made responsible for automating those beneath it.* In a Human Interaction Management System, this can be done by adding a task of a specific type, *Do Automated Role Instances*, to certain Roles in the tree (the task is included by default in a new Role definition, and can then be removed if required). What happens when a Role carries out an activity containing such a task? The parent will look at each of its children in turn. If the child is itself set to allow automation, the parent will see whether the child has any:

- Activities that the definition of the child Role specifies *should be* automated;

- Tasks within such an activity that can, *in principle*, be automated, such as a Web service call, calculation, interaction message delivery/receipt, or any other work that does not require human involvement.

For each such automation tasks found in a child Role, the parent Role will then carry out the task in the background. There are some interesting properties of this arrangement.

- Considering automation from a parent Role's perspective, the Do *Auto-*

mated Role Instances task can itself be placed in an automatable activity. So the children can be automated without the User needing to get involved directly—automation of the children just happens in the background as and when required. This provides a means of automation that doesn't impinge at all on the User of the parent Role—the parent Role elf will just get on with automating the children on the parent's behalf.

- Considering automation from a child Role's perspective, a task of type *Do Automated Role Instances* can itself be placed in an automatable activity. In other words, the child will, when an automation cycle happens, automate its own children (the grandchildren of the parent). In effect, automation can be made to cascade down the tree ad infinitum. Such an arrangement means that automation can be turned on and off at any branch of the tree—and when it turned off or on, it is turned off or on for *all* children beneath that branch. Administration of automation is not only decentralized, but nested to as many levels as required.

- Automation can be enabled or disabled in a variety of ways, for any branch of the tree. The *Do Automated Role Instances* task can be removed from any parent, or placed under manual control by making its activity *not automatable*. Similarly, a Role can itself be made automatable or not automatable, which will then apply to all activities within it. An activity containing a *Do Automated Role Instances* task can even be assigned a precondition, so that the children can only be automated under a certain state of affairs. Such a state of affairs may be true for some Roles of a certain type, and not for others. For a particular Role, it may be true at certain times only.

With respect to this latter property of automation in a Human Interaction Management System, we start to see how automation is no longer a matter for system administration at all, however decentralized. The way in which automation operates is *as much to do with process enactment as with process definition*.

This concept is totally unlike the automation facilities normally configured for process support, where making an activity interactive or non-interactive is decided during process definition, then facilitated by configuring middleware technologies such as messaging systems and application servers. With a Human Interaction Management System, we need to make things more dynamic, since we cannot always know at process definition time what should be automated and when. Apart from anything else, the very activities in a process can and are likely to change during process enactment.

So far, we have discussed how a Human Interaction Management System knows what should be automated. We have not discussed when and how the automation is actually carried out. This could be implemented in a variety of ways. There could be a background automation cycle in the Human Interaction Management System that can be configured to run at preset intervals—via the use of clustering techniques as described below, different automation cycles can then even be applied to different parts of the Role tree. There could also be a mechanism by which a User triggers an automation cycle of a Role whenever he or she visits it via the Web—a feature enabled by default, but which could be disabled generally, or just for certain parts of the Role tree.

Automation is a complex problem. Automation presents deep architectural issues, raising concerns such as:

- *Performance*—too much happening at once may drain a system of available processing power and memory, unless steps are taken to avoid this.

- *Transaction context*—the effects of an activity carried out by a Role may change the truth or falsehood of conditions controlling the enablement of other activities.

- *Concurrency*—where more than one Role may access the same resources (a database, for example), it is possible to reach blockage situations (*deadlock*, for example) where neither can proceed because the many requests for access are waiting for the others to finish, or the even more dangerous *livelock*, where each party cycles through the same series of actions in response to actions taken by the other.

It is necessary to design a Human Interaction Management System very carefully in order to eliminate the risks inherent in such problems. For example, performance issues can be managed via the use of clustering techniques—for example, it is possible to make background automation the responsibility of specific application servers in a cluster, and control the division of computing resources so as to ensure that interactive performance is unaffected by the amount of automation going on. Transaction context can be dealt with by using software design patterns and algorithms that support a changing process context. Concurrency can be managed via judicious use of configurable timeouts.

However, such solutions are intimately tied to the design of a particular Human Interaction Management System. Approaches that work for one HIMS may not work for others, and different approaches may need to be applied.

Moreover, the dynamic nature of a Role tree is such that its behavior, just like human behavior, is very hard to predict in advance. Especially when a Role-based process support system becomes very large, it will start to have *emergent* properties. It is the kind of system, known as *chaotic*, where small actions can have a large impact.

Consider, for example, a market research Role that included an activity to collate data from the Internet—listings of every reference to a company's products, for example. The Role might search the Web using specific criteria, retrieve the data into its own private resources, and then put an extract from the data into a database table for use by others when running analysis reports. If a large amount of data is retrieved, the action of updating the table could slow down the database generally—perhaps even the machine running the database. Depending on how the database and machine are involved in the work of other Roles, the effect on performance could be felt company-wide.

It is not possible to remove such situations entirely by careful design of a Human Interaction Management System, because they arise as a result of process characteristics. However, negative performance situations can be prevented from crashing the system. It is necessary when testing a process support system to ensure that hundreds if not thousands of Roles can run simultaneously, without causing the servers and databases concerned to grind to a halt. For example, early system testing of one Human Interaction Management System revealed caching problems that were not anticipated during design, yet would have caused performance to degrade dramatically once a large number of Roles were created.

It is necessary to resolve such design flaws *before* the system goes into production usage. It is generally easy to fix bugs when no one is yet using the system, but harder and more painful all round when thousands of users on different customer sites are relying on the software. This may seem like obvious advice, but many people with experience using enterprise software may suspect that the advice is not always followed by vendors.

Categorizing collaboration

We discussed in *Resources* how some resources within a Role are not bits, but atoms—an *offline Entity* is a physical, real-world object such as a key to machinery or printed policy document. We also discussed in *Interactions* how some notional Users of a system may never actually log onto the process support system. An *offline User* may work for another company, for example, and not have access to the process support system via an extranet.

The existence of offline Entities and Users complicates matters when it comes to implementing interactions, since it affects the way a message is delivered and acknowledged. In the discussion of interactions, we saw how delivery of an offline Entity from an offline User must be signified by the receiver, since there is no other way for the system to detect that it has happened.

However, in most cases, it is still possible to deliver messages. For instance, it is possible to send information to an offline User—even if they are not using the process support system, they will generally be accessible by some computerized means, even if it is only email. Hence, it is necessary to provide facilities in a Human Interaction Management System to record what should be done in such cases.

A Human Interaction Management System should allow a *messaging protocol* to be specified as part of each interaction channel, whether for sending or receipt. Messaging protocols should be customizable—typical examples are email, fax, Web service, a dedicated messaging product such as IBM MQSeries®, mobile phone text messaging, and so on. When the interaction is carried out, this protocol is matched against details of the User in question to identify exactly how the information should be transferred.

Each Human Interaction Management System must provide its own solution for such requirements. However, we can make some general comments with regard to system architecture. The use of external messaging protocols brings with it resourcing issues that must be managed.

For instance, the use of mobile phones can be a major cost for large companies. Therefore a process support system that implemented human interactions via text messaging could add dramatically to this cost. Such an addition might well be justified, if it cut down the cost of other forms of communication, such as voice calls or postage. However, the cost needs to be identified and tracked in order to make a cost/benefit analysis in the first place.

Similarly, the use of Web services might place a strain on the gateways that provided the text-messaging facility. In this case, cost might not be an issue—but system performance could be degraded, possibly with an impact on other applications. Again, if this effect is to be assessed and managed, for example by increasing the computing resources available to the gateway, the communications concerned must be monitored.

In general, such issues can be resolved one by one, but there are also high-level considerations that should be taken into account. When allocating resources (whether time, money or effort) into facilitating specific types of in-process communication, it is necessary to ask whether the solution adopted is the most sensible in business terms, as well as being the most cost-effective from an IT point of view.

Suppose the process in question is to design and build a new type of airplane wing. Should design changes be sent to materials suppliers via email or Web service call? Should the changes be sent all at once weekly, or as and when each design change is made? Should the changes be sent in detailed form, or as summaries with Web links to detailed information?

To answer such questions, we need a way of *categorizing* the interactions carried out in a particular process, for use as a basis when deciding how to implement each one. Given in Table 4: Collaboration Categorization Metrics are criteria against which forms of collaboration can be assessed, in order to provide architectural guidelines for process system implementation. For each criterion, we give example indicators that can be tracked, in order to provide metrics that permit interaction improvement against that criterion.

Table 4: Collaboration Categorization Metrics

Interaction Metric	Description	Example Indicators
Variance	How likely the interaction is to carry widely varying types of message.	Are there standard message formats that can be determined in advance? Will it be necessary to transfer binary data? For text data, will there ever be special characters, or information in foreign languages?

Interaction Metric	Description	Example Indicators
Bandwidth	Volume of traffic. Large messages may have an impact on cost and efficiency, for instance, or even stop certain communication methods from working properly. Such considerations are particularly important if an approach such as mobile phone text messaging is being considered.	How large are messages likely to get? Are many Roles likely to access the communication channel at precisely the same moment? What is the maximum number of messages that will be carried in each time period?
Dynamism	How adaptable the channel is to process changes	Will many different organizations take part in the interaction? Will it ever be necessary to change the sender or recipient of a message? Do such changes need to be made by non-technical people, from within a process?
Significance	Impact on the organization	What is the business impact of failed delivery? What is the business impact of late delivery? What is the business impact of message corruption?
Chaos	Whether there are *tipping points*, at which the nature of the interaction may change	Will usage of the interaction be restricted to a few Roles at first, then scale up suddenly? Will the volume of data sent over the interaction ever change suddenly, for example

Interaction Metric	Description	Example Indicators
		at busy trading periods such as Christmas? What effects would typical process changes have on the interaction, insofar as these can be predicted?
Burstiness	Traffic in some interactions will be relatively constant—in others it will have peaks and troughs	How does the level of communication vary from day to night? From weekday to weekend? From month to month during the year? At different times during the process lifecycle?
Quality	How important it is to have input that is guaranteed to be fit for purpose	Will data passed across be highly structured? Does the structure of the data sent and received cater to the format preferences of business partners? Is it necessary to apply validation checks on either sending or receipt? What is the effect of some data being omitted, or unexpected data included?
Security	How important it is to authenticate the transmission	Does the data represent or affect a financial transaction? Will the interaction be used for confidential documents? Will the interaction be used for exchange of contracts?

The key point is that, when implementing in-process interactions that involve communication outside the scope of the process support system itself, there are various architectural issues affecting not only IT resource usage but also business performance. The value and nature of an interaction must be assessed both in technical and in business terms, in order that the IT architect can judge how best to implement it.

Transactions

We have discussed throughout this book how activities in a Role are enabled by *preconditions* and validated by *postconditions*. When the precondition of an activity becomes true, the User (or an automation cycle) is free to carry out the activity. If, after doing so, the postcondition is true, all updates made to the information resources of the Role will be preserved; otherwise all effects of the activity will be undone.

In order to provide process support that implements this latter functionality—undoing the effects of an activity—it is necessary to treat each activity as a separate *transaction*. In other words, however many tasks are carried out as part of an activity, and whatever their impact on the Role resources, this must all be undone as a whole if the postcondition is violated on completion.

Transactions are a standard part of database theory, and conventionally their architectural properties are described as "ACID." The data changes that form the transaction should satisfy the following criteria:

- *Atomicity*—the changes should either all be made together or none be made at all

- *Consistency*—the changes should leave the system they belong to in a stable state

- *Isolation*—the changes should remain invisible to any other part of the system until the transaction is over

- *Durability*—the changes should be committed to permanent storage on completion.

This data-oriented concept of transaction is quite different from the *collaborative transactions* depicted in Figure 18: Role Activity Diagram for a concurrent design sub-project. Our concept of a *collaborative transaction* is a flexible, dynamic pattern that allows several parties all to *know where they are in the process*. Once you have communicated via the upper bound interaction, all parties know that a certain collaborative activity is underway. Once you have communicated via the lower bound transaction, all parties know how the activity worked out. Because the pattern can be nested, you can split the collaboration into pieces according to the components of the work itself. Moreover, you can decide to complete a transaction even if the job is not yet finished, starting another one if necessary for the remaining work.

Our concept of collaborative transaction is closer in spirit to the long-running business activities dealt with by protocols such as WS-BusinessActivity.[14] However, such protocols are intended for use in co-ordinating groups of machines—hence, they are focused on support of notions such as *compensation,* which extends the notion of database rollback to define how the effects of an interdependent group of tasks can be automatically undone if the activity as a whole fails. However, when groups of humans are collaborating, it is neither useful nor possible to define automated compensation mechanisms—people neither wish to nor are able to "forget" something that has already happened. They may need to take corrective action if a collaborative transaction goes awry, but this must be done via the process management techniques described above. You cannot define in advance how to get a human-driven process back on track.

Hence we are interested here only in two specific kinds of transaction, one that is standard in database theory, and one that is specific to the theory of Human Interactions. The first kind of transaction—the ACID kind—is implemented within a process support engine, and allows activities to be undone on completion if their postcondition is violated. The second kind—the collaborative kind—is a process pattern that appears whenever you have a problem formed of sub-problems, which may or may not be interdependent. Both kinds of transaction are required to support human-driven processes, but one is the responsibility of the software developers who implement your Human Interaction Management System, and the other the responsibility of the business analysts and experts who design and manage your processes.

Service-oriented architecture

Ever since the first ideas which would lead to object-oriented programming were developed back in the 1960s, the software development world has been moving closer toward general acceptance of what is now called *service-oriented architecture,* but originally went by the name of *loose-coupling* or simply *modularity.* The idea is to build a system out of components which are independent of one another, the aim being to simplify maintenance, and permit re-use of individual components in a different context. The components communicate by sending each other messages—nowadays this is seen as *requesting services* from one another.

The approach has taken a particular direction in recent years with the emergence of Internet technologies, since the universal adoption of the key protocols HTTP (for web browsing) and XML (for data formatting) has made them de facto standards. This ubiquity of these protocols has led to more and more software developers using them to send messages to and from software components. A *Web service* is simply a message sent to a software component using HTTP, possibly using XML to format the contents. There are other ways to send such messages—to *request services*—but HTTP and XML have an advantage which is important in many situations: they are platform-neutral. Hence the sender and receiver of a *Web service call* may live on different operating systems (Windows and Linux, say), or be constructed using different technologies (J2EE and .NET, say).

We conclude this chapter with a short discussion of Web services. As mentioned, there are currently two approaches competing for mindshare in the IT world:

- The *SOAP* protocol[15] is a standard permitting highly structured data to be exchanged and validated

- *REST*[16] is a simpler and more general purpose architectural style, whereby the standard Web browsing protocol HTTP is used to Create, Read, Update and Delete documents of any kind.

The debate between SOAP and REST basically comes down to where you put the complexity. Should the definition of the communication include the structure of the messages, as permitted by SOAP? Or should this be left for the systems at each end to deal with?

SOAP requires automated validation of message structures to be embedded into the Web service call itself. This is an enabler for e-commerce transactions, since these days there is pressure for such communications to conform to standard protocols. SOAP allows e-commerce transactions to be implemented using dedicated middleware, whose purpose in life is simply to enable, route, and validate Web service calls. However, this level of implementation complexity makes Web-based communication harder to put in place, less flexible, and harder to change. REST proponents would argue that the systems at each end need to include such validation anyway, so there is no need to implement it in more than one place.

A Human Interaction Management System must support both protocols. However, REST may be of more common use in human-driven processes. By and large, there is no need for humans to exchange data whose format is absolutely guaranteed in detail. A basic human skill is in the deciphering of incomplete data. We are naturally good at interpreting messages or documents that leave out details, are poorly written, abbreviated all over the place, include hints and suggestions, and so on. Moreover, we need to exchange such information in order to carry out our work—show an incomplete first draft of a design to a colleague for feedback, for example, or suggest a way forward for partnership that leaves room for negotiation.

Moreover, SOAP is currently embroiled in a level of standards debate that may hold up progress on Web-based interaction. At the time of this writing, there were over 60 Web services standards under discussion in the industry.[17] Many of these are aimed at creating business agility via dynamic networks of computer systems, in which participating machines can make decisions *without human involvement* about which Web services to use in certain situations.

However, success in letting groups of machines run things on their own is by no means guaranteed. The current attempt to do this has an uncomfortable resonance with the 1980s trend in financial markets toward automated trading based on Artificial Intelligence techniques that is widely blamed for "Black Monday," the stock market crash of 1987.[18] Two decades on, the new Web services standards are dealing with this danger by placing more and more levels of restriction and conformance on machine interactions.

This has brought a degree of complexity to machine-level process implementation that we do not need to be concerned with for the purposes of Human Interaction Management. It is the province of conventional process support and Enterprise Application Integration systems to grapple with the issues involved in making a fully automated yet dynamic framework for supply chain, financial settlement or logistics—our interest in this book is not in networks of machines so much as in networks of humans, and we argue that networks of both types are essential for the development of next generation business operations.

For us, human decision-making is the essential component in the management of complex distributed processes—and the fundamental ingredient in enabling this is not a raft of complex standards but a better understanding of the nature of work itself. A Human Interaction Management System needs to support interaction via the Web, but the simpler the better, and REST is more than enough in most cases with regard to Web services.

Unlike groups of machines, success in letting groups of humans run things is all about enablement. Computers will generally do the wrong thing unless explicitly instructed how to behave down to the very last detail. The only things that people need in order to perform to their best are *incentives* and *help*.

Supporting people with machines doesn't have to mean treating them like machines.

How to build a Human Interaction Management System

In this last section of the chapter, we address the question of how to actually go about constructing a HIMS. What sort of software development techniques do you need? We will see that the answer is not straightforward, and requires us to delve deep into the nature of a Human Interaction Management System.

Before we can do this, we need to provide the definition in technical terms of what a HIMS actually *is*—the specification for such a software system. A HIMS is:

> A process modeling and enactment system that provides *native support for the six Role Activity Theory object types* (Role, Entity, Activity, User, State and Interaction), uses a *state-based approach* to Activity enablement and validation, permits Interactions to be composed of *multiple asynchronous channels*, and supports *management of process change* by allowing any process component to be created and configured as a natural part of process execution—not just objects of the six fundamental types, but also the user interfaces by which they are presented (screens, for example) and the means by which they interact with other systems (Web service calls, for example).

A Human Interaction Management System can be likened to a *world* containing objects of several sorts. At the top level of the world there are objects representing Users, Role types, Role instances, Interaction types, Interaction instances, and Entity types—and other sorts of top-level object may also be required, depending on the system design. Objects have a mixture of human-driven and automated behavior. Some objects know about each other, and some objects communicate with each other. And all of them change, the whole time—a fundamental principle underlying a Human Interaction Management System is that the very fabric of each process can and will evolve as it takes place. Indeed, a large part of human behavior is directly concerned with guiding and agreeing on how processes evolve—this is what much of our daily work is *about*.

The Role concept, in particular, is fundamental. Some form of Role notion is available by default in many process support systems, since they allow tasks to be allocated to specific roles within an organization. However, the Role concept implicit in a Human Interaction Management System is richer than these notions—a Role in a Human Interaction Management System is an independent object, separate from the User assigned to it at any given time, and in possession of a *private information space*. This information space includes both *properties* that capture data held internally to the Role, and *references* to other independent objects in the Human Interaction Management System—Users, other Roles, and so on. The Role uses the references as a means both of communicating with and of manipulating the other objects in the world. A Role may also have references to objects that are actually stored outside the process support system, for example documents—this permits them to be created, exchanged, viewed, edited, downloaded and uploaded via the Web in the manner of groupware or knowledge management systems (indeed, such systems may be utilized behind the scenes), yet under full process control.

Further, all the various objects in a Human Interaction Management System, not just Roles, are related to one another in different ways, such as:

- *Composition*—for example, an Entity instance may acquire other Entity instances as contents

- *Specialization*—for example, one Role type may be a sub-type of another

- *Instantiation*—for example, an Interaction instance may be created from an Interaction type

Some of these relationships are to do with the existence of both types and instances in a Human Interaction Management System, which brings yet further complication. Each type needs to know about both its instances and any sub-types made from it, just as each instance needs to know what type it is. It is often sensible to use a successful process as the basis for others, which means utilizing instances effectively as types. And returning to the principle of continual evolution described above, everything in a Human Interaction Management System may change, including object types. Not only may a type be *altered*, but it may become *unavailable* (since a Human Interaction Management System world is distributed across multiple machines, possibly in separate locations and belonging to separate organizations) or even *obsolete*—in all these cases you must then manage the consequent impact on any existing instances.

What sort of technology do we need in order to build such a world?

One fundamental requirement that follows from the above discussion is the ability for *objects to acquire and retain information about each other*. This information is not restricted to enumerating specific properties of an object, but relates also to the object's general nature—what sort of thing it is, what it can do, and how it does it. In fact, objects in a Human Interaction Management System often need such information about *themselves* as well as about others—for example, it is common in a Human Interaction Management System for a Role to change its own behavior as a result of circumstances. The ability of objects to "introspect" themselves and others in this way is provided in conventional object-oriented programming languages—in Java, for example, this ability is known as *reflection*.

Another fundamental enabler for construction of a Human Interaction Management System is the ability to *create objects that are really extensions of other objects*. For example, the many task types in a Human Interaction Management System can be divided into groups—some create Roles, others configure Interactions, yet others maintain Users, and so on. It is much easier to put such groups of task types in place if each member can draw from behavior defined in a generic task type that underlies the whole group. Otherwise, the same behavior must be defined again and again for each member, which makes maintenance of changes to the core behavior complex and error-prone. Again, the ability of objects to base themselves on others in this way is provided in conventional object-oriented programming languages—in this case the ability is known as *inheritance*.

Hence, when considering how best to implement a Human Interaction Management System, we should look for software development tools capable of providing object-oriented programming features such as reflection and inheritance. Ideally these features will be there by default, in the toolset itself. Otherwise you will effectively end up trying to recreate them for yourself as you go about building a Human Interaction

Management System—a route forced upon you by the nature of the system you are trying to construct.

Recreating such features may not actually be *possible*, if the development tools you choose are insufficiently powerful. Even if the development tools you choose are powerful enough in theory to build object-oriented programming features from scratch, it is necessary to appreciate at the start that you are embarking on a wheel re-invention program of quite phenomenal scale.

In practice, you can build any software system in a variety of ways. However, IT is ultimately an engineering discipline, and the choice of tools for system construction is a decision that should be based on engineering principles. What will get you there fastest, cheapest, most reliably, and—crucially—in the most *maintainable* way?

Putting it all together

To summarize this chapter, we have shown what a Human Interaction Management System looks like, and compared it to a set of helpful elves (Roles) rather than to the toolbox interface used by current enterprise systems.

We then went on to discuss certain aspects of process support implementation in detail:

- *Content management*—how the private information resources of a Role can be implemented via eXtensible Markup Language (XML)

- *Automation*—the interdependent techniques necessary if machines are to share the workload with people in carrying out human-driven processes

- *Categorizing collaboration*—criteria against which forms of interaction can be assessed, in order to provide architectural guidelines for their implementation via specific messaging protocols

- *Transactions*—the differences between the database-style transactions required to maintain the integrity of private information within a Role, and collaborative transactions that orchestrate human activities at a higher level

- *Service-oriented architecture*—how Web services can be implemented within the context of a Human Interaction Management System

- *How to build a Human Interaction Management System*—the definition in technical terms of what a HIMS actually *is*, and the sort of technology you need to construct one

We have now completed our journey to the next stage of process understanding—at least insofar we are able to do in this book. The next chapter is a short recap of everything we have discussed.

References.

[1] Wolf, C., Harmon, P., 2004, "Business Process Trends in 2005," http://www.bptrends.com/deliver_file.cfm?fileType=publication&fileName=bp temailadvisor122104%2Epdf

[2] Whitehead, R., 2003, "The Intangible meets The Imponderable," http://www.bpmg.org/downloads/LookingAskance/Looking_Askance_2.pdf

[3] Verhoef, C., "Quantitative IT Portfolio Management," Free University of Amsterdam, Department of Mathematics and Computer Science, http://www.cs.vu.nl/%7Ex/ipm/ipm.pdf

[4] http://www.w3.org/XML/

[5] http://www.w3.org/TR/xquery/

[6] http://www.w3.org/TR/xsl/

[7] See, for example, http://xml.apache.org/fop/

[8] RADRunner does this natively for any relational database, while some databases offer built-in support for data access via XML (for example, Oracle— http://www.oracle.com/technology/products/database/application_developme nt/sqlxml)

[9] http://dublincore.org/

[10] A matter of choosing the right tool for the right job

[11] Actually you would specify the address of the WSDL (Web Service Definition Language) file for the Web service, which describes how to use it. See http://www.w3.org/TR/wsdl.

[12] Simple Object Access Protocol—see http://www.w3.org/TR/soap/

[13] REpresentational State Transfer—first described in Fielding, R.T., 2000, "Architectural Styles and the Design of Network-based Software Architectures," Doctoral dissertation, University of California, Irvine, http://www.ics.uci.edu/~fielding/pubs/dissertation/introduction.htm

[14] [WS-BusinessActivity] provides the definition of the business activity coordination type that is to be used with the extensible coordination framework described in the WS-Coordination specification. The specification defines two specific agreement coordination protocols for the business activity coordination type: BusinessAgreementWithParticipantCompletion and BusinessAgreementWithCoordinatorCompletion. Developers can use any or all of these protocols when building applications that require consistent agreement on the outcome of long-running distributed activities.
http://www-106.ibm.com/developerworks/library/specification/ws-tx/

[15] Simple Object Access Protocol—see http://www.w3.org/TR/soap/

[16] REpresentational State Transfer—first described in Fielding, R.T., 2000, ibid.

[17] See, for instance, the summary at
http://roadmap.cbdiforum.com/reports/protocols/summary.php

[18] REMEMBER Black Monday? On October 19th 1987, the Dow Jones plunged 23%, wiping hundreds of billions of dollars off share values. The crash was blamed on the big brokerage houses' automated trading programs, which magnified a bad day into a calamity.
http://www.economist.com/surveys/displayStory.cfm?Story_id=949129

In searching for the cause of the crash, many analysts found fault with "program" trading by large institutional investing companies. This is where computers were programmed to automatically order large stock trades when certain market trends prevailed.
http://www.computerweekly.com/Article112706.htm

Seven

Human Interactions in a nutshell

There is common consensus that a modern business, if it wishes to stay competitive, must put in place efficient systems for management of its *processes*. Here is the process view of an enterprise:

Routinized, regulated, automated, mechanistic activity

Flexible, innovative, collaborative, human activity

Figure 29: The process iceberg

Current approaches to analysis of business processes deal very well with the part above the water, and hardly at all with the part below. Human activity, where it is covered at all, is treated as if it *was* mechanistic—which is probably worse than leaving it alone. Hence, businesses are competing on only a small part of the activity they carry out: the routinized, regulated, mechanistic part. How much advantage could be gained by competing on the human activity as well?

Understanding how humans carry out their work—the *patterns underly-*

ing what they do—allows an enterprise to better structure, measure and control this work. Such understanding also paves the way for implementation of computerized support, and such systems are starting to appear. Whether or not human processes are facilitated with software, it is the early adopters of human-driven process management who will reap the greatest benefits.

Here are the five main features of human working activity, together with an outline explanation of how they can be managed.

1. *Connection visibility.* In automated processes, the ultimate aim is to render the distribution of data, logic and control arbitrary. However, in human collaborative situations, quite the opposite is true. A human process creates meaningful connections between participants whose skills, responsibilities, authorities and resources are quite distinct and probably very different. To work with people, you need to know who they are and what they can do. Therefore, collaborative technology must provide a strong representation of *process participants*, the *roles* they play and the *private information resources* that belong to each of them. We do this using Role Activity Diagrams (RADs)—a simple graphical approach to depicting processes that anyone can understand in moments with no need for training. An example RAD is shown in Figure 30: A Role Activity Diagram for an engineering design process. It shows a Manager in the engineering design field, assigning work to some Designers.

2. *Structured messaging.* Messaging is an enabling force for human-computer interaction, yet typically results in efficiency losses as well as gains. For example, the volume of email received by organizational workers is an increasing problem—sorting it by relevance and priority alone can consume much of a working day. If we are to manage our interactions with others better, they must be structured for us, under process control. Role Activity Diagrams are again a way forward, because they allow us to show not only the communications between process participants, but also to impose structure on them—by showing their *intention*, describing the *content* of the message, and showing the interaction *in a process context* so that its dependencies and impacts can be understood.

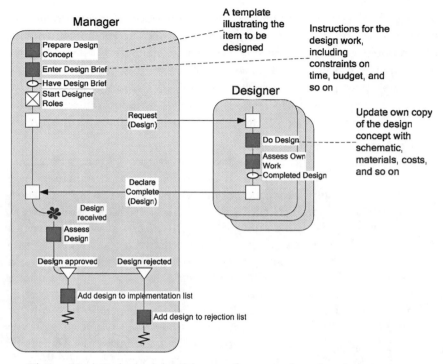

Figure 30: A Role Activity Diagram for an engineering design process

3. *Support for mental work.* A large part of what humans do has little concrete output—at least, not the kind of concrete output that is easily
measured by existing management techniques or computer systems. Yet
the time and mental effort invested in researching, comparing, considering, deciding, and generally *responding to information*—turning it into
knowledge and ideas—is a critical part of the job of an interaction
worker. Mental effort along with all other human activity can be described via a simple and generic pattern Research Evaluate Analyze
Constrain Task, or REACT (where Research has a sub-pattern Access,
Identify, Memorize, or AIM). REACT and AIM repeated, interleaved,
nested, and split across process participants can be used to create process descriptions that reflect the reality of human activity. We also identify a pattern for *collaborative transactions* that allows a complex problem
to be managed as a group of simpler ones, with the necessary dependencies automatically catered for. All of these patterns can be depicted
via Role Activity Diagrams.

4. *Supportive rather than prescriptive activity management.* Humans do not sequence their activities in the manner of a procedural computer program—"after doing x, I either do y or z, only depending on the outcome of x." A person that worked like this would *be* a machine. On the contrary, people take action in different ways on different days, in response to their dealings with others, to changes in the state of resources to which they have access, and—if we're realistic—to their mood at the time. We can support this in a simple way by changing the way we read a Role Activity Diagram. We say that a particular activity or interaction has a *precondition* (a state of affairs in which it becomes available) and a *postcondition* (a state of affairs that is guaranteed to be the case on completion). We then allow people to carry out any activity for which the precondition is true, at any time—no matter what activities they just did previously. We also insist that any activity whose results violate the postcondition must be completely undone, so as to prevent it derailing the process.

5. *Processes change processes.* Human activities are concerned often with solving problems, or making something happen. Such activities routinely start in the same fashion—by establishing a way of proceeding. Before you can design your new widget, or develop your marketing plan, you need to work out *how* you are going to do so—which methodology to use, which tools are required, which people should be consulted, and so on. In other words, process definition is an intrinsic part of the process itself. Further, this is not a one-time thing—it happens continually throughout the life of the process. Hence actions and interactions in human-driven processes cause *continual change to the process itself.* We deal with this by developing a new approach to process management. The principle of *separation of control* allows us to distinguish *management control* (day-to-day facilitation of human activity, carried out as part of the process itself—ongoing resourcing, monitoring and process re-design) from *executive control* (exercise of authority over the process, via determination of its primary Roles, interactions and deliverables). Process evolution can be implemented under management control via the establishment of consensus among certain participants, based on *how they would proceed from now on*—we term such a consensus an *agreement.* Each successive agreement can be documented and shared via an updated Role Activity Diagram.

This approach to understanding and depicting processes is radically different from that taken by current process analysis techniques. It deals head on with the greatest nightmare of current process support systems—*process change*—and the approach adopted allows a formal, mathematical basis to be developed for process analysis, something that is necessary for process support to have long-term success.

More immediately, human-driven process management offers the chance to gain massive competitive advantage by taking control of the hidden activity inside the organization—human work. The opportunities provided by such improvement of process control range from intangibles such as better human relations through to fundamental aspects of corporate life such as quality management, project planning and confidentiality.

In all cases, there is significant impact on both the bottom line and on customer satisfaction, as well as on something crucial to general organizational health—the welfare and commitment of its employees.

Finally, Human Interaction Management permits suppliers to establish a fundamental integration with the needs of their customers, by engaging directly with the human-centered processes for which their products will be used. In the twenty-first century, where customers are bewildered by choice and seek *understanding* from a supplier as well as low price and efficient delivery, such integration may be a necessity. Customers will find a supplier that they trust, engage with them, and stick with them. Anyone can compete in this heady new world—but to keep the customers you gain, you need Human Interaction Management.

Readers of this book are invited to take part in the development of Human Interaction Management, by *instigating a real-world proof-of-concept project* based on the ideas in this book, and *encouraging their Business Process Management vendors to extend or enhance their application suite* along the lines we've described.

Readers may also wish to participate in the debate on how to advance computer support of human co-operative work. Membership in the Web forum *Role Based Process Support* is open to all, and the reader is encouraged to join. See: http://www.smartgroups.com/groups/roles/

Epilogue

The future of process support

First published as "Human Interactions: No Cheese is Made of Chalk" in In Search Of Business Process Management Excellence, Business Process Management Group, Meghan-Kiffer Press, 2005. This essay shows how and why conventional process modeling techniques are not suited to support of interactive, human driven processes. Hence, its focus is mainly on issues related to enterprise IT, a subject in which some readers of this book may have only a tangential interest. The general reader should feel free to skip the essay entirely.

KEY POINTS: There is common consensus that a modern business, if it wishes to stay competitive, must put in place efficient systems for management of its processes. It seems to go almost without saying that the solution lies in computer systems for Business Process Management. After all, re-arrange the words slightly, and the problem becomes the solution. If you need to sand a floor, you buy a floor sander. If you need to paper a wall, you buy wallpaper. If you need to manage business processes, you buy a Business Process Management system. And, for an appropriate price, there will always be skilled people willing to do the work itself.

But is it always so simple? What if you need to build a reseller network in Asia? Improve in-house design skills? Control the flow of commercially sensitive information outside the company? There are processes involved, certainly. However, it would take a particularly hard-nosed Business Process Management vendor to stand up and say to a board of directors that its software caters in itself to such problems. Existing process languages, for all their power, do not in themselves capture the human issues crucial to such activities. Why is this? And what else do you need?

Vendors of advanced process support software rightly claim that their products expose processes in order to render them more manageable. However, we will show that the processes typically exposed by such systems are of a specific type: centered on software applications. Hence, the benefit of expressing such processes via such systems is largely that you can then make better use of the software applications concerned—to re-use legacy applications, for example, or provide more sophisticated automation that joins up diverse applications. Is this the best we can hope for from process management? To answer this, we must deal with the underlying question—are all business processes about software applications? Are business processes just about executing transactions and keeping records?

Unlike cats, not all processes are grey in the dark. Every business person knows that not all the activity in the enterprise takes place within a computer. There are two major types of business processes, and these require different forms of treatment, both by managers and by computer systems. Unlike the mechanistic processes conventionally handled by process support systems, many business processes are essentially human phenomena—driven by people rather than by machines. There is a major new source of competitive advantage out there, just waiting for a new type of process management software—the Human Interaction Management System.

What is a process made of?

No cheese is made of chalk.
Three Voices, Lewis Carroll.

If we are to understand what current process modeling techniques can do, and what they can't do, we need to understand what they *are*. In particular, we cannot fairly judge the utility of these techniques unless we have a true understanding of what those who employ them mean when they talk about "processes"—since this may not be the same as we take them to mean. What are the nuts and bolts from which such a process is actually made?

Look at the Web site of a typical process support vendor and you will see a range of product descriptions, ranging from prophetic claims of step-changes in IT thinking, through to sturdy reassurances of scalability and robustness. You will get support for massive parallelism, transparent messaging both within and across organizations, automatic handling of failure conditions, Old Uncle Tom Cobley[1] and all. But what is being run in parallel? What messages are being sent? Failures in what, exactly, are being handled so well?

It is necessary to pull back the wizard's curtain, and look at the fundamental components of the typical business processes implemented by current enterprise systems. This is possible since all mainstream process languages, standards and protocols share the same basic constructs. We can see this by looking at a graphical notation recently devised for diagramming processes, the Business Process Modeling Notation (BPMN)[2]. This notation sets out specifically to be a way of depicting business processes that is *universal*—applicable to any business process whatsoever. BPMN lets a process modeler specify that:

- Specific things happen at specific times (Event triggers);

- A sequence of activities should be automated (Control flow);

- A big process is made out of smaller ones (Composition); and

- More than one thing can happen at the same time (Parallelism).

This is certainly useful, but nothing new. A process represented by BPMN can be coded directly using any modern, low-level programming language—Java, for instance, for which there is now a huge range of mature and effective tools and methodologies. So why use a process support system at all?

The benefits of defining processes as separate entities have been promoted by business theorists for a long time now, but until recently, technology did not permit end-to-end implementation of processes on an enterprise scale. A common perception of Business Process Management is as workflow "grown up"—*enhanced* to cater for fuller automation (perhaps by incorporating Enterprise Application Integration tools) and *extended* across (and between) organizations.[3] Some software vendors go even further than this, and claim that their systems operate fundamentally at a *business* level. These vendors assert that their systems can be configured to get work done simply by "calling down" into lower-level components of the technology stack and, ultimately, application programs—thus obscuring low-level technology details from the business user entirely.

In other words, the IT department is not intended to remain in control of how the technology stack is used, but to pass control over to the business. Moreover, process support systems, once built, are supposed to be easy to change—because they are expressed at such a high-level, essentially that of the business itself, and you can map business changes directly onto new process definitions. Well, perhaps. And perhaps not yet.

Typical process support systems, in their current incarnation, are unlikely to fulfill this vision, since the underlying process languages from which they are constructed aren't designed for such purposes. Consider BPEL,[4] for instance, a process language with the support of several major incumbent IT vendors, and therefore a likely candidate for future standard. Languages such as BPEL were designed to help technicians build automated process execution engines, capable of orchestrating distributed computing resources of various kinds—such languages were not intended to supply the semantics needed by a business analyst to carry out high-level process work. In fact, current work on BPEL is focused on driving down further into the technology stack rather than up into the business, with the creation of a low-level add-on that programmers can use to do even more detailed technical work.[5] For now at least, the high-level business-oriented process tier is having to wait, while the process world focuses on empowering IT developers to build business processes via programming techniques. For now at least, the users of standard process languages are not business people, they are not even business analysts—they are IT developers.

In fact, we see the same principle at work with another hot topic in IT, *Web services*. Much is made of the way in which advanced process support systems can call (or preferably, "orchestrate") Web services to create business processes. What *is* a Web service? It's a piece of function, generally implemented in some low-level programming language, and made available via the Web. Here again, low-level programs are the building blocks of supposedly high-level business processes. This has all sorts of implications, of which, two in particular jump out as having direct impact on the business. First, not many business analysts want to write computer programs, so the programmers are back in the picture. Second, once you have low-level programs as part of your process system, the sort of freewheeling on-the-fly responsiveness to business needs promised by process support vendors is just not going to happen—it's back to the IT department with a change request if you want something to work differently, with the usual consequent haggling over the delivery schedule.

Hence, most of today's process implementations are not, in fact, contained neatly in their own top tiers of the enterprise architecture, providing a simple translation from business needs to process implementations. Rather, the current Business Process Management *stack* is scattered across different levels of infrastructure as its designers require. Moreover, any serious process support implementation needs to make use of a range of other enterprise technologies—enterprise application integration, secure messaging, directory services, data management, and all the rest. It thus becomes part of a complex technology backbone, dependent on a range of other systems. Process support systems, as proffered by some IT vendors, are, in fact, new management techniques that help technicians handle the technology stack.

So, does this detract from the value of current process support systems? Not at all. Features such as *process projection*—linking individual functions in legacy systems together to create new processes—have enormous potential for cost-saving. Process projection provides the enterprise with the ability to migrate more easily to new versions of old systems, or to new systems entirely. Process projection also offers the chance to make the best possible use of existing applications by transitioning away from the processes that were originally hard-coded within them, toward a more adaptive framework that exposes processes and allows them to be changed as necessary.

Moreover, while enterprise systems have always been constructed from a range of technologies, we have always needed consistent interfaces, and standard technologies for federating and managing enterprise technologies. As the Business Process Management industry matures, it is driving the adoption of such interfaces and standards.

However, appreciating that a typical process support system is part of a more general technical framework does have deeper implications. Suppose one accepts that, as shown above, a typical business process implementation is essentially a new, higher-level approach to automation—essentially, a different way of creating and changing *programs*. Then some light is shed on the original question: What do most process support vendors, and most business process analysts, mean when they talk about "processes?" We can now see that the usual meaning of "process" is something very specific: *a sequence of activities driven by, and mostly carried out by, machines.*

In the book that spearheaded the Business Process Management movement, Smith and Fingar define a business process as: "the complete and dynamically coordinated set of collaborative and transactional activities that deliver value to customers." [6]

What we have shown is that current process modeling techniques and tools are geared toward activities that are transactional. So, what about the activities that are collaborative?

Straight away both the benefits and limitations of current approaches to process support are made clear. They let us *automate* as much of our business operations as we care to, and *routinize* other aspects via traditional workflow techniques. However, they do not deal with things that cannot be so easily automated or routinized—the dynamic, innovative, *collaborative* processes driven by humans. We know, however, that such activities exist. After all, if you are reading this, your job is concerned with them. But what characterizes them?

Human-driven processes

Processes don't do work, people do.
The People Are the Company, John Seely Brown and Estee Solomon Gray.[7]

We have seen how the underpinnings of current process implementations are essentially the same as the underpinnings of any modern computer program. A process suitable for expression in a process support system is assumed to concern *mechanistic transactions*. The basic principle is that you can understand processes by understanding the tasks carried out, the data operated on, and how they interrelate. This may be true for some business behavior, but surely is not true for all.

The mechanistic modeling approach works very well for certain processes. Many of the current Business Process Management success stories are drawn from areas such as manufacturing replenishment, factory control, financial transaction management, and logistics. Here the aim is to reduce human involvement to the minimum—not only to cut costs, but also to free up workers so as to allow more productive use of their knowledge and skills. As described above, the significant advances being made by process support vendors are to enable more complete automation of routine work and transactional activities.

However, there are other types of process in which human involvement should not, and perhaps cannot, be automated away. We might best describe these as *human-driven processes*. Consider, for example, complex sales, marketing, product design, negotiation, project management, and process design itself. Not only is it unfeasible to exclude humans from these activities; they are indeed the lynchpins of commercial success or failure. If you're good at such processes, you're probably good at business.

So, don't such processes deserve effective computer support, a Human Interaction Management System? For one thing, you cannot improve something unless you are able to measure it—so measurement tools for processes of the *human kind* should be of great value. In addition, even if automation is not the most important thing in these cases, computerized aid might still be of great value. Just to take a single example, *sales* is a critical activity in any business. Yet many salespeople feel they are poorly supported by the Customer Relationship Management (CRM) systems provided for their use.[8]

The underlying problem with systems such as CRM is that their aim is simply to provide information believed to be of value to those carrying out the processes concerned. There is no attempt to *manage* the processes. Hence, such a system offers no visibility of bottlenecks, communication failures, dependencies, goals, competencies, or any of the other aspects that an executive responsible for the process is concerned with.

This shortcoming seems a drastic one, given the importance of the processes. What can be the reason for this gap in process support technology?

Modeling the why and how

The red plague rid you for learning me your language.
The Tempest, Shakespeare.

The problem of computer support for human-driven processes may simply be that business analysts lack terms suitable for describing them. There are many management techniques based on understanding human behavior, ranging from human resources methods[9] through to project management theories.[10] However, not only is there a bewildering variety of such approaches, but no one approach sets out to provide a generic way of describing human-driven *processes*.

Hence, if you are responsible for a process such as complex sales, marketing, product design, negotiation, project management, or process design, you must find your own way to define and manage it. If you want business support tools, you must devise them too, either from scratch or by purchasing a package that has some in-built assumptions about how the process works. This situation is exactly what first workflow, and then Business Process Management, set out to change.

However, most current process implementations don't cater to such processes. As described above, process support systems have generally been used only for the support of processes that could be characterized as *machine-driven*—sequences of tasks, sequenced and constrained via techniques drawn from programming languages. So, when business analysts come to analyze a business in terms of process, as often as not, human-driven processes are simply left out of the picture. Even on the occasions when an attempt is made to understand these processes, it is unlikely to succeed, because the terms available to describe such activities leave out so much of their essential nature.

Moreover, it is not possible to use conventional process modeling techniques to implement collaborative human-driven processes. In order to support human activity, a computer system must in some basic sense *mirror it*—provide a free-wheeling world of independent entities that know about each other, understand key aspects of the world with which they interact, are capable of communicating to each other this knowledge and understanding, and support any conceivable change on-the-fly. Such aspects of human activity cannot be captured via techniques designed primarily to specify the execution of tasks in predefined, if-then-else sequences, where the choice of what to do and when is made in advance by the process designer. To build support for human-driven processes, you need to use tools that make fewer assumptions about the world. In the words of Lewis Carroll, "no cheese is made of chalk." The stuff in current process modeling frameworks is simply not the same stuff found in human interactions.

So, what *is* the essential nature of a human-driven process? In machine-driven processes, it is useful to focus on *what* happens. By contrast, in human-driven processes, it is as important, if not more so, to look at *why* people do things, and *how* they carry them out. This is because, when people do knowledge work, the observed sequence of actions is just a corollary of why and how the actions are carried out. Unless you model the why and how, you will fail to understand the way in which processes can be carried out differently on different occasions. People tend to repeat, interleave and loop actions in ways that are not at all amenable to traditional analysis in "programmatic" terms.

Managing people as if they were machines is like trying to teach small children table manners. As soon as you've finished designing a process, the users will try to deviate from the expected behavior—usually when you least expect it, and with results that only create more work for their managers.

A step in the right direction is to think about actions as caused by business rules, rather than simply as a result of what has gone before.[11] Business rules are much more akin to the way people think about their everyday work than the programmatic "control flow" inherent in most process modeling techniques. In general, interaction workers do things *if and when* they need doing. They don't carry out fixed sequences of activities in the same order every day.

However, this provides only a small part of the answer. There are a number of other base concepts necessary to model human-driven processes. In particular, it is important to understand the *Roles* assigned to process participants. The Role notion is absolutely fundamental to human behavior. We all play multiple Roles in everyday life, and adjust our behavior accordingly. A single job title generally conceals a number of different Roles—typically such different responsibilities as line management, client account management, financial reporting, operational activities, product direction, project management, and so on may be taken on by the same person at different times. These Roles need to be separated out if the underlying processes are to be understood.

Moreover, it is also vital to distinguish between a *Role* and its *User*— the person, organization or machine assigned to it. The choice of Users to play the Roles in a process has a fundamental impact on how that process will be carried out. Roles and Users are both important, and have quite different—although sometimes parallel—characteristics. For example, they both have *capabilities* and *authority*, but the terms do not refer to the same thing for a Role as they do for a User. The interrelationship between Role and User is critical to understanding how to manage human-driven processes. However carefully designed the Roles are in a process, it is likely to flounder unless the users playing those Roles are appropriately chosen.

To provide an overview of some of the fundamental concepts in human-driven processes, here is a list of example issues as they relate to a Role and to a User. This is illustrated by reference to *Complex Sales*, a process involving multiple vendor Roles such as Account Manager, Technical Support, Marketing, Sales Director, and so on (for simplicity, we leave out client-side Roles).

Role:

- *Goals* (the Account Manager tries to make his or her personal target).

- *Responsibilities* (the Technical Support must answer questions correctly and in a timely fashion).

- *Interests* (the Sales Director wishes to keep track of key sales).

- *Agreements* (between vendor and client there exist contracts, specifications, informal understandings, etc).

- *Private information resources* (the Account Manager maintains varied information about the client).

- *References to other Roles* (the Sales Director knows who his or her Account Managers are, each Account Manager knows how to get hold of the Marketing department if required).

- *Capabilities* in terms of actions that can be carried out (only certain Account Managers can grant high levels of discount).

- *Process authority* (Marketing has the final say on what promotional literature can be distributed).

User:

- *Identity* (a Sales Director will not entrust a key account to just anybody—they need to know that an appropriate person is taking on the Role).

- *Physical location* (the time zone of the user assigned to Technical Support may be important if phone calls in office hours are required).

- *Virtual location* (if it is necessary to get hold at short notice of the Sales Director, his or her mobile number and email address must be known).

- *Relationships* with others (it would not be sensible to assign to a client an Account Manager who is known to get on badly with someone in his or her organization; conversely it is wise to build upon existing working relationships where possible).

- *Behavioral tendencies* (a client whose preference is for extended and repeated meetings preparatory to purchase should be assigned an Account Manager with the necessary patience).

- *Capabilities* in terms of knowledge and experience (the user assigned to Technical Support should have the necessary skills).

- *Organizational authority* (a major client may feel slighted unless his or her Account Manager has a senior position in the vendor's organization).

The concepts above, as they apply to a *Role* (process participant) or *User* (the person, machine, or organization that drives a Role), find no place in conventional Business Process Management systems. Yet they are fundamental to the proper support of human-driven processes.

Having said this, some of the above concepts are catered for by existing modeling techniques based on role-based analysis of processes,[12] for which there now exist corresponding process enactment software and even a Business Process Management methodology.[13] However, in order to provide full support for human-driven processes, a process modeling technique alone is not enough. It is also necessary to understand *what sort of things go on* in a human-driven process.

Small talk

Human language can be used to inform or mislead, to clarify one's own thoughts or to display one's cleverness, or simply for play.
Language and Mind, Noam Chomsky, 1968.

We have seen that a fundamental aspect of human-driven processes is *collaboration*—human interactions, in which people co-operate to achieve individual and shared goals. So, if we seek to understand human-driven processes, we must ask, "What sort of things go on within a collaborative activity?"

A pointer in the right direction can be found in the theory of *speech acts.*[14] This is a way of describing human interactions that classifies them into a fixed set of types. There turn out to be a surprisingly small number of types that recur often in business. Most interactions can be classified as *request/promise, offer/acceptance,* or *report/acknowledgement.* Combinations of such "speech acts" can be built up to make "conversations" that capture much of what goes on in a business activity. A negotiation, for example, can be expressed as a conversation comprising a number of speech acts.

This approach, in itself, offers a useful device for analysis and support of human-driven processes, and software tools to support speech acts have been around for a long time. However, speech acts on their own cannot be used to model human-driven processes, or support them fully with software:

- First, there is no place in speech act theory for the aspects of Role and User discussed above. Without these concepts, each conversation effectively happens in limbo, without providing any of the information or insight that might allow management for improvement.

- Second, conversations cannot be defined in advance, then set into play like mechanical automata. Much of what happens in a human-driven process is concerned with deciding what to do next—in other words, the conversation is made up as it goes along. You might start with a basic notion of how the story will play out, but this doesn't last long.

For instance, suppose a specific team of designers is tasked to create a new type of switch for use in a car dashboard. Almost as soon as they get going, everything changes. The switch is actually made of multiple parts—so they split the team to work on each part separately, with the intention of integrating the parts at the end. Then some necessary expertise turns out to be missing, so new designers need to be brought in. They discover that some sub-components can be bought in rather then designed, although minor customization is necessary, so dealings with suppliers get complex. Just as integration is completed, there turns out to be a safety issue that affects other components. On rectifying this, someone notices that there is a fault in a component of the switch itself. And so on.

This situation is not a special case, but the norm. All human-driven processes have this character. Once you set a human-driven process in motion, it generates one sibling- or sub-process after another. These child processes then do the same. And all the processes pass information back and forth among themselves. In speech act terms, they ask for things, deliver things, and bring things to each others attention. However, speech acts on their own do not provide enough information to make sense of this—for you need to understand the *things* that are being requested, delivered and reported.

Returning to the dashboard switch, the designers will end up creating a number of drawings for different parts of the switch, interfaces between sub-components, interfaces between the switch and the rest of the dashboard, etc. They will also maintain fault logs, benchmarks, cost analyses, and so on. There are complex inter-relationships between these objects—so changes to some objects inevitably affect others. It is no good designing a sub-component that does not match the interface expected of it. Unless you can track dependencies, and understand the impact of changes, across a complex web of process information, you cannot manage the process at all.

So you need to know not only what sorts of conversations are taking place, but understand *what they are about*. In other words, you must understand the information that the process uses and creates, and the relationships between different pieces of this information. But if the process itself is a moving target, how can we possibly get a handle on the information that it generates?

To answer this question, we need to get away from current enterprise computing approaches to data management, and look at the way we humans really work, day to day.

All information is personal

Today's conventional operating systems force you to give every document a name, which is a nuisance and a waste of time.
The *Aesthetics of Computing*, David Gelernter, 1998.

Modern enterprise systems, in general, are founded on the separation of control flow from data. This follows from a general assumption, now standard in enterprise IT, that any and all business data should "live" in a centralized corporate repository, such as a database, data warehouse, file server, document/content management system or directory. Storing data in this way allows retrieval, maintenance and analysis tools to conceal the data's actual location from the business user, which makes it much easier for IT staff to maintain that data and keep it consistent. From the point of view of computerized process support, a process activity can make use of any such repository by invoking a tool to access it. In theory, this is a fundamental enabler, since it makes it possible to define processes without having to manage the data they operate upon.

That's the theory. In practice, only certain types of information are really centralized in this manner. Human-driven processes typically involve collaboration, innovation, discussion, negotiation—and such activities tend to result in a large number of document versions, notes, text messages, emails, letters, and telephone calls. All these are forms of information, highly relevant to the business, and potentially an important audit trail—yet no one would claim that all these are faithfully filed away in the appropriate corporate repository, grouped according to the process of which they form a part.

How could they be? There is an instinctive understanding that, in such human-driven activities, information is *personal*. Each participant builds up his or her own store of knowledge, and shares parts of this, now and then, with the others involved. Only in this way can the process move forward, since the nature of a human process is that we meet, go off and do different things, meet, go off and do different things, meet, ... and so on. The "different things" that we do when apart create information personal to each participant.

Could one insist that all participants start to keep everything they create—from a jotted down note to a text message to a revised document draft—in a single central repository? For a start, this would run the risk of imposing a stifling and unnatural block on progress, since the effort to file and maintain the varied pieces of information thus created would be an overhead no one wants. Moreover, even if you tried to enforce such a discipline, and accepted the consequent overhead, process participants may well be unwilling to work with it. This is for all sorts of reasons, not just the sheer amount of extra work that would be created and perceived as unnecessary by process participants. The most important reasons are to do with basic human nature. In such processes, we do not always wish to openly share everything we do the whole time. There are considerations of politics, courtesy, confidentiality, intellectual property, and just "readiness"—when you are first developing an idea, of any kind, it is natural to keep early versions private, or show them only in a certain form, only to a few chosen people.

You have to allow for this personal aspect of data both in your description of human-driven processes, and in the corresponding computer support. Otherwise, all that will happen is that people will bypass the system and do things the old way. It is an old adage of the IT industry that the success of any software is dependent on whether people "buy into" it. If a new system makes things that people need to do harder rather than easier, at best, they will pay it lip service; at worst, they will ignore it. Either way, the system will wither on the vine and never deliver on its promise.

So, suppose one accepts that personalized data is a feature of human-driven processes. A host of other considerations then come into play. Where is the audit trail of a process? How are document versions managed? What should be done about dependencies between different pieces of information? How can the enterprise know which document should be used for which purpose? What should happen when a document is discovered to contain errors or gives rise to problems? And, most importantly of all, how can process participants work together, if they each have their own, different data stores?

These problems seem very hard. Yet we cannot ignore them. After all, the same issues are there now, every day, as people work in precisely the way described above. These very real process problems are just brushed under the carpet, because at present there is no general attempt to manage such processes in a consistent or computer-assisted way. If we want to move forward, and look for what could be huge competitive advantage in dealing better with human-driven processes, it is necessary to grasp the bull by the horns.

What we need is some way to untangle the web of data—a simple approach to process definition that allows us to make sense of how personalized information is treated within the process as a whole. How can we sort the mess out?

Knowing what you know

To my surprise, it was my wife, I took down to Lamorna
Lamorna, English folk song.

We can get part of the way there by looking back at one of the notions central to human-driven processes: Role. In a human-driven process, personalized information can be handled simply by attaching it to a Role. Copies can be passed from one Role to another—and the original deleted if no longer required by the sender. Each Role can keep all versions of a particular document that it possesses, or just certain versions.

This gives us a way of storing information that is more appropriate to human-driven processes than using enterprise repositories. However, it does *not* give us a way to tell which documents are to be used for what. Returning to the dashboard switch, "Which designs should we base the final product on? What do we need to change if a particular supplier goes out of business? What actions should we take if a fault becomes apparent?"

Perhaps we need a "document relationship management" system to track all this. Hold on though—we must be careful not to fall again into the CRM trap. Document relationship management can provide us with vital facilities such as audit trails—which are a *legal* requirement in some areas. In safety engineering, for example, a crash investigation may require production of all written material, down to notes in a log book, as evidence in a court of law. This "product assurance" requirement is so stringent that engineering companies commonly resort to handling it by deleting any extraneous data, which only hinders problem identification and resolution.

This drastic approach to dealing with the problem is forced on the engineering industry, since just keeping copies of everything is not enough on its own—it doesn't tell you enough about what was used where, how, and for what reason. Unless document management is intimately tied into the *processes* that create and use the documents, it will be an expensive waste of time. For example, the answers to all the questions above about the dashboard switch depend on what exactly is going on in the switch design process, and those related to it—what version(s) of the switch is (are) in production, what arrangements we have in place with suppliers, who is using the switch and for what.

So, in order to manage our documents, we need to know "what is going on" in the process—"where we are," if you like. What deliverables have been accepted, problems identified, resolution strategies put in place, information requested, services contracted to customers—it is these *agreements* that determine the relationship between documents.

It's not *document* relationship management that we need—it's *interaction* relationship management. If we are to manage human-driven processes, we need to get a handle on the information generated by these processes, which means tracking, at a detailed level, what happens in the interactions between the Roles that own this information. What benefits will accrue from this?

Getting on better with each other

The only source of war is politics—the intercourse of governments and peoples.
On War, Clausewitz, 1832.

In principle, people seek to work well together, and managers seek to enable this. In practice, however, working well together is hard to achieve. Even in the best human interactions, there is often a lot of wasted time and effort, as people have to repeat requests for the same information, end up in meetings to which they have nothing to contribute, wonder whether or not they have made themselves clear, and so on. People may try to take this kind of thing, annoying as it can be, with a good grace—but things more detrimental to the business can be the norm. In the worst (but common) case, people don't understand the actions of others; they can only feel they are being treated unfairly; they start responding poorly to other process participants—and you get a vicious circle that is hard to break.

If we are to genuinely improve human-driven processes—and deliver competitive advantage from the activities of the workers who carry them out—it is necessary to put in place an environment in which each participant is able to *understand the actions of the others*. This means understanding the *interactions* in the process—for, by definition, these are the only points of contact between participants. Hence, interactions are the only time at which one participant can gain knowledge about the others.

Focusing on interactions and their content, rather than on tasks (as in conventional process analysis) or on data (as in CRM), instantly suggests all sort of ways in which human relations can be improved:

- *Cultural clashes can be minimized, as can clashes of personality.* Both these manifest themselves in a variety of ways ranging from the order in which actions are carried out, to the way in which documents are written, to "token" gestures that may carry great significance.

- *Incentivization can be re-engineered.* In many organizations, it is only sales staff and their managers who are given additional compensation on an ongoing basis in accordance with the results of their work. This can lead to resentment among other staff, (for example, the technical support team who were the critical enabler of a sale), but even if no one minds, how much better would all concerned perform if they too were compensated fairly? Taking a process view of human relations even permits the fair allocation of reward to third parties such as suppliers, if that is desired.

- *Meetings can be streamlined.* Whether a meeting is a physical get-together or an electronic (audio, video or Web) conference, all too often many of those involved are not really required, at least not all of the time. Or the meeting accomplishes less than intended because someone who is not there should be. And who hasn't attended a meeting that had no clearly defined aim? Better meeting planning can only be achieved via better understanding of the interaction(s) represented by each meeting.

- *Communication within a team can be improved.* In many collaborative efforts, a number of those involved feel they should be privy to information that others alone possess. Sometimes this is inevitable, but often it is just an oversight, because there is no way to see "who knows what." Feeling that you are out of the loop is disempowering, and can cause not only discontent but also resentment. Moreover, a very common cause of problems is that someone wasn't informed of something they needed to know.

- And so on.

Any good manager sees it as his or her duty to resolve these sorts of issues. But without an interaction management system that caters for Roles, Users, and the information that each of them owns, achieving this is at best a black art, and unlikely to happen.

Managing human interactions

You better start swimming
Or you'll sink like a stone
For the times they are a-changin'
The Times They Are A-Changin', Bob Dylan, 1963.

So, what is the *nature* of Human Interaction Management? In order to answer this, let's summarize the fundamental features of human-driven processes that require support from computer systems:

- *Connection visibility.* Collaborative technology must provide a strong representation of *process participants,* the *roles* they play and the *private information resources* that belong to each of them.

- *Structured messaging.* In the future, our interactions may still take place via email, the Web, or any other standard protocol, but if we are to manage them better, they must be structured for us, under process control, by software.

- *Support for mental work.* Human-driven process support must act to recognize the value of the information processing done in people's heads, and offer ways to manage and recompense it like any other form of activity.

- *Supportive rather than prescriptive activity management.* People take action in different ways on different days. One should not seek to change human nature, but to make the best of it by supporting such behavior patterns.

- *Processes change processes.* Actions and interactions in human-driven processes must be able to effect *continual change to the process itself.*

In order to provide systems to support these features, we need a corresponding theory of processes, one that forms a complete modeling framework for human-driven processes. This is Role-based—it enhances and extends the existing notation known as Role Activity Diagrams, both to change some basic principles appropriately and to combine these principles with concepts drawn from social systems theory, organizational theory, cognitive theory, computer science and mathematics. We draw together key lines of thinking, old and new, theoretical and practical, to synthesize *social computing* with *mainstream information technology*.

Providing computer assistance for human interactions has many and varied benefits—not least that it brings along a new concept of *process management* that caters naturally for the monitoring of, and control over, the most persistent problem of the business world—*process change*. The theory of human-driven processes allows complex problems to be made simpler, responsibilities to be assigned where they belong, and process support to be given a formal underpinning that allows an analyst not just to define and implement a process, but also to *reason about it*.

In a world where government regulations, such as the Sarbanes-Oxley Act, are putting corporate transparency at the top of the board-level priority list, businesses are grappling with the need to support change on a daily basis. Businesses require a formal underpinning for process support that deals head on with continuous change, and provides guarantees that systems will perform as expected. Such reassurance is not just a nice-to-have; in today's business world it's a sine qua non.

Robust, scalable, certified Human Interaction Management software already exists, and more such systems will follow in due course. These systems are required to complement existing transaction-oriented process implementations, if we are to deal with the full range of processes that exist in every business.

The techniques and tools via which business processes are currently implemented embody a sequenced activity approach to computation that's not designed to support the free-wheeling interactions of humans. Consider what industry veteran, Paul Harmon, wrote about the main contender for a standard process language, BPEL:

> "Most people assume that a BPM system should be able to manage a business process that includes employee activities, as well as wholly automated activities. The current version of BPEL can only manage automated activities! Thus, although BPEL can function as an EAI component in a BPM Suite, it cannot function as the primary BPM engine. In other words, no BPM Suite, today, can rely on BPEL as its primary language. This completely undermines the possibility of using BPEL as a way of passing process descriptions from one tool to another, or of passing a

company's process description to its business partners."[15]

A process language such as BPEL cannot of itself support human-driven processes—it has different uses, for which it is well-adapted. In order to cater for human-driven processes, the *collaborative* as opposed to *transactional* face of business, similarly well-adapted tools and techniques are required.

This new category of enterprise system—the Human Interaction Management System—is a player that will sit alongside transactional process support systems to complete the business process picture. Human Interaction Management will *overarch* enterprise technologies to support human-driven processes, just as conventional process support tools and techniques *underarch* enterprise technologies to support machine-driven processes. The two approaches to process support will cooperate naturally with each other and with all other forms of enterprise software to realize the vision of the process management pioneers—to make processes the foundation of the enterprise IT architecture.

The Human Interaction Management System has emerged in response to the need for control over human-driven processes. It is the missing link in enterprise IT required to fill the gap left by today's transaction-oriented systems—and the early adopters will be the ones to reap the most competitive advantage.

Putting it all together

We are seeing the transformation of corporations into "real-time enterprises" that place as much emphasis on providing great product services as on making great products. A real-time enterprise accomplishes its work and innovates via a dynamic supply network (rather than a static supply chain) with lightning-fast response to ever-changing customer needs. In this new world, companies are competing on their processes. So, let us suppose that *human-driven* processes are truly the next step in process management, thus driving competitive advantage. What then will lead a company to industry domination?

Human-driven processes can only be understood—and hence managed—via the interactions between their Roles, and the Users that drive them. To do this, you need to manage:

- Both Roles and their Users,
- The information within the Roles,

- How this information is used in the tasks and conversations that constitute human-driven processes, and

- How each human-driven process evolves as it is carried out.

In the real-time age, the process-managed enterprise will dominate by implementing radically new means of support for human interactions. Winning companies will deploy innovative information technology tools to manage Roles and Users, capture information deeply personal to Roles, and help process participants use this information both individually and *collaboratively*. A new breed of software, the Human Interaction Management System, will provide the freedom that interaction workers need so that they are helped, and not hindered, by *the system*. With Human Interaction Management, smart companies will be able to optimize the human-driven processes that are, in the end, their people's jobs—and the next source of competitive advantage.

Human Interaction Management permits suppliers to establish a fundamental integration with the needs of their customers, by engaging directly with the human-centered processes for which their products will be used. In the twenty-first century, where customers are bewildered by choice and seek *understanding* from a supplier as well as low price and efficient delivery, such integration may be a necessity. Customers will find a supplier that they trust, engage with them, and stick with them. Anyone can compete in this heady new world—but to keep the customers you gain, you need Human Interaction Management.

Now is the time for companies determined to dominate their industries in the decade ahead to embrace the future of process support.

References.

---

[1] The English folk song *Widecombe Fair* is about a horse, borrowed by people who don't understand her capabilities, and who thoughtlessly overload her with "Bill Brewer, Jan Stewer, Peter Gurney, Peter Davy, Dan'l Whiddon, Harry Hawke, Old Uncle Tom Cobley and all." Eventually the poor horse just keels over and gives up, returning to haunt the moors as a ghost.

[2] Business Process Modeling Notation (BPMN)—see
http://www.bpmn.org/Documents/BPMN V1-0 May 3 2004.pdf

[3] While Business Process Management has its heritage in workflow there are two key differences:

1. Workflow focused mainly on document based processes where people performed the process steps. Business Process Management manages processes that encompass steps performed by both people and systems.

2. Workflow automated processes that existed with an individual department. Business Process Management addresses processes that can span the enterprise. Business Process Management technology must therefore provide far higher degrees of scalability than workflow.
(http://www.staffware.com/software/process_management/bpmfaqs.jsp?m=c6 #5)

[4] OASIS Web Services Business Process Execution Language (WSBPEL), commonly known as BPEL
(http://www.oasis-open.org/committees/documents.php?wg_abbrev=wsbpel)

[5] BPEL is geared toward programming in the large, which supports the logic of business processes. These business processes are self-contained applications that use Web services as activities that implement business functions. BPEL does not try to be a general-purpose programming language. Instead, it is assumed that BPEL will be combined with other languages which are used to implement business functions (programming in the small).
…
BPELJ enables Java and BPEL to cooperate by allowing sections of Java code, called Java snippets, to be included in BPEL process definitions.
(http://www-106.ibm.com/developerworks/webservices/library/ws-bpelj/)

[6] Smith, H., Fingar, P., 2003, "Business Process Management: The Third Wave," Meghan-Kiffer Press

[7] http://www.fastcompany.com/online/01/people.html

[8] To make a CRM system effective you must rely on, say, the sales executive doggedly entering data about product, opportunity, target industry and so on for each prospect. And they have to re-enter this information time and time again. No sales staff are tempted by the idea of spending a day on the road then another two hours entering what happened that day into the CRM system. Reward systems are another hazard. Seddon suggests that it will always be difficult to make sales people use CRM systems because "they are incentivised individually. So they don 't want to put their information in the public domain." In this climate, sales people will even falsify data to hide what they re up to. Many CRM installations are designed to monitor the sales staff as much as the customers. Not a happy situation for either the system or the people using it.
(http://www.themanufacturer.com/content_detail.html?contents_id=2732&t=

manufacturer&header=reports)

[9] such as Belbin team roles (http://www.belbin.info/)

[10] for example, Coplien's organizational patterns (http://users.rcn.com/jcoplien/)

[11] This is known as *state-based workflow.*

[12] in particular, Role Activity Diagramming (RAD)

[13] Riva (http://www.mkpress.com/OULDdesc.html)

[14] See, for example, "Using a Language Action Framework to Extend Organizational Process Modeling" (http://www.cems.uwe.ac.uk/~sjgreen/UKAIS2003.pdf), which shows how speech acts can be layered on top of Role Activity Diagrams to provide a deeper understanding of interaction dynamics.

[15] Harmon, P., 2005, "BPEL and BPM," http://www.bptrends.com/deliver_file.cfm?fileType=publication&fileName=bptemailadvisor012505%2Epdf

Index

About the Author

You can reach the author by email:
human.interactions@rolemodellers.com

KEITH HARRISON-BRONINSKI obtained a BA Hons in Mathematics (starred double first, 1985) and MSc Computation (1986) from Oxford University. His first assignment in the IT industry was to create the central conceptual model for the UK government-sponsored IPSE2.5 project that pioneered the take-up of Role Activity Diagrams for process support in the late 1980s. Keith then spent many years as an independent IT and management consultant, working in a wide range of sectors, technologies and countries. His primary interest has always been to integrate advanced software implementations with social workplace issues.

Keith is the CTO of Role Modelers Ltd (rolemodellers.com), whose mission is to develop the ideas necessary to support human-driven processes, and implement software applications to support them. Keith designed the Human Interaction Management System, *RADRunner*, a dynamic process enactment engine based on Roles and interactions, and is currently working on a suite of visual tools for human-driven process modeling, monitoring, simulation, analysis, and archival.

Keith is also the instigator of the Web forum Role Based Process Support, whose purpose is to discuss and synthesize work on human-driven processes (www.smartgroups.com/groups/roles). Forum members are drawn from varied academic and industry backgrounds, and debate approaches to social analysis of business processes. If you are interested to take a look and/or enter the debate on how to advance computer support of human co-operative work, membership is open to all and you are encouraged to join.

Keith is married with two children and lives in the South-West of England countryside. In his spare time, he plays jazz piano, composes jazz/classical fusion music, and runs with wife Ann an offbeat arts event in their village (www.nunneyjazzcafe.org).

Watch for forthcoming titles.

Meghan-Kiffer Press
Tampa, Florida, USA
www.mkpress.com
Innovation at the Intersection of Business and Technology